English in Modern Times

English in Modern Times 1700–1945

JOAN C. BEAL
Sheffield University, UK

HODDER
EDUCATION
PART OF HACHETTE LIVRE UK

First published in Great Britain in 2004 by
Hodder Education, part of Hachette Livre UK,
338 Euston Road, London NW1 3BH

www.hoddereducation.com

British Library Cataloguing in Publication Data
A catalogue record for this book is available from the British Library

Library of Congress Cataloging-in-Publication Data
A catalog record for this book is available from the Library of Congress

ISBN: 978 0 340 76117 5

Typeset in 10/13 Sabon by Phoenix Photosetting, Chatham, Kent

What do you think about this book? Or any other Hodder Education title?
Please send your comments to educationenquiries@hodder.co.uk

Contents

Figures

Preface

'Modern times': the study of Later Modern English

In my (1999) book on English pronunciation in the eighteenth century, I bemoaned the scholarly neglect of the Later Modern English period by historical linguists, and concurred with Charles Jones in describing the eighteenth and nineteenth centuries as 'the Cinderellas of English historical linguistic study' (1989: 279). Whilst welcoming the appearance of Richard Bailey's (1996) textbook on nineteenth-century English, and anticipating the publication of volumes III (1476–1776) and IV (1776–1976) of the *Cambridge History of the English Language*, I stated that 'there is still no sign of an undergraduate textbook equivalent to Görlach (1991) for the eighteenth century'.

The turn of the millennium has seen considerable improvement in the status of Later Modern English studies. Manfred Görlach has produced two excellent textbooks dedicated to the eighteenth and nineteenth centuries respectively (2001, 1999). As in his (1991) book on Early Modern English, approximately half of each of these volumes is taken up by texts from a wide variety of genres, which exemplify the points made in the chapters and provide materials for exercises. The two relevant volumes of the *Cambridge History* have been published (Romaine, 1998; Lass, 1999) and the first international conference dedicated to Later Modern English took place at the University of Edinburgh in September 2001. The latter event provided ample evidence for the transformation of this particular Cinderella, with delegates from three continents, and 39 papers from both established and up-and-coming scholars on a wide range of topics. The proceedings of the conference have been published as Dossena and Jones (2003).

How can this change in attitudes to Later Modern English be explained? Perhaps the most obvious clue is in the millennium itself: the nineteenth century is no longer 'the last century', so that there is the perception that a 'safe' distance now exists between the 'Later Modern' period and the present day. As Jones (1989: 279) points out:

> There has always been a suggestion . . . especially among those scholars writing in the first half of the twentieth century, that phonological and syntactic change is only properly observable at a great distance and that somehow the eighteenth, and especially the nineteenth centuries, are 'too close' chronologically for any meaningful observations concerning language change to be made.

As the 'distance' between the 'present' and the nineteenth century grows, scholars will feel that they have a clearer perspective on the later modern period.

A second explanation for the recent upsurge in interest in this period lies in the change of emphasis within historical linguistics from the purely theoretical to socio-historical and corpus-based approaches to the study of language. I pointed out (1999: 19) that it was precisely those scholars who were 'willing to recognize the importance of socio-historical factors in linguistic change and the existence of gradual (in the sense of 'socially and lexically diffusing') changes who paid most attention to the eighteenth century in their accounts. This type of scholar is exemplified by Barbara Strang, who, in apparent contradiction to the 'uniformitarian principle', suggests that different forces were at work in the period from 1770 to 1970:

> In the past two hundred years changes in pronunciation are predominantly due, not, as in the past, to evolution of the system, but to what, in a very broad sense, we may call the interplay of different varieties, and to the complex analogical relationship between different parts of the language (1970: 78–9).

This view is echoed by David Denison in his chapter on syntactic change in volume IV of the *Cambridge History*:

> Since relatively few categorical losses or innovations have occurred in the last two centuries, syntactic change has more often been statistical in nature, with a given construction occurring throughout the period and either becoming more or less common generally or in particular registers. The overall, rather elusive effect can seem more a matter of stylistic than syntactic change (1998: 93).

Sadly, Barbara Strang's untimely death in 1982 meant that she was unable to take advantage of the electronic resources which make it possible to track the 'interplay of different varieties' across corpora consisting of thousands and even millions of words. Her last paper (1982) attempted to do 'by hand' precisely the kind of statistical study which has come to the fore recently. The availability of the Chadwyck–Healey literary databases has done away with the need for hand-written index cards (see, for instance, Rohdenburg (2001) for an example of an investigation using the Chadwyck–Healey databases as corpora of Later Modern English). More recently, new corpora such as the *Corpus of Nineteenth-Century English* (CONCE), the *Corpus of Public and Private Writing* (PPW) and the extension of the *Corpus of Early English Correspondence* (CEEC) into the eighteenth century, are yielding useful results and will provide rich material for future investigations (see, for instance, Kytö, Rudanko and Smitterberg, 2000; Grund and Walker, 2001; Nevala, 2001; and Oldireva, 2001).

The time is ripe, then, for a volume that will introduce readers to the major themes and developments in the study of Later Modern English and provide them with an overview of the period. As the title suggests, the main theme of this book is that it is in this (later modern) period that the English language becomes recognizably 'modern' in the sense of 'like that of the present day'. The approach that I take here is socio-historical, maintaining that social changes in the Anglophone world need to be taken into account if we are to understand the linguistic changes taking place in Later Modern English. In this respect, I agree with Jeremy Smith, who states that:

> The various changes at an intralinguistic level ... cannot be meaningfully accounted for without reference to the extra-linguistic contexts (historical, geographical, sociological) in which these phenomena are situated ... If we attempt to explain language change entirely intralinguistically, without ultimate reference to extralinguistic factors, then ... [we] will ultimately fail (1996: 3).

Chapter 1 sets out the 'extra-linguistic contexts' in which the changes and developments at various linguistic levels are situated. Chapters 2–7 are arranged in pairs: for each linguistic level (lexis, syntax/morphology, phonology) there is a chapter reviewing the efforts of those who sought 'some Method ... for *ascertaining* and *fixing* our Language for ever' (Swift, 1712: 31), and one describing the changes which occurred despite (or sometimes because of) such efforts. This counterpoise confirms the truth of Dr Johnson's observation that no lexicographer (or, for that matter, grammarian or elocutionist) 'can embalm his language, and secure it from corruption and decay' (1755: C2ʳ). What it also demonstrates, though, is that the binary division into prescriptive/descriptive that has become a commonplace of modern linguistics is not always useful with regard to later modern texts. The so-called 'prescriptive' authors of the eighteenth century were often describing real usage, whilst the 'descriptive' scholars of the late nineteenth and early twentieth centuries played their part in the normative agenda by choosing to 'describe' only Standard English and/or RP.

Whilst discussion in these chapters is not confined to writers and developments based in England, or London, Chapter 8 focuses more specifically on attitudes to, and use of, non-standard ('provincial') varieties of British English, and the emerging extraterritorial Englishes. In concluding with an overview of extraterritorial varieties, I hope to show that, by the end of the later modern period, if not at the beginning, the English language is no longer 'owned' by the English.

Acknowledgements

This book has been several years in the writing, so I have accumulated a large number of favours and debts which must be acknowledged. First of all, I am grateful to the Arts and Humanities Research Board for the Research Leave grant which allowed me to begin work on this project in earnest. I am likewise grateful to the British Academy/Association of Commonwealth Universities for the grant which allowed me to collaborate with Carol Percy on the 'Grammars of the People' project, ideas from which have informed Chapter 5 in particular.

In the course of writing this book, I moved from the University of Newcastle upon Tyne to the University of Sheffield. I have been privileged to spend all my working life at these two great northern universities, and owe a debt to many of my colleagues in both places for their friendship and encouragement.

Especial thanks must go to Karen Corrigan for friendship, power breakfasts and sharing the joke about turnpikes, to Hermann Moisl for helping me keep things in perspective, and to April McMahon for support and understanding through difficult times.

I have also had help and encouragement from many colleagues around the world who have answered e-mails and commented on draft chapters: Rowena Fowler, Malcolm Jones, Maria Rodriguez Gil, Carol Percy Massimo Sturiale and Ingrid Tieken have all provided comment and/or information. I am always grateful to Roger Lass for helping me to believe that my work is worthwhile.

Anthony Grant deserves an accolade for his work as a research assistant in the middle of this project: Chapters 1–4 have benefited from his work, but I owe him thanks particularly for his continuing interest and encouragement.

I am, as always, grateful to my husband Ninian and my daughters Madeleine and Alice for coffee, wine, love and tolerance. I have not been easy to live with in the last few months of this project, but they have stayed with me. Hodder Arnold, too, have kept faith in me despite several delays, and I am grateful for all their help and forbearance.

Finally, thanks are due to the University of Sheffield for permission to reproduce the photograph on the cover, and to Carl Winter for permission to reproduce the page from the *Chronological English Dictionary* which appears as Figure 2.2.

1

Modern English and modern times

1.1 Introduction: Defining 'modern times'

'Modern times' in this book are defined as the years from the beginning of the eighteenth century through to the end of World War II. This more or less coincides with the period generally referred to in more recent histories of English (e.g. Blake, 1996) as 'Later Modern English'. Dates are always contentious in histories of English, and the boundaries of 'Modern' and 'Later Modern' English have long been, and are still, a matter of debate. In this chapter, I intend to demonstrate that the period covered is one in which the characteristics of both 'Modern' English and the modern world evolve.

The term 'Modern English' with reference to a historical period seems to have been coined by Sweet in a lecture delivered to the Philological Society in 1873 and published in the society's *Transactions* for 1873–4: 'I propose . . . to start with the three main divisions of *Old, Middle* and *Modern*, based mainly on the inflectional characteristics of each stage' (1873–4: 620). Since Sweet defined 'Modern English' as the period of lost inflections, there would be no need in his view for any further subdivision of this period, since the only inflection lost after the seventeenth century is the second-person singular *-st*. Writing at the beginning of the twentieth century, Wyld proposes a modification of Sweet's threefold division, with Early Modern English 'from 1400 or so to the middle of the sixteenth century' and 'Present-day English' from the beginning of the eighteenth century to the time of writing (1920). Wyld is fairly typical of writers from the first half of the twentieth century in viewing the period from 1700 to what for them was 'the present' as coherent. Poutsma is perhaps the first to use the designation 'Late Modern English' in his title, but it is clear that he intends this work to be an account of the synchronic grammar of his own day: 'a methodical description of the English Language as it presents itself in the printed documents of the last few generations' (1914: viii). Even today, many would agree with McArthur (1992: xx) who, in his entry for 'Modern English', defines 'Late/Later Modern English' as stretching from 1700 to the present day.

Of course, it would be foolish to suggest that any such period could be homogeneous or that the boundaries would not be fuzzy. The starting-point of 1700 is particularly arbitrary, especially since, as Schlauch (1959: 122–5), Blake (1996: 4–5) and Bailey (2003: 22) suggest, the obvious political turning-point which might mark the Early/Late Modern English boundary is the restoration of the monarchy in 1660. This coincides with the view of historians that the 'long' eighteenth century extends roughly from the restoration of the English monarchy (1660) to the fall of Napoleon (1815). On the other hand, the 'long' nineteenth-century in European history is generally acknowledged as beginning with what Schlauch calls 'the great bourgeois French Revolution' of 1789 (1959: 122) and concluding with the end of World War I in 1918 (see, for instance, Blackbourne, 1998). So the period covered by this volume would be recognized by historians as coinciding with the 'long' eighteenth and nineteenth centuries. The questions to be addressed in this chapter are: what are the social, political and intellectual 'movements' which define the 'later modern' period in British history, and how do these affect the development of 'Later Modern English'?

1.2   Politics

We have already noted that the beginning of our period is marked by the Restoration (1660). The word 'restoration' is something of a misnomer here because, whilst the accession of Charles II marked the return of the monarchy after Cromwell's Commonwealth, the monarch was never again to enjoy the power or autonomy wielded by his predecessors. Charles II had been invited to return by parliament, and the so-called 'Glorious Revolution' of 1688 was to usher in the system of constitutional monarchy that still exists in Britain today. The Bill of Rights (1689) removed the right of the monarch to raise taxes or suspend laws without the consent of parliament: the days of divine right were over and, as Porter (2000) acknowledges, England gained the reputation of being a 'free nation'. We might characterize the later modern period in England, and later Britain, as an age of increasing democratization, starting with the 'Glorious Revolution', continuing with the Reform Acts of 1832, 1867 and 1884, and culminating in the granting of universal male and female suffrage in 1918 and 1928, respectively. Whilst Britain remains a constitutional monarchy, in the year of writing, that of Queen Elizabeth II's golden jubilee, republicanism is a growing force in several Commonwealth countries (most notably Australia) and even in Britain.

1.3 Science

As well as marking the date of the Restoration, 1660 also saw the foundation of the Royal Society, promoting scientific and rational discourse. The publication of Newton's *Principia* in 1687 is seen by many (e.g. Porter, 2000; Lass, 1996) as marking the dawn of the Enlightenment in England. This period was one in which faith was no longer solely placed in an omnipotent God, but in humanity's capacity for rational thinking. This did not mean that religion was abandoned, but, just as belief in divine right had been replaced by the constitutional monarchy, so belief in God was tempered by faith in science and reason. Newton's role in this was acknowledged by his contemporaries: his *Opticks* (1704) explained the principles of light itself. Alexander Pope equates this great scientist symbolically with the Enlightenment and with the Creator himself: 'Nature, and Nature's Laws, lay hid in Night: God said, *Let Newton be! And All was Light*' (1720, in Butt, 1965: 808). Porter points out that 'the affinities between the Newtonian cosmos and the post-1688 polity were played up'. He notes that J. T. Desaguliers, in *The Newtonian System of the World: The Best Model of Government, an allegorical Poem*, describes God as 'a kind of constitutional monarch': 'His Pow'r, coerc'd by Laws, still leaves them free / Directs, but not Destroys their Liberty'(1728, quoted in Porter, 2000: 137). Newton's *Opticks* and other scientific treatises by the Royal Society's members paved the way for the technological innovations of the Industrial Revolution in the later eighteenth century. Wedgewood installed the first steam engine in his factory in 1782 and the power loom followed in 1785, heralding a mechanization of labour which would transform the lives of working men and women and make the fortunes of the new plutocracy. In the nineteenth century, the advance of science was so rapid that this period was termed 'the wonderful century' by Wallace in his eponymous work of 1898. As we shall see in Chapter 2, new words were coined at a rate not seen since the sixteenth century, largely to provide names for the discoveries being made every day in a wide range of scientific fields. Victorian Britons saw their time as 'wonderful', because many of these discoveries and innovations brought genuine improvements to their quality of life. In the medical field, the introduction of vaccination (1776), the stethoscope (1816) and anaesthesia in surgery (1842) vastly improved chances of survival, whilst other inventions such as gas (1792), and, later, electric (1879) lighting, improved the quality of that life. Of course scientific progress in all these fields continued, indeed accelerated, in the twentieth century, but towards the end of our period, doubts are expressed about the value of 'progress'. Even at the end of the nineteenth century, these misgivings are expressed by Wells in works such as *A Story of the Days to Come* (1897) and *When the Sleeper Wakes* (1899). In the early twentieth century, the 'progress' celebrated in Haldane's *Daedalus* (1924) is questioned by Russell's *Icarus, or The Future of Science* (1924), and in dystopian literature such as Huxley's *Brave New World* (1932) and Orwell's *1984* (1949). The ultimate proof that progress is a two-edged sword was, of course, provided on 6 August 1945, when the first atomic bomb wiped out the city of Hiroshima. The nuclear age, and the Cold War which followed World War II, brought fears that the ingenuity of human beings might cause their destruction. Although scientific progress continues unabated throughout the second half of the twentieth century and into the twenty-first, the value of this 'progress' is questioned by many. The anti-nuclear movement began with the Campaign for Nuclear Disarmament's first march in 1956, and, whilst the collapse of the Soviet empire has diminished the perceived threat of nuclear war, distrust of science continues to be expressed. At the time of writing, the advances made by Pasteur are being spurned by parents throughout the developed world, who treat vaccination with fear and the medical profession with suspicion. In this post-scientific age, educated and affluent people turn to alternative practitioners, some of whom combine modern technology, such as websites, with the pre-Enlightenment physiology of humours. An example of this can be found in the *Observer* Magazine, 14 April 2002. In response to a reader who fears that her forgetfulness might be a symptom of Alzheimer's disease, the 'Barefoot Doctor' writes:

> At the deepest of levels, there seems to be a confusion between the elements of fire and water and earth. This relates to your heart, kidney and spleen, and does not indicate a possibility of Alzheimer's, the very thought/fear of which is indicative of this imbalance.

So, with regard to science and popular views of science, the period covered by this book begins with the optimism of the Enlightenment, when the medieval world-view was discarded, continues with the Victorian age of 'progress' and ends with the scepticism of the post-war era.

1.4   Society

Just as the later modern period exchanges divine right for constitutional monarchy and faith in God for faith in human reason, so power in British society shifts from those who held it by privilege of birth to those who had gained influence through wealth. The Industrial Revolution brought prosperity for self-taught, self-made men, some of whom actually rose to the peerage. Examples of such men are the engineer William (later Lord) Armstrong in Newcastle, and Lever (later Viscount Leverhulme), the soap manufacturer from Bolton, Lancashire, who founded the model village of Port Sunlight on the Wirral.

Whilst eighteenth-century novels are full of expressions of disdain towards those 'in trade', by the end of the nineteenth century, the aristocracy of Britain had become a plutocracy. Even so, 'new money' was no guarantee of class, but money could buy access to the public schools which were the breeding ground for Received Pronunciation (RP), that peculiarly English sociolect which reached the zenith of its importance in the early twentieth century.

Moving down the social scale, to the upper middle class, the nineteenth century saw the rise of new professions, such as engineering. The new professional class was educated in new universities established to teach a more scientific curriculum. The first of these was Durham, established in 1832, followed by London (1836), Manchester (1851), Birmingham (1874) and Liverpool (1881). It was no coincidence that most of these new 'red-brick' universities were in the same provincial cities that had been the engine-rooms of the Industrial Revolution.

These provincial towns and cities had a tradition of practical education reaching back to the eighteenth century, when the dissenting academies in medium-sized towns such as Warrington, Gloucester, Northampton and Hinckley provided a more scientific curriculum for the sons of tradesmen and artisans. The emphasis here was on reading and writing in English rather than Latin, together with arithmetic, geography and science. Teachers at these academies included men like Joseph Priestley, who, as well as conducting the scientific experiments for which he is best known, produced his *Rudiments of English Grammar* (1761) whilst teaching at the Warrington Academy. The lower middle class was to expand in the nineteenth century, when the increase in trade and commerce created clerical and service jobs for both men and women. The introduction of universal elementary education in 1870 meant that these people had the required skills in writing and arithmetic. As well as being moderately educated, members of this class were required to be 'respectable' in dress, manners and speech. They created a demand for 'penny manuals' which distilled the proscriptions of eighteenth-century grammarians and elocutionists into brief lists of 'dos and don'ts'. (See Mugglestone, 1995 for a full discussion of these manuals.)

The lower classes were increasingly engaged in industrial rather than agricultural labour. The later nineteenth century saw the emergence of an urban working class which was politicized through organized labour movements, such as the Trades Union Congress, formed in 1868, and the Labour Party, formed in 1900. This working-class consciousness also led to an appreciation of the newly emerging urban dialects, whose 'covert prestige' acted as a counterbalance to the influence of RP. In music halls and mechanics' institutes, entertainers such as George 'Geordie' Ridley and Tommy Armstrong sang songs written in dialect, some of which were to become anthems of local and class identity. An example of this is Ridley's *The Blaydon Races*, which was sung by soldiers from the north-east of England in the trenches of World War I, and is still heard today from fans of Newcastle United Football Club (see Beal, 2000 for further discussion of this).

1.5   Urbanization

We have already noted that the scientific advances of the eighteenth century had profound effects on the lives of both working people and the plutocrats who became their employers. Britain from the mid-eighteenth century was the first country to embark upon the Industrial Revolution and it continued to benefit from this head start. By the middle of the nineteenth century Britain had become the first country in which the urban population outnumbered the rural population.

Before 1750 only London had a sizeable population: other urban centres were mere market towns, the largest of which was Norwich. By 1801, there were seven cities in Britain with a population of more than 50,000: London (1.1m), Edinburgh, Glasgow, Birmingham, Manchester, Liverpool and Bristol. By 1851 there were other sizeable towns clustered around the cities, especially in Lancashire and Yorkshire where towns such as Burnley, Huddersfield and Halifax and cities such as Bradford grew up to serve the textile industries. Other twenty-first-century cities such as Sheffield, Newcastle, Sunderland and the major towns and cities of South Wales grew in the later nineteenth century to service the steel, coal and shipbuilding industries. This process of urbanization was complete by the early twentieth century: by 1911, 80 per cent of the population of Britain lived in towns. After 1945 this movement from rural to urban areas levelled off, with subsequent movement between urban areas, from 'inner city' to suburb or 'new town'. More recently, the trend is for more affluent citizens to seek a better lifestyle in small villages, but rather than repopulating the countryside this has only led to more out-migration from working-class 'natives' forced out by rising house prices and lack of employment in 'desirable' areas.

1.6 Transport and communications

Of course workers could move from rural areas to the newly emerging towns of the Industrial Revolution because of the dramatic improvements that had taken place in both the means of transport and the routes by which they could travel. Between the 1730s and the 1780s, the Turnpike Trusts would provide more and better roads, cutting journey times dramatically. For instance, the journey from York to London was reduced from three days to one. This meant that travel could become a leisure pursuit, at least for the moderately wealthy. Eighteenth- and nineteenth-century literature contains many accounts of such journeys, such as Elizabeth Bennett's trip to Derbyshire in *Pride and Prejudice*. The travelogue is an important literary genre of this period, examples being Celia Fiennes' accounts of her travels through England and Scotland in the 1690s, Defoe's *A Tour Thro' the Whole Island of Great Britain* (1724–7), Johnson's *Journey to the Western Isles of Scotland* (1755) and Cobbett's *Rural Rides* (1830). These journeys were made by carriage, but later inventions were to improve the means of transport, particularly in and between urban centres. Trams, first used in 1881, improved access between cities and the suburbs which housed the middle classes. The automobile was invented in 1885, and patented in 1886, but was not generally available until 1908, when the Model T Ford was designed for mass ownership. Production in Britain lagged behind that in the USA and France, but after World War I cars became more affordable, although it was not until the last quarter of the twentieth century that car ownership in Britain became viewed as a necessity. Automotive transport did become the norm, though, with lorries and buses used for cargo and passengers respectively. In Britain, expansion and improvement of the road system continued with trunk roads ('A' roads) built from the 1930s, to be superseded by motorways from 1959. As was the case with scientific advances, the later twentieth century, at least in Britain, saw people questioning the value of this expansion. Concerns about pollution and the destruction of wildlife habitats led to the protests of the 1990s, and, at the time of writing, several British cities are reinstating tram networks and imposing tolls on car users entering the city limits.

Roads were by no means the only transport routes in this period: the canal network was extensive by the 1830s, though mainly in the north-west and midlands of England, where these routes served industry. Coastal shipping had provided transport for passengers as well as cargo since Tudor times. From 1716 to 1914 coal was the most important cargo and the busiest route was from Newcastle to London. Sailing ships of increasing sophistication were developed for use both in battle and exploration throughout the eighteenth and early nineteenth centuries. When steam was introduced, it was as a supplement to sail, but the development of Charles Parsons' steam turbine in 1897 made possible both the battleships of World Wars I and II and the transatlantic liners of the early twentieth century.

Perhaps the most important development in transport, at least for the lower and middle classes, was the railway. In Britain, the first railway line was the Stockton and Darlington Railway, opened in 1825, with its first train drawn by George Stephenson's *Locomotion No. 1*. The rail network in Britain grew dramatically in the 1830s and 1840s and rose steadily in importance, only to decline after World War II, especially after the closures ordered by Lord Beeching in the 1960s. In an age when cars were beyond the means of ordinary people, trains provided comfortable and affordable transport, opening up leisure travel to the middle and lower classes. These people took advantage of more generous holidays to visit coastal resorts such as Blackpool, Southport, Whitley Bay and Scarborough, which could be visited on day trips from the industrial heartlands of Lancashire, Tyneside and Yorkshire.

Experiments with air transport began as early as 1783, when the first successful manned balloon flight was made in France. This led to the development of dirigible airships from 1852, first in France, and later as fighting and passenger craft by Count Ferdinand von Zeppelin from 1900 (the eponymous Zeppelin was to be used with considerable effect in World War I). Meanwhile, in the USA, Wilbur and Orville Wright were developing the aeroplane in which Orville was to make the first successful flight in 1903. Both world wars saw aeroplanes engaged in conflict, but commercial air travel was to remain very much a means of transport for the elite until after World War II, when the development of the jet engine made long-distance travel feasible. By the end of the twentieth century, air travel had become affordable to all but the very poor in Britain, and holidays abroad came to be viewed as the norm.

The effect of all these advances in transport has been to make travel within the British Isles, and later between Britain and other countries, increasingly comfortable and affordable. Travel brings speakers of different dialects and languages together, increasing their awareness of these differences, and opening the way to mutual influence. Eighteenth-century travellers such as Defoe remarked on the dialect of outlandish places such as Northumberland and Cornwall and, as we shall see in Chapter 2, travels further afield brought words into the vocabulary of English from an increasingly wide variety of languages throughout the nineteenth and twentieth centuries.

1.7 Communications

Of course, in the modern age, people do not have to meet face to face in order to communicate with each other and influence each other's language. This period saw advances in the means and media of written and spoken communication which, as the period progressed, were to facilitate interaction on a global scale. All the advances in transport mentioned in the previous section allowed letters, as well as people, to be carried from place to place more easily. However, in Britain, the real revolution in written communication came with the introduction of the Penny Post in 1840. Before this date, 82 million letters a year were sent in Britain, but within 30 years this number had risen to 917 million. This cheap and efficient service, together with the expansion of education in the nineteenth century, led to more people writing English in this period. Most of these letters were written in Standard English, and the nineteenth century saw a proliferation of manuals designed to teach the 'proper' way to write letters. However, as we shall see in Chapter 4, the relatively informal style of personal letters allowed new syntactic structures to be introduced into the written medium, even as grammarians were railing against them.

The Penny Post only facilitated letter-writing within Britain: communication between British speakers of English and their correspondents in the USA and other English-speaking countries still had to be delivered by ships until the introduction of the electric telegraph in 1837. The first transatlantic cable was laid in 1858, and by 1872 most of the world's cities were in contact by telegraph. For the first time rapid communication was possible right across the globe. This communication was, however, written and truncated. The introduction of the telephone in 1876 allowed spoken communication to take place over vast distances, whilst the invention of the phonograph in 1877 allowed speech to be recorded and preserved. For the first time, people could hear the voices of speakers from other parts of Britain, and even from other countries, without having to travel and meet them face to face.

The real revolution in spoken communications came with the invention of radio in 1895 and, in Britain, the establishment of the BBC in 1927. As we shall see in Chapter 7, the BBC's policy of only employing announcers who spoke RP was to secure the position of this superordinate variety of British English, bringing it into most homes as the 'voice of authority'. On the other hand, the introduction of 'talkies' from 1927 and television (demonstrated in 1926, broadcast by the BBC in 1936, but suspended during World War II) brought American voices to the attention of ordinary British people. The first 'talkie' was *The Jazz Singer* and British TV schedules of the 1950s included American westerns and crime series. These media, along with the presence of American troops in Britain during World War II ('overpaid, oversexed and over here'), established American English as an important influence and as an aspirational variety, at least for young people in Britain. Strang (1970: 36–7) presents a guide for American servicemen stationed in Britain during World War II which gives 'translations' of several US-English words and phrases for which British English used different terms. The extent of American influence on British English is shown by the quaintness, to late twentieth/early twenty-first-century readers, of such supposedly 'British' terms as *shocker* for *thriller* and *buttered eggs* for *scrambled eggs*.

1.8   Britain and the British Empire

The prestige of American English towards the end of our period was, of course, due not only to contact between British and American speakers of English, but to the change in the respective positions of these two nations on the world stage. The period between 1700 and 1945 saw the rise and fall of the British Empire, the American War of Independence (or Revolution, depending on which side of the Atlantic you stand), and the rise of the USA as the most powerful nation on earth.

Britain itself did not exist as a political entity until the Act of Union (1707). This Act united England and Scotland, abolishing the Scottish parliament, and sending 16 Scottish peers and 45 MPs to Westminster. When Scottish accents were first heard in this august gathering, they were ridiculed. As we shall see in Chapter 7, guides to 'correct' pronunciation in the eighteenth century were often written by and for Scots, containing lists of 'Scotticisms' to be avoided by those who wished to pass as 'British'. The word 'British' was politically loaded in the eighteenth century, often appearing in the titles of works which advocated a uniform standard of speech and grammar as a unifying force: e.g. *The British Grammar* (Buchanan, 1762) and *British Education; or The Source of the Disorders of Great Britain* (Sheridan, 1756). The Union with Ireland (1801) was to complete the 'British Isles', but this particular Union was to prove much less stable and was eventually dissolved with the partitioning of Ireland in 1920 and the creation of the Irish Free State in the south in 1921.

Although the British colonies in America were lost after the War of Independence (1776) the British Empire began to expand in the late eighteenth century. Indeed, American independence itself led directly to the establishment of British rule in two major English-speaking nations. Ten thousand loyalists fled from the USA to Canada, consolidating British power in that nation, whilst, at the same time, establishing the 'American' basis of the English spoken, at least in the heartlands of Ontario. Meanwhile, the loss of the Virginia plantations as a suitable place for the transportation of criminals came only six years after Captain James Cook's landing at Botany Bay, Australia. In 1788, the first settlement of 750 convicts and 250 free settlers marked the introduction of British rule, and the English language, to Australia. In the nineteenth century, Britain established further colonies in South Africa and New Zealand, and expanded its influence throughout the world, culminating in Queen Victoria being declared Empress of India (1877). By 1914, the British Empire held territories in every continent: Canada in North America; British Guyana in South America; extensive territories in Africa including the Gold Coast (now Ghana), Nigeria, the Sudan and South Africa; India, Burma and Malaya as well as Hong Kong in Asia; and, of course, Australia and New Zealand. In the twentieth century, the colonies settled by British migrants gained a measure of independence as dominions in the Commonwealth (Australia 1901, New Zealand 1907, South Africa 1910). After World War II independence was granted to almost all former colonies, beginning with India (1947), the most recent being Hong Kong, which was returned to China in 1997. The end of our period thus coincides with the end of the British Empire and with the establishment of the Scottish National Party (1934) and Plaid Cymru (1925), perhaps the beginning of the end for Britain itself.

The British Empire established English as the dominant language throughout the world. Where British settlers had been in the majority, in Canada, Australia and New Zealand, distinct national varieties of English emerged. At first these were viewed as inferior to Standard (English) English, but, as in the case of the USA, political independence was followed by linguistic independence, and the publication of national dictionaries for all these varieties. The loss of the Empire did not lead to any decline in the influence of English. By the time nations such as India and Nigeria gained independence, English had long been established as a second language and entrenched as the language of education and government, whilst its continued prestige on the world stage was ensured by the rise of the USA, another English-speaking nation.

1.9 Modern times and Modern English

In this brief historical introduction, I have attempted to demonstrate that the period between 1660 and 1945, covering what historians would call the 'long' eighteenth and nineteenth centuries, but stretching beyond the latter to the end of World War II, can be viewed as a coherent period, at least in British history. Within this period we see the rise of the constitutional monarchy, the British Empire, the Industrial Revolution and the consequent urbanization of society, the scientific thinking of the Enlightenment and universal education. After World War II, Britain, and its place in the world, is changed again: the Empire breaks up, science and 'progress' are viewed with scepticism, and industry declines, leaving us in a post-colonial, post-scientific and post-industrial age, which we might characterize as 'post-modern times'.

Of course the focus of this volume is not on history per se, but on the history of the English language. Although Sweet divided this history into three periods on internal linguistic grounds alone, more recent histories of English have paid much more attention to 'external' factors. What we need to consider here, and in all the chapters that follow, is how the historical events and movements outlined above affected the development of the English language in 'modern times'.

Sweet could only characterize Modern English as the period of lost inflections. If this were all that could be said about the history of Later Modern English, there would be no justification for a volume of this size. However, whilst it might be fair to say that the strictly 'linguistic', i.e. structural, foundations of Modern English had been laid down by 1700, the socio-linguistic foundations were the product of the later modern period. This period sees the rise of RP, the genesis of urban dialects, the corresponding decline of 'traditional' rural dialects, and the growth of separate national varieties of English in the USA, Canada, Australia, New Zealand and South Africa. These developments are the result of the social and political factors discussed above: industrialization, urbanization and mobility forging the urban dialects, plutocracy and social mobility leading to the conditions in which RP could evolve and flourish, and colonization followed by the loss of Empire causing in turn the creation and subsequent separation of the 'extraterritorial' Englishes.

The later modern period, and more specifically the eighteenth century, has often been characterized as the 'Age of Correctness': a period in which the English language goes through what Haugen (1971) would term the *codification* and *acceptance* stages of standardization. Grammarians, lexicographers and elocutionists attempted to formulate and impose rules for 'correct' usage in books which were bought and read especially by the upwardly mobile population of provincial towns and cities. Both these aspiring middle classes, and the flourishing towns that they inhabited, were the product of the historical developments outlined above.

'External' factors can also affect the 'internal' history of the language: whilst the syntactic developments discussed in Chapter 4 and the phonological changes outlined in Chapter 6 can certainly be explained in terms of the internal development of the language, external factors come into play in their diffusion from spoken to written English and from 'vulgar' to 'educated' English respectively. In both cases, education and social mobility are the key factors.

The influence of 'external' historical events on the 'internal' structure of a language is nowhere more transparent than in the lexicon. Interaction between speakers of English and those of other languages, whether through trade, colonization or warfare, brings words from those languages into English, whilst innovations in science and technology create the need for new words, sometimes introducing new morphological patterns into the language. This will be the focus of the next chapter.

2

The vocabulary of Later Modern English

2.1. Introduction

We have seen in Chapter 1 that the later modern period was one in which speakers of English were exposed to a vast number of new experiences. Technological and scientific inventions, trade, exploration and colonization all brought speakers of English into contact with phenomena which had not previously been named in their language. We might expect to see a steady growth in the vocabulary of English throughout this period, as the pace of 'progress' accelerates. However, as Figure 2.1 shows, the progress of lexical innovation in this period is not so straightforward. There appears to be a 'trough' which bottoms out in the middle of the eighteenth century, followed by a steep rise between 1780 and 1840 and a fall in the last 20 years of the nineteenth century. How can this be explained?

The first thing to bear in mind is the source of the data on which Figure 2.1 is based. The numbers of lexical innovations for each decade are taken from the *Chronological English Dictionary* (*CED*), which in turn took its information from the *Shorter Oxford English Dictionary* (*SOED*). The *CED*

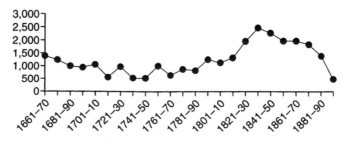

Fig. 2.1   Numbers of first citations in the *SOED*, by decade, 1661–1990

has proved immensely useful to historians of English, as it reorganizes entries in the *SOED* by year of first citation and provides a numerical code to indicate the etymology of each word. For each year, the total number of first citations is given at the end of the table. Figure 2.2 reproduces the *CED* entry for 1749, a year at the bottom of the trough in Figure 2.1. We can see that there are only 38 first citations from this year, of which ten have the code 042 (Latin) and nine have the code 026 (French). The designation *ALD* marks

1749	ACADEMICIAN		N,	026	ALD
	ALKALIZE		VB,	026	
	BANTAM		N,	100	ALD
	BRANCHIOSTEGAL		ADJ	026	
	BUFFER	4	N,	000	ALD
	CARICATURE	2	VB,	026	ALD
	COMBINABLE		ADJ	042	
	DEMI-REP		N,	042	
	DOWD	2	N,	000	
	EBULLIENCE		N,	042	ALD
	ELECTROMETER		N,	042	
	EMPRESSMENT		N,	026	
	ETONIAN		N,	101	
	FROST-BIT		ADJ,	019	
	GENTLEMAN-FARMER		N,	056	
	GOUTIFY		VB,	056	
	HACKNEYED		ADJ	056	ALD
	HAVERSACK		N,	026	ALD
	HURDY-GURDY		N,	000	ALD
	INEFFICIENCY		N,	042	ALD
	IRRETENTIVE		ADJ	056	
	KALON		N,	032	
	LEFT-HANDINESS		N,	019	*
	LEYDEN		N,	101	*
	LOGE		N,	026	
	MINIONETTE	2	ADJ,	026	
	NERVE	2	VB,	042	ALD
	PECULATE		VB,	042	ALD
	PSALMODIC		ADJ	042	
	PYROMETER		N,	032	
	SENSORY	2	ADJ	042	
	SENTIMENTAL		ADJ	056	ALD
	SLACK-ROPE		N,	019	
	SPECTACLE	2	N,	026	
	TOWNLY		ADJ	019	
	TRYGON		N,	042	
	ULLAGE	2	VB,	098	
	WYANDOTTE		N,	004	*
	(38)				

Fig. 2.2 A page from the *CED*

those words which are found in the *Advanced Learner's Dictionary of Current English*. This, together with the designation *GSL* (*General Service List of English Words*) is intended to provide 'an indication of the role or importance of a word in 20th century English' (Finkenstaedt, Leisi and Wolff, 1970: ix). By this criterion, from the words in Figure 2.2, only 12 are in common use today: *academician, bantam, buffer, caricature, ebullience, hackneyed, haversack, hurdy-gurdy, inefficiency, nerve, peculate* and *sentimental*. Other innovations have either fallen out of use or are confined to technical registers. *Branchiostegal* is a zoological term, defined in the *OED* as 'pertaining to the membrane which protects a gill chamber'. *Empressement*, 'animated display of cordiality' seems never to have been naturalized, occurring in italics in its first citation and in quotes in its second (there are only three) whilst *minionette* 'small and pretty', has a single citation from Walpole. These latter two words of French origin are cited from letters, and seem to have been conscious Gallicisms on the part of the authors. This brief examination of the entry for one year has already provided a good deal of information about such lexical innovation as did occur in the mid eighteenth-century 'trough', and we shall consider these points further in Section 2.2. However, the authors of the *CED* themselves admit that their work has limitations, largely due to its being based on the *SOED*. Most importantly for our purposes, they acknowledge that 'the vocabulary of the twentieth century is less systematically represented than that of the preceding periods' (1970: xi). This almost certainly accounts for the steep drop shown in Figure 2.1 from the end of the nineteenth century onwards: since the *SOED* is based on the first edition of the *OED*, it reflects the coverage of the latter, which was, as we shall see in Chapter 3, very much a product of the nineteenth century. In order to examine the nature and extent of lexical innovation in the first half of the twentieth century, I have therefore based Figure 2.5 and the discussion in Section 2.5 on information from the *OED* online (http://www.oed.com).

2.2   Innovation and resistance, 1660–1800

We have already noted that Figure 2.1 shows a 'trough' in the mid-eighteenth century, during which period lexical innovation seems to be minimal. In this section we shall examine the factors which may have led to this slump, as well as the characteristics of such innovations as were recorded from this period. Figure 2.1 shows a downturn in lexical innovation from 1660 to 1750. If we had looked further back in history, we would have seen that this is the continuation of a steady decline from a peak of 3,300 first citations from the last decade of the sixteenth century (see Schäffer, 1980). The late sixteenth and early seventeenth centuries (the years in which Shakespeare was at the height of his powers) are characterized as a period of exuberant lexical innovation, hardly tempered by the criticism of Latinate 'inkhorn' terms. This innovation was to some extent necessary, as English was taking over 'higher' functions which had previously been the domain of Latin (science, religion, medicine, philosophy), and needed a swift and large injection of vocabulary in order to cope. By the end of the seventeenth century, this gap in the vocabulary of English had been filled, and so it is hardly surprising that lexical growth slowed down.

Another factor which may have contributed to this deceleration is the linguistic conservatism of this period. Writers such as Swift and Addison used the new vehicle of periodicals to rail against what they saw as affectation. In the *Tatler*, 26–28 September 1710, Swift produces a fictitious letter designed to exemplify all the 'false refinements' of language to which he objects. He draws attention here to three types of lexical innovation, all equally objectionable in his eyes. Firstly, he mentions the clippings which produced slang words such as *mob, hipps, pozz,* and *rep,* and were guilty of 'overloading' English with 'monosyllables, which are the disgrace of our language'. He seems to blame this spate of lexical innovation on the war (the War of the Spanish Succession 1702–13), which was also the source of equally objectionable polysyllables: *speculations, operations, preliminaries, ambassadors, palisadoes, communications, circumvallations, battalions*: 'as numerous as they are, if they attack us too frequently in our coffee-houses, we shall certainly put them to flight, and cut off their rear'. The third category of 'refinement' mentioned by Swift is that of 'certain words invented by some pretty fellows': *banter, bamboozle, country put* and *kidney* (as in 'others of that kidney'). These are either words of unknown etymology, or involve semantic shift: Swift seems to object to them because they are fashionable, or have their origin in cant. Later in the same article, Swift comments on 'young readers in our churches' who 'in their sermons . . . use all the modern terms of art, *sham, banter, mob, bubble, bully, cutting, shuffling* and *palming*'. Like today's 'trendy vicars', the young readers of Swift's time were attempting to display what would now be termed 'street cred' by their use of slang terms, all of which could be found in the 'cant' dictionaries of the time.

Swift's conservatism is echoed by Addison in the *Spectator* 165, 8 September 1711. Like Swift, Addison uses a letter as a means of satirizing the fashion for adopting French words, and blames the war for this. Addison produces a letter written to his father by a young man serving in the army. The letter contains a number of words of French origin, including *corps, hauteur, Gasconade, Fossé, Chamade,* but *Charte Blanche* and *Gens d'Armes* are marked out as particularly 'alien' by being printed in italics.

The father is particularly perplexed by *Charte Blanche*, and asks advice of the curate, who judges the letter to be 'neither fish, flesh, nor good red herring'. The father concludes from an earlier letter that his son is capable of writing in plain English when he needs money. However, he later sees 'all the prints about three days after filled with the same terms of art, and that Charles only wrote like other men'. Addison here is rather more accurate than Swift in targeting lexical innovations: whilst Swift's *preliminaries* had been used in this military sense by Cromwell in 1656, the first citation of *corps* in the *OED* is from this very article by Addison. The term *carte blanche* is cited first in 1707, and Addison uses it again in 1712: 'I threw her a *Charte Blanche* as our News Papers call it' (*Spectator* 299: 2). Addison first pokes fun at the lexical innovation, then uses it, whilst distancing himself by putting it in italics and adding the phrase 'as our News Papers call it', acknowledging and blaming the role of the press in introducing French loan-words. Then, as now, the press acted as both an agent of change and a medium for critics of change: newspapers brought dispatches from the front and used the language of the enemy either out of necessity, to describe innovations, or in order to provide authenticity.

War also, by necessity, brings innovations in weaponry and military techniques. A review of Le Blond's *Military Engineer* in 1759 concedes that 'the French are so much acknowledged superior to other nations' in siege warfare 'that their technical terms are adopted by all the continent; insomuch that a general can neither give instructions to his officers, nor make a report of military operations to his sovereign, without using a multitude of French words and phrases'. However, the reviewer goes on to complain:

> Why ... should we be so complaisant to the French, as to use their terms of *carcasse, cavalier, chamade, chauffe-trappe, bivoac, chevaux de fries, abatement, enfilade, feu-razant, manoevre* and *coup de main*; when we can say *fire-ball, mount, parley, crow's foot, blocking guard, turnspikes, tree-felling, flanking-fire, grazing-fire, operation* and *bold stroke* (Anon, 1759: 178).

As is so often the case, the English calques never caught on, and it is ironic that the reviewer suggested as an 'English' alternative, the much older French loan *parley* (first citation in the *OED* in 1581). Complaints about French military terms continue throughout the eighteenth century: in the *Critical Review*, April 1789, a reviewer of Edwin Hugill's translation of *The Field Engineer* writes:

> He seems frequently to consider himself as translating the work into French, for so many French words occur, as to render his version unpleasing to an English ear, and inconvenient to a mere English reader ... We acknowledge

that tactics, as a science, exists chiefly in the French language and that many of the words are almost naturalized by adoption; but it surely need not be crowded with those which admit of a translation, as the terms we have mentioned, and many others, which we have marked would do (Anon, 1789: 329–30).

Britain's relationship with France fluctuated throughout the eighteenth century, but the tendency for English to adopt French loans, and of critics to oppose this, continued unabated. In the 1770s, Britain and France were at peace, between the Seven Years' War (1756–63) and France's entry on the American side to the War of Independence (1781). However, objections to French borrowings are as strident as they had been in times of war. In 1771 the *Monthly Review* takes issue with those who use *rôle* for *part* or *penchant* instead of *the passion of love*. The critic goes on to write that 'the offended ear of the unfrenchified reader sickens at the sound' of these words. In 1775, the *Critical Review* comments that 'we are obliged to the French for a great number of terms and phrases, some of them used by men of taste and learning; others only by the *coxcombs* of both sexes, who *affect* to speak à la Mode de Paris'. Words listed here are: *connoisseur, premier, etiquette, vis à vis, tête à tête, fracas, bon mot, billet doux, bagatelle, manoeuvre, je ne sçais quoi, jeu d'esprit, mauvais (honte), éclaircissement, à propos, bon ton, rouge, dishabillé, ragoût, fricassé, tour, route, levée, finesse, foible, caprice, douceur, embonpoint*. What is noticeable about these words, most of which are still in use, is that they have, for the most part, not been anglicized. Phrases such as *je ne sais quoi* and *billet doux* remain conscious Gallicisms. Blount has *je ne scay quoi* in his *Glossographia* in 1656, and it is still marked as 'alien' by the use of quotes or italics today. The writer in the *Critical Review* is not necessarily complaining about innovations so much as the tendency to use French terms in a self-consciously 'fashionable' manner, an affectation of the aspiring classes of English speakers since the Norman Conquest, captured in the current phrase: 'Pretentious? Moi?'

The period between the late seventeenth and early eighteenth centuries is often referred to as the 'Augustan Age', because of the veneration of classical literature during this period: Dryden famously translated his writing into Latin to ensure that it was good English. It is therefore somewhat surprising to find critics of Latinate borrowings in this period. In some cases, religious prejudice seems to play a part: Withers in *Aristarcus* writes: 'I would sooner appeal to modern Rome for the truth of my creed as to antient Rome for the Propriety of my Diction'. Other eighteenth-century objectors echo the 'inkhorn' debate of the sixteenth century in their calls for plain English. In 1798, reviews of Charles Cooke's *History of England* complain of his 'continually deriving assistance from the Latin language' and that he is 'fearful of using terms which are familiar to the reader'. As was so often the case with the critics of inkhornisms, the list of objectionable Latinisms is entirely made up of words that have since found a niche in the English language: *anticipative, nudity, quadrupeds, reciprocation, incipient, insurrection, immolation, Hibernian, pleb[e]ian, senatorial*. In fact, the only word in this list that was new in 1798 is *senatorial*, first cited in the *OED* from Cowper's translation of the *Iliad* (1791). The reviewers here are perhaps objecting to Cooke's lexical choice rather than innovation per se. As we shall see in Chapter 3, Dr Johnson was an important conservative influence in the mid-eighteenth century, admitting to his *Dictionary* only such foreign words as he deemed worthy of citizenship, yet even he was criticized for his use of Latinisms. The *Critical Review* of 1795 complains that 'instead of adding to the improvement of style in modern times' Johnson had 'professed to delight in cloathing a common sentiment in the splendour of words, and in building his tome on an inflated diction'. Here again, the point made is that 'splendid' words, usually of Latin origin, obscure the sense of writing in English, a point still being made today by the Plain English campaign.

This conservatism on the part of eighteenth-century writers may go some way towards explaining the relatively small number of lexical innovations in the period, but the very fact that they could find objectionable words proves that innovation occurred. Figure 2.1 shows that the 'trough' in lexical innovation bottoms out between 1741 and 1760, but even within this 20-year period there are relatively productive years, usually coinciding with major publications. Figure 2.3 shows the number of lexical innovations per year between 1741 and 1760. What is evident

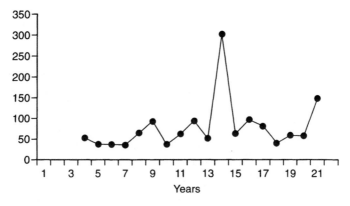

Fig. 2.3   Lexical innovation by year, 1741–1760

from Figure 2.3 is that one year in this 'trough' bucks the trend: 298 words have their first citations in 1753, accounting for 19 per cent of the innovations in the entire 20-year period. This 'blip' can be explained by the fact that the supplement to Chambers' *Cyclopaedia* was published in this year. Of these 298 words, 135 are marked in the *CED* as of Latin origin and 36 of Greek origin, accounting for 45 per cent and 11 per cent of the total respectively. The words cited from Chambers are almost all of a scientific nature, reflecting the interest in botany, zoology and medicine in this scientific age. Examples are *adarticulation, aeronautics, azalea, ballistics, hydrangea, primula, sphagnum* and *trifoliate* from Latin (although *aeronautics, azalea, ballistics, hydrangea* and *sphagnum* themselves derive from Greek roots) and *anthropomorphism, eczema, mnemonic* and *urology* from Greek. This large-scale importation of scientific vocabulary from the learned languages is, as we shall see in Section 2.3, more typical of the nineteenth century. Such innovations were acceptable even in this more conservative age, because of the typically eighteenth-century belief that everything in nature must have a name: words which filled gaps in the vocabulary and which added to the clarity of nomenclature were welcomed. Many of the French words first cited in 1753 are likewise scientific: *aerostatics* and *ballon* reflect French supremacy in *aeronautics* in these early years of experiments with air travel by balloon, whilst *anticatharral* and *cellular*, classified as French by the *CED*, probably belong with the Latin scientific words. A few more fashionable words are brought in by men of letters: *soubrette* (a serving maid) and *vis-à-vis* (a carriage in which passengers sit facing each other) are cited from Walpole, who was particularly innovative in his choice of vocabulary, creating nonce-forms such as *gloomth* and *greenth* (by analogy with *breadth*), also in 1753. Other tendencies in the innovations introduced by Chambers, which likewise foreshadow trends of the nineteenth century, are the scattering of words from 'exotic' languages to describe the findings of explorers and plant hunters, and the appearance of eponyms which name the object after its discoverer or inventor. Examples of the former are *jacaranda* and *jacare* (an alligator), both from Tupi, whilst the eponyms include *camellia* (named after the Moravian Jesuit botanist Josef Kamell) and *fuchsia* (from the German botanist Fuchs).

2.3   Invention and innovation, 1800–1900

We saw in Figure 2.1 that the mid-eighteenth century trough was followed by a sharp increase in lexical innovation, reaching a peak in the mid-nineteenth century, between 1831 and 1850. From these two decades, the *CED* lists 2,481 first citations between 1831 and 1840, and 2,291 between 1841 and 1850. This compares favourably with the two decades in which lexical innovation reached its highest peak according to these statistics: 1591–1600 (3,270 first citations) and 1601–10 (2,710 first citations). The figures from the early modern period have been called into question by Schäfer (1980) and Mackie (1936). Both these authors point out that Shakespeare's works (most of which were written between 1590 and 1610) are over-represented in the *OED*, and that several innovations attributed to Shakespeare can be pre-dated. For instance, *Uncomfortable*, listed under 1592 in the *CED*, and attributed to Shakespeare's *Romeo and Juliet*, is, according to Mackie, found in Walton's translation of Boethius (1410). However, recent work on the third edition of the *OED* has revealed far more 'new' sixteenth-century first citations and antedatings within the sixteenth century than items which can no longer be given sixteenth-century first citations due to ante-dating (Durkin 2002).

As we noted in Section 2.1, the apparent decline in lexical innovation towards the end of the nineteenth century is entirely due to the fact that the *OED* was being composed during this period. The compilers of the *OED* were aware of this neglect of contemporary material, and produced the 1927 *Supplement* to rectify this. However, not all of the words in the *Supplement* are found in the *CED*. To test this, I have taken 12 words at random from the B section of the *Supplement* and looked for them in the *CED* under the year of their first citation. The words are (year of first citation in brackets): *bouton* (1851), *beige* (1858), *bodagh* (1865), *berghaan* (1867), *bauxite* (1872), *Bundesrat* (1879), *batik* (1880), *boongary* (1889), *bahai, bola* (both 1892), *bel canto* and *briquettage* (both 1908). Of these, only *beige* and *bauxite* appear in the *CED*. Whilst such a haphazard sample cannot be seen as in any way statistically significant, two out of 12, or 17 per cent, is a very small proportion. Such under-representation of lexical innovation from the later nineteenth and early twentieth centuries would certainly explain the sharp down-turn shown in Figure 2.1.

If we look at comments on language in the nineteenth century, we find a range of opinions remarkably similar to those expressed during the 'inkhorn' controversy of the late sixteenth/early seventeenth centuries. On the one hand, there were complaints about the number of new words coined from Latin and Greek. Richard Grant White writes:

> In no way is our language more wronged than by a weak readiness with which many of those who, having neither a hearty love nor a ready mastery of it, or lacking both, fly readily to the Latin tongue or to the Greek for help in naming

a new thought or thing, or the partial concealment of an old one . . . By doing
so they help to deface the characteristic traits of our mother tongue, and to
mar and stunt its kindly growth (1872: 22, cited in Bailey, 1996: 141–2).

Others objected to the profusion of technical and scientific vocabulary,
again mainly from Greek and Latin sources. R. Chenevix Trench wrote
(1860: 57–8) that these were 'not, for the most part, except by an abuse of
language, words at all, but signs: having been deliberately invented as the
nomenclature and, so to speak, the algebraic notation of some special art
or science'. Trench was referring here to the tendency, from at least the
time of Linnaeus (1707–78), to use words or morphemes from the
classical languages as building blocks in scientific terminology. This
provides an international scientific vocabulary, and the analogy with
algebra is just, since the individual elements do represent stable values to
an extent that is not normally the case in everyday vocabulary. To the
non-specialist, though, many of these words might as well be algebraic
formulae. To take a twenty-first-century example at random, I picked up a
tube of antiseptic cream from my bathroom. This contains *polyoxyethylene stearyl ethers* as well as the colours E124 and E110. To me, and, I
suspect, to most readers, the words modifying *ethers* and the European
numeric codes for artificial colourings ('E-numbers') are equally obscure,
but a pharmacist would know exactly what each element represents and
could use morphemes such as *poly-* and *oxy-* to create names for newly
discovered chemicals. Indeed, these individual elements may be familiar to
educated laypersons: some readers may once have taught or studied at a
polytechnic (first cited 1805), or favour the *polygenetic* (1861) explanation of the origin of language, and so guess that that there is more than
one of something in my antiseptic cream. They could not live without
oxygen (1790) and so would probably guess that the *oxy-* element relates
to this, and may even know that *ethyl* (1840) is the base of alcohol, and
that *ether* (1757) was an early form of anaesthetic. All this might lead
them to the conclusion that *polyoxyethylene stearyl ethers* constitute the
'local anaesthetic' promised on the front of the tube. It is worth noting
that, whilst *polyoxyethylene stearyl ethers* might well be an invention of
the late twentieth century, all the elements in this phrase were first cited in
the eighteenth and nineteenth centuries. The *OED* has *oxy-* as a head-
word, and tells us that 'the *oxy-*, or rather *hydroxy-* organic compounds
are unlimited in number'. It gives a sample of these compounds with first
citations from the nineteenth century, including this from *Nature*: 'By the
action of boiling 60 per cent nitric acid, cellulose is converted into an
amorphous substance $C_{12}H_{26}O_{16}$, *oxycellulose*' (1882, XXVII: 118.2).

What is notable here is that the writer gives the chemical code before the newly coined word: the two are equivalent.

Trench was perhaps justified in his view that such neo-classical compounds did nothing to augment the vocabulary of most speakers of English. Indeed, some critics were concerned that the over-use of words coined from the classical languages would prove a barrier to those without a classical education, i.e. the lower classes. William Barnes, the Dorset poet who was a staunch advocate of dialect, complained that 'the Latinish and Greekish wording is a hindrance to the teaching of the homely poor, or at least the landfolk' (1878: 88), in language which echoes the 'purist' side in the inkhorn debate. However, just as in the sixteenth and seventeenth centuries, whilst some, such as Alford (1870), deplored the dilution of the 'fine manly Saxon', others took nationalistic pride in the augmentation of the vocabulary. Charles Mackay was of this opinion:

> The English-speaking people of the nineteenth century, whether they live at home in the British Isles, emigrate to America, Australia, New Zealand, or the Cape, or are the descendants of Englishmen, Scotchmen, and Irishmen who have emigrated a hundred or two hundred years ago, are continually making additions to their admirable mother tongue. The English Language is endowed with a higher vitality than any other now spoken on the globe, and begs, borrows, steals, and assimilates words wherever it can find them without any other rule of accretion than that the new word shall either express a new idea or render an old one more tersely and completely than before (1867: 399, cited in Bailey, 1996: 161).

The imperialist overtones of Mackay's writing are very obvious in the post-colonial age: English in the nineteenth century could borrow, steal and assimilate words, just as British archaeologists felt justified in doing to the treasures of Greece or Egypt, and the Empire wished to assimilate peoples. The same link between the superiority of the English language and its speakers was made by Richard Carew in 1595. Here, he plays on national stereotypes to illustrate *The Excellency of the English Tongue*:

> I com nowe to the last and sweetest point of the sweetnes of our tongue, which shall appeare the more plainelye, yf . . . wee match it with our neighboures. The Italyan is pleasante but without synewes, as to stillye fleeting water, the French delicate, but ouer nice as a woman scarce daring to open her lipps for feare of marring her countenance, the Spanish maiesticall, but fullsome, runninge to muche on the .O. and terrible like the deuill in a playe, the Dutch manlike, but withall very harshe, as one ready at euery worde to picke a

quarrell. Now we in borrowing from them geue the strength of Consonantes to the Italyan, the fulle sounde of wordes to the French, and ye mollifieinge of more vowells to the Dutch, and soe (like bees) gather the honye of their good properties and leaue the dreggs to themselues (cited in Görlach, 1991: 244).

Carew was writing in the time of Elizabeth I, Mackay in that of Victoria: in both cases, confidence in the language matches the imperial ambitions of the nation and its sovereign.

Closer examination of the sources of lexical innovation in the nineteenth century reveals that both White and Mackay were to a certain extent justified in their opinions. Figure 2.4 shows the etymological sources of the 350 words listed in the *CED* as first cited in 1835, a year which I have chosen as falling within the 'peak' shown in Figure 2.1.

White's view that English speakers tended to 'fly readily to the Latin tongue or to the Greek' is to a certain extent borne out here by the predominance of those two classical languages, which taken together account for more than two-thirds of the words cited for this year in the *CED*. Of the 155 words with Latin etymologies, many are technical, having the 'algebraic' qualities complained of by Trench. Examples of these are: *bicrenate, brachiate* and *capilliform* – all botanical terms unknown to non-specialists. However, others, such as *conjunctivitis, myelitis* and *synovitis* are medical terms, which have become more familiar to laypeople. Indeed, the very formulaic nature of these words has led to the proliferation of the suffix *-itis*. According to Bailey, 'early in the century, medical doctors

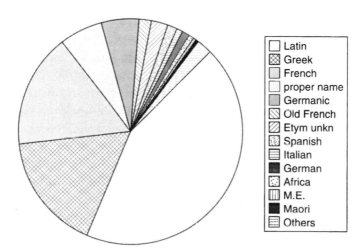

Fig. 2.4 Source of 350 words first recorded in 1835 (*CED*)

were especially active in naming inflammations of various organs' (1996: 140). Other Latin-derived words first cited in 1835 are less technical, examples being, *abnormal* (replacing French *anormal*), *intensifier, gradualism, paraffin* and *revolver.*

Fifty-seven of the 350 words listed under 1835 in the *CED* are of (ancient) Greek origin. Whilst Greek had been recognized as a language of learning for centuries, it was not until the nineteenth century that large numbers of neologisms were formed from etymologically Greek words and elements. Indeed, Bailey (1996: 144) points out that 70 per cent of the Greek words in the 80,000-word core vocabulary of English appeared after 1800. As was the case with the Latin-derived words, those from Greek tend to have technical and/or scientific referents, and some are obscure to laypeople. Examples of these are the botanical terms *campylotropous* and *cyclosis.* Others, such as *acne* (which started out as a misspelling of *acme*), *creosote, eclecticism, ideograph, phonograph* and *telephone* have become much more commonly used, and the last two in particular illustrate the tendency for elements of Greek (as well as Latin) to be used as 'building blocks' in the creation of neo-classical compounds whose referents did not exist in classical times.

French has been a major source of lexical innovation in English at all times since the Norman Conquest, and the nineteenth century is no exception. Fifty-eight words of French origin are listed under 1835 in the *CED*, making the role of French very slightly greater than that of Greek. However, the referential nature of the words borrowed from French is different to that of those modelled on Greek elements. Many of the words of French origin come from the field of fashion, examples being *lingerie, négligé, organdie* and *peignoir.* All of these were recorded in the *Court Magazine* of 1835, clearly the *Hello* magazine of the Victorian era. Other French loans are in the semantic fields of politics and philosophy (*conservatism, guillotinade, individualism*) medicine (*antibilious*), zoology (*campagnol* – 'a short-tailed field mouse'), and chemistry (*methylate*). In some of these latter cases, as Görlach points out, although the immediate source of the word is French, the same process of neo-classical formation has clearly gone into the coining of the French term, as was the case with *myelitis* and *ideograph* discussed above. Görlach goes so far as to suggest that the 'etymological classification used' by the *CED* 'leads to grievous misinterpretations' and an over-representation of the contribution of French to lexical innovation in nineteenth-century English (1999: 111). Although French was, then as now, the most widely taught foreign language in Britain, there was in the nineteenth century, as there had been in the eighteenth, criticism of the excessive use of French loans for fashion's sake.

G. F. Graham, for instance, writes disparagingly of the 'French words and forms which would-be fashionable people so delight in' (1869, quoted in Crowley, 1991: 164). Thomas Martin goes so far as to decry the teaching of French literature:

> Will not the Englishman stagger with amazement when he finds his countrymen recommending that language which has wrought the work of desolation in almost every European nation, and which has recently threatened to overthrow our own *a second time*? (1824: 276, emphasis in the original).

Most of the words of Latin and Greek origin and some of the French loans were created to name new inventions or discoveries in this 'wonderful century'. The desire to commemorate or honour the inventor or discoverer often led to the creation of eponyms – words formed from proper names, a method of word-formation which becomes prominent in the nineteenth century. Examples from the *CED's* list for 1835 include *bromlite, lanarkite, leadhillite, proustite, smithsonite, stromeyerite, troostite, uralite* and *voltzite*. These all refer to minerals which were named after either the area in which the mineral was found (Bromley Hill in Lanarkshire, the Lead Hills, the Urals) or the discoverer (Proust, Smithson, Stromeyer, Troost, Voltz). These words were all coined to the same formula of personal name + *-ite*, which was to become the standard method of naming minerals in the new science of geology. Bailey notes:

> The names of newly discovered or freshly classified natural objects, particularly minerals and fossils, gave great productivity to the suffix *-ite*. Murray described it as having produced a 'vast number of modern names in which *-ite* is added to an element expressing colour, structure, physical characteristics or affinities, or to the name of a locality, discoverer, mineralologist, distinguished scientist, or other person whom the discoverer may have desired to commemorate' (1996: 146–7, citing *OED*, volume V, 1901, pp. 520–1, under *-ite*).

Other eponyms cited in 1835 include *jacquard* and *mackintosh*, both words from the field of fashion, but here perhaps demonstrating the increasing importance of commerce and advertising in nineteenth-century Britain.

Words derived from the classical languages, French and eponyms together account for the vast majority of first citations recorded for the year 1835 in the *CED*. The only other category of any size is that which the *CED* designates as 'Germanic'. This label is somewhat misleading, for the words in this category are not introductions from Germanic languages, but words whose base morpheme is of 'Germanic' (usually English or Common Germanic) origin, from which a new word has been created either by compounding or derivation. (The same could be said for the *CED*'s categories of 'Old French' and 'Middle English': clearly whole words are not introduced into English from these sources in 1835!) The 17 words of this category recorded in 1835 include the compounds *all-fired, dapple-bay, free church, god-fearing, hole-and-corner, runway, side-track, snow line, underclothing* and *underfed*, and the derived forms *disenshroud, dribbler, stepper* and *stumpage*. Since compounding and derivation have existed as means of lexical innovation throughout the history of English, it is not surprising to see an eclectic mixture of words from various semantic fields here. *Runway* here is used in the sense of 'the customary track of an animal', not, of course, in the later aeronautical sense.

Whilst there are no other major sources of lexical innovation represented in the *CED*'s list of first citations for 1835, the remainder of the chart in Figure 2.4 represents words from a wide variety of languages, no single one of which is a major source. Some of these are European languages which have been minor sources of innovation for centuries, whilst the presence of other, more 'exotic' languages testifies to the widening experience of English speakers as a result of exploration and colonization. Spanish and Italian each contribute four words to this list: *cubica, donnish, lariat* and *silo* from the former and *basset-horn, vistaed, lavic* and *phantasmascope* from the latter. From this list, *lavic* and *phantasmascope* are based on Italian and Greek roots respectively which were already established in English, *donnish* and *vistaed* were created by adding English suffixes to the established loans *don* and *vista*, and *basset-horn* is a compound with an English second element, so only *cubica* and *lariat* would have appeared 'foreign'. Much more exotic to nineteenth-century readers would be the three words imported from Maori: *kiwi, rata* and *tui*. Although Cook had encountered Maori as early as 1769, extensive British settlement in New Zealand did not take place until the nineteenth century, and the Treaty of Waitangi was signed by a group of Maori chiefs and representatives of the British government in 1840. The presence of these three words (including *kiwi*, here referring to a bird but eventually to become a nickname for New Zealanders) is a testimony to growing British interest in New Zealand.

The category 'others' in Figure 2.4 includes a geographically wide range of languages, each represented by a single word in the *CED*'s list for 1835. Apart from the single Irish word *brogan*, these are recorded in English as a result of colonization and exploration. All are the names of 'exotic' flora or fauna, 'native' tribes or artefacts. Following the *SOED*, the *CED* here refers to 'native languages of Africa', etc., a phrase which has a distinctly imperialist ring to it today, but I have identified the donor language more precisely wherever possible. From Africa we have *chacma* (from Nama) and *kroo* (the ethnonym of a Liberian tribe); from India *fulwa*, the Bengali word for the butter tree; from South America (Tupi/Guarani) *nandu*; and from the Native American language Lakhota *tepee*.

This examination of the *CED*'s list of first citations for 1835 thus provides a snapshot of trends in lexical innovation in the early to mid-nineteenth century. The vast majority of these words are formed from Latin or Greek roots to provide labels for scientific innovations, so that White's accusation that speakers of English 'fly readily to the Latin tongue or to the Greek for help in naming a new thought or thing' (quoted above, p. 22), seems justified. The large number of eponyms, like the words derived from classical languages, reflect the extent of scientific invention and discovery in this period, whilst the wide range of languages each contributing small numbers of words signal the effect of exploration and colonization on the language.

2.4   Wars and rumours of wars: 1900–1945

Whilst the nineteenth century in Britain can be seen as an age of invention, exploration and colonization, all of which are reflected in the lexical innovations of the period, the first half of the twentieth century in British history is dominated by the two world wars, in 1914–18 and 1939–45. Detailed examination of the extent to which the events and experiences of this period are reflected in the lexicon of British English has not been possible until very recently. The release of the online edition of the *OED* has made it possible to find quickly the number of first citations in any given year and, since this edition is based on the second edition of the *OED* and is continually being updated, it provides a much fuller picture of lexical innovation in more recent times than the *SOED* or the *CED* could. We saw in Figure 2.1 that the *CED* appeared to show a steep decline in lexical innovation towards the end of the nineteenth century, with only 522 first citations recorded in the decade 1891–1900. However, it was acknowledged that this was an artifice of the *CED*'s ultimate dependence on the first edition of the *OED*, which was not able to include as much information from this period as from the earlier part of the century. Figure 2.5 confirms that the 'trough' in Figure 2.1 is misleading. The *OED* online includes no fewer than 571 first citations for the year 1900 alone, more than the total for 1891–1900 in the *CED*.

Figure 2.5 shows the number of first citations recorded in the *OED* online for each year between 1900 and 1952. The upper line represents the total number of first citations recorded, whilst the lower line shows the number of

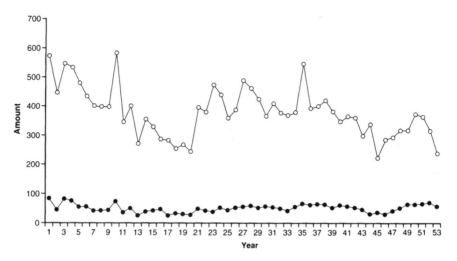

Fig. 2.5   First attestations, 1900–1952

these which were first recorded in the second edition of the *OED*. What is apparent here is that lexical innovation continues at a healthy level throughout the first half of the twentieth century, with no fewer than 200 first citations in any single year. However, there are two obvious 'peaks' in 1909 (581) and 1934 (546), and four 'troughs' in which the total dips below 300 per year, in 1912, 1915–19 inclusive, 1944–6 inclusive, and the last year represented here, 1952. The 'peaks' can be explained by the publication in each of those years of a major dictionary from which the *OED* has in turn taken citations. In each of these years an edition of *Webster's International Dictionary of the English Language* was published, that in 1909 edited by W.T. Harris and F.S. Allen, and the edition published in 1934 edited by W.A. Neilson, T.A. Knott and F.W. Carhart. Furthermore, in 1909, a supplement to the *Century Dictionary and Cyclopedia* (originally published in 1889–91) appeared. The supplement to the *Century Dictionary and Cyclopedia* provided 102 of the first citations for 1909, whilst Webster's dictionary yielded 61. If we subtract these 103 citations from the total for 1909, we would be left with 423, a figure much closer to, though still higher than, those of the preceding years. This indicates that the 'peaks' are rather artificial, since these words must have been attested elsewhere earlier than 1909, in order to be recorded in Webster's or the supplement to the *Century Dictionary and Cyclopedia*. These two dictionaries merely provided convenient datable sources of lexical innovations, for which antedatings will no doubt be provided in due course. However, the early twentieth century on the whole, like the late nineteenth century, was a period in which new fields of science and scholarship provided new terminologies. Freud's *Interpretation of Dreams* had been published in 1899, but 1909 saw the introduction of ten psychological terms from William James's *Pluralistic Universe*, including *conceptualize, abstractionsism* and *Bergsonian*, as well as *addict*, cited from Jennings' *Morphia Habit*. Our other 'peak' year, 1934, saw the introduction of a number of linguistic terms, including *pidginise* (from Priebsch and Collinson, *The German Language*), and *morphophonemic* (Morris Swadesh, in *Language*, volume 10). There are four entries in the *OED* online based on the stem *morphophon-* alone, and 13 linguistic terms in all first cited in 1934.

The 'troughs' are more difficult to explain: two of these periods, 1915–19 and 1944–45, coincide with the First and Second World Wars respectively. Although it is possible that publication of major literary works and dictionaries might suffer in wartime, in the twentieth century we might expect the activities of the press to provide a conduit for military terminology, just as the 'prints' in the eighteenth century brought the French terms satirized by Addison (see Section 2.2 above). Innovations in military strategy, the technology of warfare and servicemen's slang would all create a need for new words, whilst the languages of the allies and adversaries might be expected to provide loan-words. Indeed, works such as Zandvoort (1957) give the impression that the war years were times of lexical expansion in English. Zandvoort stresses that his work is 'not a glossary of new words or an annotated vocabulary, but a record of linguistic usage during a period when men's thoughts were constantly occupied by the war and its consequences' (1957: v). However, the methodology used here implies that the objective was, indeed, a search for wartime neologisms. Zandvoort's assistants scrutinized copies of weekly and daily newspapers printed between 1938 and 1948 for likely neologisms, which were then 'checked against the latest dictionaries' (Zandvoort, 1957). This process yielded a list of words and phrases, all in semantic fields concerned with the war, stretching to 254 pages with an average of five words per page, or approximately 1,270 entries. The OED online has 3,270 first citations from this period, but the extra 2,000 could well be explained by there being neologisms in fields not concerned with war. That neologisms were introduced during the war years is thus not in doubt, but it is clear from Figure 2.5 that the war did not stimulate higher levels of lexical innovation. Amongst Zandvoort's entries are words which are now only used in historical reference, such as *Bevin boy* (1944) and *denazification* (1945); others whose primary senses have shifted, notably *bikini* (here in the sense 'any very large explosion' (1947); and others which have become 'civilianized' and thus more widespread in usage, such as *cash and carry* (cited from 1939 in Zandvoort, but as early as 1917 in this sense in the *OED* online). What is notable about Zandvoort's list is that very few of the words are loan-words, supporting Görlach's assertion that, from the end of the nineteenth century 'the English Language, which had imported foreign words in huge quantities . . . now started to export words' (1999: 118). Apart from a few German loans such as *blitz* (shortened from *Blitzkrieg*), *panzer, stalag* and *stuka*, the wartime neologisms listed by Zandvoort are all native formations. These include compounds such as *black market, civil defence, clothing book, jet-plane, scorched earth policy*; derivations such as *bizone, compartmentalise, decontaminate*; or acronyms such as *ANZAC, NAAFI, SNAFU* (delicately glossed as 'situation normal, all fouled up') and *FLAK*. The last of these does, however, show the influence of German, as it is an acronym of *Fliegerabwehrkanone* (my emphasis). Indeed, the influence of both the 'enemy' and 'allied' languages on the vocabulary of English is slight during the war years (unless we count internal borrowing from US into British English). In the *OED* online, 127 words from German are first cited in the years 1914–18, and 142 between 1939 and 1945. Far from representing an increase in the influence of German on English, they actually show a slight decrease. In the period from 1909 to 1913, 176 first citations from German are recorded in the *OED* online, and the numbers decline further in the equivalent post-war period 1919–23, with 105 first citations recorded. Of the loans from German first cited during the war years, many are in the scientific and technical fields from which German loan-words were taken in the late nineteenth century. Examples are *polymery* (1914), *radon* (1918), *ergocryptine* (1944), and *Creutzfeldt–Jakob disease* (1939). The languages of the other 'enemy' nations provide very small numbers of loan-words during the war years of 1939–45. There are 17 Italian words first cited during these years, but none of them are military terms, examples being *pizzeria* (1943) and *espresso* (1945). Since a number of Italian prisoners of war were stationed in Britain, these loan-words could perhaps have been introduced by them, although friendly relations between the USA and Italy after the latter's surrender, and the American administration of Italy during the period when war against Germany was still continuing, may account for their presence here too. Japanese provides 15 terms in all from 1939–45, no less than nine of which relate to martial arts, e.g. *mawashi* 'a sumo wrestler's loincloth' (1940) and *dan* 'a grade in judo' (1941). (Words which we associate with Japanese involvement in World War II were in some cases introduced earlier: for instance *kamikaze* is given a first citation for 1896, when it was used to refer to the 'mystic wind' which kept the Mongols from the Sea of Japan in 1281.) These loans are not the kind we would expect when the speakers of the 'donor' and 'receiving' languages are at war: they suggest the same kind of interest in Japanese culture aroused by the orientalism of the nineteenth century or the new-ageism of the late twentieth. The only 'military' term borrowed from Japanese during the war years is *Tojo*, an Allied slang term for a Japanese soldier. Apart from French, the languages of the allies likewise provide few loan-words during the war years. There are 19 words from Russian, but only two of these, *MiG* and *Molotov* (cocktail) are military terms and both of them are eponyms, the others being from a range of semantic fields, such as the the mineral name *kurnakovite* (1940). French, of course, continues to be an important source of loan-words throughout the first half of the twentieth century, and the war years are no exception. Between 1914 and 1918, 121 French words are cited for the first time. These include *Boche, camouflage* and *poilu*, 'a regular French soldier, literally: hairy one', but most of these terms are non-military: for instance, *surrealist, musicologist* and *monetarist*. Between 1939 and 1945 there are 93 first citations from French. Again, not many of these are military terms, *maquisard*, 'member of the French Resistance', being a rare example. Mostly they are words such as *macroeconomic* (1939) which are more like the neo-classical compounds of the nineteenth century, together with a few more overtly French words such as *microfiche* (1943); no single semantic field comes close to dominating among French loans from World War II.

From the above discussion we can conclude that war does not stimulate lexical innovation: although the loan-words from allies and enemies alike are noticed during and after these conflicts, they are not great in number. There is also, throughout the twentieth century, a resurgence of lexical innovation from native English sources, whether these be British or American. Examples of such innovations from 1900 to 1945 often seem surprisingly modern. They include compounds such as *haywire* (1905), *egghead* (1907), *internal audit* (1915) and *checkup* (1921); blends such as *chunnel* (1928); eponyms such as *Cook's tour* (surprisingly late in first being attested in 1906, Thomas Cook having died in 1892); derivations such as *do-gooder* (1927) and *gritter* (1940); and invented forms such as *boffin* (1941), *gismo* (1943) and *hobbit* (1937).

This chapter has attempted to identify trends in lexical innovation between 1700 and 1945, and to explain these in terms of what we might term 'external' influences on the language, such as technical innovations, fashions and relations between speakers of English and other languages, and, indeed, between speakers of different varieties of English. In attempting to identify 'peaks' and 'troughs' in innovation, I have used statistics taken from the *CED* and the *OED* online. The latter provides us with a much fuller and more reliable picture than does the former, but I have deliberately based Figures 2.2 and 2.3 on the *CED*, so that readers with access to the *OED* online can carry out their own research using that facility and therefore discover the differences between the two resources for themselves. What must be borne in mind is that the *OED* online is a 'work in progress', and figures collated at any one point in time may well be different from those taken at a later date. As Philip Durkin (chief etymologist with the *OED*) states:

> The dates provided by historical dictionaries are the best that have been arrived at after a process of research (in the cases of both the first edition of the *OED* and *OED3*, two of the biggest research projects that have ever been undertaken in the humanities); however ... the dates given will often be susceptible to substantial revision when further systematic research is undertaken. Caution is therefore advisable when making use of such data for statistical purposes, combined if possible with an awareness of what data is available to the historical lexicographer for each period (2002: 75).

In other words, any account of lexical innovation in a given historical period can only be as good as the historical dictionaries from which information is taken. In the next chapter, we will look at the dictionaries themselves, and the development of lexicography in the later modern period.

3

Recording and regulating the lexicon: dictionaries from Dr Johnson to the *Oxford English Dictionary*

3.1 Dictionaries before Johnson

There is a popular misconception, propagated by ill-informed websites, that the first dictionary of English was Johnson's *Dictionary of the English Language* (1755). In fact, the existence of the seminal (and still unsurpassed) work on early English lexicography, Starnes and Noyes' *The English Language from Cawdrey to Johnson* (1946, new edition 1991), proves that this is not the case. The earliest English dictionary still extant is Robert Cawdrey's (1604) *A Table Alphabetical*, but, as Osselton's (1986) discovery of an earlier manuscript dictionary proves, there may well have been earlier attempts, and dictionaries of English were being planned as early as the last quarter of the sixteenth century.

Whilst there was an established tradition of bilingual dictionaries in the sixteenth century, especially Latin–English and English–Latin, the need for a monolingual English dictionary arose towards the end of this century, when, as we have seen in Section 2.1, there was a large influx of learned vocabulary, mostly adapted from Latin. These 'hard words' became the focus of the 'inkhorn controversy', a hotly contested debate between those who viewed the Latinate words as either a necessity or an ornament, and those who viewed the use of such terms as affected and/or obscurantist (see Jones, 1953; Blank, 1996 for further discussion of this). Whilst this debate produced much invective, and is the source of topical humour in works such as *Love's Labours Lost*, pedagogical authors sought to make these words accessible by producing glossaries or dictionaries. Amongst those actively considering a dictionary were a trio better known to posterity as orthoepists or spelling reformers. William Bullokar, who produced The *Booke at Large* (1580) on spelling, and the *Bref Grammar for English* (1586), tells us in the latter that he intends to produce a third volume:

> Your good acceptance of thaez painz
> wil cause me to set hand
> too perfecting a Dictionary
> the third strength of this band.
> (1586: a 4 verso)

However, Bullokar died before compiling a dictionary and without fulfilling this promise. Richard Mulcaster is known for his *Elementarie* (1582), which, like Bullokar's *Booke at Large* is mainly devoted to spelling reform. However, he writes:

> It were a thing verie praiseworthie in my opinion and no lesse profitable then praise worthie, if some one well learned and as laborious a man, wold gather all the words which we vse in our *English* tung, whether naturall or incorporate, out of all professions as well learned as not, into one Dictionarie, and beside the right writing, which is incident to the Alphabete, wold open vnto vs therein, both the natural force, and the proper vse ([1582] 1925: 274).

This is followed by a list of 8,000 words, without definitions. Another orthoepist, Edmund Coote, likewise provides a list of 'hard words' in his *English Schoole Maister* (1596), but in this case, simple definitions are provided in what is, in fact, a brief dictionary. This list, together with the 1596 edition of Thomas's Latin–English dictionary, was to provide much of the material for Cawdrey's *A Table Alphabetical* (1604), the earliest extant dictionary of English. Starnes and Noyes (1991: 17) provide a table comparing entries from these three works, which clearly indicates Cawdrey's dependence on the two earlier works. For examples *castigation* is defined by Coote as 'chastisement', and Thomas glosses *castigatio* as 'a chastising, correcting or blaming'. Cawdrey's entry for *castigation* appears to be an amalgamation of the two: 'chastisement, blaming, correction'. This dependency on earlier works is typical of the English dictionaries of the seventeenth and early eighteenth centuries. As Starnes and Noyes point out, 'in this early period lexicography progressed by plagiarism' and 'the best lexicographer was often the most discriminating plagiarist' (1946: 183). Cawdrey's *Table Alphabetical* is also typical of these early attempts at English lexicography in its emphasis on 'hard words'. As we shall see throughout this chapter, every dictionary is a product of its time, reflecting the linguistic ideas of its author and responding to the needs of its potential readers. In the early seventeenth century, the pressing need was for a guide to the new Latinate vocabulary of literary English, especially for those who had not learned Latin in school. The title page of *A Table Alphabetical* announces that this is precisely the market at which it is aimed. It is

> gathered for the benefit & helpe of Ladies, Gentlewomen, or any other un-skilfull persons. Whereby they may the more easilie and better understand many hard English words, which they shall heare or read in Scriptures, Sermons, or elswhere, and also be made able to use the same aptly themselves (1604: title page).

As the seventeenth century progressed, a number of dictionaries were produced, each of which more or less took the word list from its predecessors and added more entries. There were some innovations which extended the scope of what a dictionary might be expected to contain. Blount's *Glossographia or the Interpretation of Hard Words* (1656) made some attempt at providing etymology, so that the entry for *abbadon* has 'Heb.   *Abadh*, the Devil'. These etymologies are often fanciful, though: Blount's entry for *abbadon* goes on to state '*quasi, A bad one*' and his entry for *honeymoon* is often quoted as an amusing example of mis-guided etymologizing (for instance, by Starnes and Noyes 1991: 44): '*Hony-Moon*, applied to those married persons that love well at first, and decline in affection afterwards; it is hony now, but will change as the moon. *Min*'.

The first fully etymological dictionary, the *Gazophylacium Anglicanum*, was produced in 1689. Like many of its predecessors, it owes a debt to an earlier Latin work, in this case Skinner's *Etymologica Linguae Anglicanae* (1671), but in its acknowledgement of the Germanic origins of many more general English words, as well as catering to a more scholarly interest in the language, it anticipates the dictionaries of the eighteenth century. Another innovative dictionary of the late seventeenth century was Elisha Coles' *An English Dictionary* (1676). This was the first English dictionary to include cant and dialect words, but, in doing this, Coles was almost certainly cash-ing in on the market created by works such as Richard Head's *The Canting Academy* (1673) and John Ray's *Collection of English Words not Generally Used* (1674). Coles justifies his inclusion of cant by arguing ''tis no disparagement to understand the Canting Terms. It may chance to save your throat from being cut, or (at least) your Pocket from being pickt'. Whatever Coles' motivation for including dialect and cant, his dictionary does represent a stage in the progression of English lexicography, from the 'hard words' of the early sixteenth century to the inclusiveness of the eighteenth.

As Starnes and Noyes point out, 'Coles is therefore receptive to almost every element in the vocabulary except the everyday words – the last to be admitted into the English dictionary' (1946: 63).

The beginning of the eighteenth century saw this last category of words included for the first time in JK's *New English Dictionary* (1702). This marked a move away from the 'hard words' tradition of the seventeenth century towards the concept of a dictionary as a record of the core vocabulary of English. The *New English Dictionary* took its word list not from previous dictionaries, but from spelling books used in schools, and its primary purpose was to teach its readers to spell correctly. In bringing the emphasis on spelling out of the schoolroom and into the hands of the wider readership of dictionaries, 'JK' anticipated the emphasis on 'settling the orthography' found in Johnson's *Preface*. Indeed, it was its usefulness as a guide to spelling which brought the *New English Dictionary* its success in the first half of the eighteenth century. Isaac Watts recommended it as such in 1720 and again in 1731:

> In your younger days especially, take all proper opportunities of writing, and be careful to spell every word true: This may be done by the help of some small English *dictionary*, where the words are put down in the order of the alphabet; and if you doubt of the spelling of the dictionary, write it not without first consulting the dictionary.
>
> The best dictionary that I know for this purpose, is intitled, A New English Dictionary, &c., by *J. K.* The second edition, 1713 in a small octavo (1720).

> I am so far from disapproving that paragraph which you have reprinted from my little book of reading and writing, that even since the larger Dictionary of Mr. *Bailey* is published, which may be very entertaining and useful to persons of a polite education, yet for the bulk of mankind, this small one of *J. K.* is more convenient; and I wish it were in the hands of all young persons, to acquaint them better with their mother-tongue (1731; both passages in Starnes and Noyes 1991: 75).

However, the most successful eighteenth-century lexicographer before Johnson was undoubtedly Nathan Bailey. His *Universal Etymological English Dictionary* (1721) was pitched at a wider market than the 'Ladies, Gentlewomen, or any other unskilfull persons' who made up the readership of the seventeenth-century 'hard words' dictionaries, declaring on the title page the intention to 'entertain as well inform'. Bailey made greater advances in etymology than any of his predecessors, providing the immediate and ultimate sources of words. Thus under *citizen* we find '*citoyen* F., of *civis* L.', an etymology which we would not dispute today. According to Starnes and Noyes (1991: 102), Bailey 'established etymology as one of the requisites of any reputable dictionary'. More importantly, perhaps, he produced a dictionary which was more than just an expositor of hard words or a guide to spelling, and which the reader might pick up and browse for intellectual pleasure. In this, he perhaps acts as a bridge between the dictionaries of the seventeenth and early eighteenth centuries and Johnson. Bailey also anticipates Johnson in his treatment of old and obsolescent words, including items taken from glossaries of literary figures such as Spenser and Shakespeare, both of whom were also much cited by Johnson. Indeed, although Johnson's dictionary has become the most famous dictionary of the eighteenth century, Bailey's has more of a claim to represent that period, running as it did to 30 editions between 1721 and 1802. Bailey also introduced innovations which were to be taken up by later dictionaries: the second volume of the *Universal Etymological English Dictionary* (1727) was the first dictionary to include an indication of accentuation, and his *Dictionarium Britannicum* (1730) attempted to group related words together in an orderly fashion, with derived and related expressions. An example of this is his entry for *abstract*:

Abstract ("short Draught"), *Abstract* (with Logicians), *Abstract* (in Philosophy), An *Abstract* Idea, To *Abstract*, *Abstract* Numbers, *Abstracted* (Mathematics), *Abstracted* Nouns (Grammar), *Abstractedly*, *Abstractive*, *Abstraction* (in Philosophy) – a long discussion with examples (Starnes and Noyes 1991: 120).

Despite his dominance of the market, Bailey was not the only innovative lexicographer to emerge in this mid-eighteenth-century period. Dyche and Pardon's *New General English Dictionary* was the first to include reference to grammar. Their title page announces that words 'are not only fully explain'd, but accented on their proper syllable, to prevent a viscious Pronunciation; and mark'd with Initial Letters, to denote the Part of Speech to which each Word peculiarly belongs'. They also prefixed their dictionary with a short grammar, something which was to become a hallmark of Johnson's and subsequent dictionaries. Like Bailey's dictionaries, Dyche and Pardon's (or, rather, Dyche's, for Pardon is a shadowy figure who disappears after the sixteenth edition of 1781) was commercially successful. Where Bailey appealed to the leisured, literate browser, Dyche aimed his dictionaries at the 'unlearned' readers formerly served by the 'hard words' dictionaries. Between them, Bailey and Dyche introduced all the innovations necessary to make a dictionary a more complete guide to English usage. This leads us to ask why Johnson's dictionary has been viewed by the ignorant as the 'first' dictionary of English, and by the less ignorant as somehow presenting a new concept of a dictionary.

3.2   Johnson's *Dictionary of the English Language* (1755): the first 'modern' dictionary?

Both Starnes and Noyes (1991) and Osselton (1983) put forward the view that the middle of the eighteenth century sees a new departure in lexicography, most prominently (though not exclusively) marked by the appearance of Johnson's *Dictionary of the English Language* in 1755. Summing up their account of dictionaries before Johnson, Starnes and Noyes come to the following conclusions:

1.   In this early period lexicography progressed by plagiarism;
2.   The best lexicographer was often the most discriminating plagiarist;
3.   A good dictionary was its own justification, whatever the method of compilation (1991: 183).

They go on to point out that, although Johnson clearly made use of Bailey's *Dictionarium Britannicum*, he did this in a discriminating manner, deliberately excluding whole classes of words such as 'obsolete terms, proper names, and such highly specialized scientific, religious and other terms as seemed to Johnson more suitable for treatment in an encyclopaedia' (1991: 185). Far from being 'the most discriminating plagiarist', though, Johnson actually acknowledges Bailey as the source of certain words: for instance, 'Sturk, the young of an ox or heifer. Bailey', or

ABA'SED. *Adj.* [with heralds] is a term used of the wings of eagles, when the top looks downwards towards the point of the shield; or when the wings are shut; the natural way of bearing them being spread with the top pointing to the chief of the angle. *Bailey. Chambers.*

But very often Bailey's work was simply cited as *Dict.*, as these three consecutive entries from his dictionary show:

ABANNI'TION. *n. s.* [*abannitio*, Lat.] Abanishment for one or two years, among the ancients, for manslaughter. *Dict.*

A'BARCY *n. s.* Insatiableness. *Dict.*

TO A'BARE, *v. a.* [abarian. Sax.] To make bare, uncover, or disclose. *Dict.*

In Section 3.1, I presented the development of lexicography in the seventeenth and early eighteenth centuries as a progression towards a modern type of dictionary, from lists of 'hard words' to a more inclusive vocabulary, with information on grammar and pronunciation added. However, as Osselton points out, this was largely because each lexicographer added some new selling-point to the word list taken from his predecessors, rather than any conscious attempt to redefine the genre.

> Before 1750 there was ... no theoretical basis whatever for lexicographical practice: nobody had ever sat down and asked 'what is a dictionary?' ... Dictionaries happened; they grew by a process of accretion, and without reflection on what it was leading to (1983: 17).

Osselton sees the century from 1750 to 1850 as the period in which the dictionary takes on its modern form. He suggests that in this period a dictionary became:

1. A scholarly record of the whole language;
2. Based on, or derived from, a corpus;
3. Put emphasis on literary, rather than technical language;
4. Assumed an authoritarian or normative function.

If we take these points in order, we can determine the extent to which Johnson's *Dictionary* did or did not mark a radically new departure in lexicography. It is probably fair to say that, after Johnson, readers expected a dictionary to provide 'a scholarly record of the whole language', but, as we have seen in Section 3.1, a great deal of progress towards this ideal had been made by the time Dyche and Pardon's (1735) *New General English Dictionary* appeared. However, Johnson can be seen to have completed this process by adding a history of the English language as well as a grammar and notes on pronunciation. More importantly, the mid-eighteenth century brought a new, systematic and scholarly approach to definition. Whether Johnson was the first to take this approach is difficult to determine, because, between the publication of Johnson's *Plan of a Dictionary* (1747) and his *Dictionary of the English Language* (1755), there appeared another innovative and 'scholarly' dictionary: Benjamin Martin's *Lingua Britannica Reformata* (1749).

It is clear from Martin's preface that it is his dictionary rather than Johnson's that is the first to have been produced to a plan rather than by a process of accretion: in Osselton's terms, Martin certainly did sit down and think 'What is a dictionary?' Martin outlines 'the Requisitions of a Genuine English Dictionary'. This should be 'Universal ... to avoid a Redundancy of useless and obsolete words' and to include 'all the words in Use'. It should offer 'a sure Guide to the modern Orthography', and should provide a guide to orthoepy, with indications of accentuation and 'silent' letters. Most importantly, though, Martin noted the need for a new approach to definition:

A Critical and accurate Enumeration and Distinction of the several Significations of each respective Word must be allowed by all to be indispensably the chiefest Care of every Writer of Dictionaries. And yet nothing is more certain, than that all our English Dictionaries are more notoriously deficient in this important Particular than in any other (Martin, 1749: vii–viii).

Martin goes on to lay down the following order for the various definitions of a word:

1. The etymological or original meaning
2. The general and popular
3. The figurative or metaphorical
4. The humorous, poetical and burlesque
5. Scientifical adaptations
6. Compounds and phraseologies or idioms.

Martin gives as an example his definitions of the word *keen*:

1. sharp, that cuts well
2. sharp or subtle
3. cold or severe
4. eager or ardent
5. pungent or satirical
6. sharp or hungry.

This approach to definition is very similar to that outlined in Johnson's *Plan of a Dictionary* (1747). Here, Johnson outlines his proposed order of definitions, using *arrive* as an example: first comes the 'natural & primitive signification' as 'to reach the shore'; then the 'consequential meaning . . . to reach any place'; then the 'metaphorical sense . . . to obtain anything desired' such as 'he *arrived* at a peerage'. Johnson goes on to state that he will then:

mention any observation that arises from the comparison of one meaning with another; as it may be remarked of the word *arrive*, that in consequence of its original and etymological sense, it cannot properly be applied but to words signifying something desirable; thus, we say a man *arrived* at happiness, but cannot say without a mixture of irony, he *arrived* at misery (Johnson, 1747: 22).

Thus it is difficult to determine who was the first to institute this methodical approach to definition. Johnson was the first to suggest it in his *Plan*, but Martin was the first to put it into practice, since his dictionary was published six years earlier than Johnson's, and one year before Osselton's watershed of 1750.

If we take Osselton's second point, that it was not until after 1750 that dictionaries were based on corpora rather than accreted word lists, Johnson has a better claim to be the pioneer. As Osselton points out, in the *Preface* Johnson states clearly the period from which his words are taken to be between 1560 and 1660, and gives reasons for excluding certain types of words: self-explaining compounds, specialized technical terms, swear words, many dialect words, proverbs and proper names. In fact, although Johnson does claim to have 'endeavoured to collect examples and authorities from the writers before the restoration' (i.e. 1660) and to have 'fixed Sidney's work for the boundary' (1755: c recto) beyond which he takes few earlier words, he does not adhere strictly to these rules. Contemporary authors such as Addison are cited, and a number of dialect words from Ray's *Collection of English Words not Generally Used* (1674) also find their way in, along with a few spurious 'dictionary' words taken from Bailey. Nevertheless, Johnson's *Plan* does, as Osselton suggests, constitute an attempt to set boundaries from within which the words will be chosen and so, in a sense, defines a corpus. Osselton's third point is that dictionaries after 1750 were based on literary, rather than technical usage. We have seen in Section 3.1 that, in fact, Bailey introduced a literary element to his *Universal Etymological English Dictionary* (1721) by including words taken from glossaries of Shakespeare and Spenser. What marks Johnson out as an innovator is that he is the first English lexicographer to allow the reader to deduce meanings from literary quotations. Moreover, he is very selective in the authors from whose works his citations are taken. Osselton points out that one third of all Johnson's quotations are taken from the works of just four authors: first comes Shakespeare with 15 per cent of all quotes, then Dryden (11 per cent), Milton (5 per cent) and Addison (5 per cent). Together with Bacon, Pope and the Bible, these authors contribute 50 per cent of all Johnson's illustrative quotations. Whilst Johnson was not the first English lexicographer to introduce literary language, he was the first to give such a prominent place to citations from 'respected' authors, and to establish this as a hallmark of a 'good' dictionary. It is Johnson's use of quotations, above all, that makes his *Dictionary* look more like a 'modern' dictionary such as the *Oxford English Dictionary*.

So far, then, we have only partially supported Osselton's claim that 1750, or rather 1755, was a watershed in English lexicography, for some of Johnson's 'innovations' appear to have been at least partially introduced by Martin and, to a lesser extent, Bailey. When we come to Osselton's fourth characteristic of dictionaries produced between 1750 and 1850, we are on more solid ground, for it would be hard to deny that Johnson's dictionary was the first that 'assumed an authoritarian or normative function'. Whilst seventeenth century dictionaries were produced to satisfy a demand for guides to 'hard words', and those of the early eighteenth century were produced for a variety of readerships, by the middle of the eighteenth century, several influential figures were calling for a dictionary that would be the English counterpart to the *Dictionnaire de l'Académie Française* (2nd edn, 1718). In 1747, Warburton complained that English was 'yet destitute of a Test or Standard to apply to, in cases of doubt or difficulty . . . For we have neither Grammar nor Dictionary, neither Chart nor Compass, to guide us through this wide sea of words' (preface to the Warburton and Pope edition of the works of Shakespeare, 1747). In fact, we have already seen that there was a number of dictionaries by 1747, and, as we shall see in Chapter 4, there were likewise several grammars. What Warburton is calling for here, though, is a dictionary which will prescribe 'correct' and proscribe 'incorrect' usage. This is exactly what Johnson set out to do in his *Plan of a Dictionary*:

> This . . . is my idea of an English Dictionary, a dictionary by which the pronunciation of our language may be fixed, and its attainment facilitated, by which its purity may be preserved, its use ascertained, and its duration lengthened.

The key words here are *fixed* and *ascertained*: Johnson was answering a demand amongst educated readers for a dictionary that would rescue the language from the vagaries of linguistic change, and which would make explicit the rules of correct usage. Lord Chesterfield, Johnson's original patron, uses a revealing political metaphor in his recommendation of the as yet unpublished *Dictionary*:

> Good order and authority are now necessary. But where shall we find them, and at the same time, the obedience due to them? We must have recourse to the old Roman expedient in time of confusion, and choose a dictator. Upon this principle, I give my vote for Mr. Johnson to fill that great and arduous post. And I hereby declare, that I make a total surrender of all my rights and privileges in the English Language, as a free-born British subject, to the said Mr. Johnson during the term of his dictatorship (letter in *The World*, 28 November 1754).

As Crowley (1991: 43) points out, Johnson himself uses the metaphor of citizenship in describing his criteria for including words of foreign origin in his dictionary: he sees himself as setting the boundaries of the English language, with the intention of repelling invaders as far as possible. In fact, by the time Johnson's *Dictionary* was published, its author had become resigned to more modest and pragmatic ambitions:

> If the changes that we fear be thus irresistible, what remains but to acquiesce with silence, as in the other insurmountable distresses of humanity? It remains that we retard what we cannot repel, that we palliate what we cannot cure.

Even so, Johnson took the view that 'every language has . . . its improprieties and absurdities, which it is the duty of the lexicographer to correct or proscribe'. In particular, 'barbarous or impure words or expressions may be branded with some note of infamy, as they are carefully to be eradicated, wherever they are found'. Examples of Johnson's proscriptions are *bamboozle*, 'a cant word not used in pure or grave writings'; *banter*, 'a barbarous word, without etymology'; and *clever*, 'a low word, scarcely ever used but in burlesque or conversation'. Sledd and Kolb (1955: 37) point out that, in the case of these and other words (800 in all) 'branded with some note of infamy' by Johnson 'evidence provided by the OED reveals that Johnson's condemnation was no death warrant'. However, for Johnson's contemporaries, it was this very prescriptiveness that was to prove the major selling-point. Thomas Sheridan, the renowned elocutionist (of whom we shall have more to say in Chapter 7) wrote in 1756 that 'if our language should ever be fixed' Johnson 'must be considered by all posterity as the founder, and his dictionary as the cornerstone' (Sheridan 1756: 376).

3.3 After Johnson: English dictionaries in the nineteenth century

Johnson's *Dictionary* was to set the pattern for English lexicography for well over a century. Although major dictionaries were produced throughout the nineteenth century, both in Britain and in America, Johnson's dictionary, revised and extended by Todd (1818) continued to be, in Sheridan's words, the 'cornerstone' of English lexicography. It is Johnson's dictionary that Becky Sharp tosses away after leaving school in *Vanity Fair*, and, as we shall see in Chapter 6, when pronouncing dictionaries such as Sheridan's (1780) and Walker's (1791) were produced, these tended to take their lexical entries from Johnson. Indeed, Charles Richardson, in the preface to his *New Dictionary of the English Language* complains:

> Had the Dictionary of the English Language been the production of any writer of less name, a period of eighty years would not have been permitted to elapse without the appearance of a rival. And so far the name of Johnson has been an obstacle to the advancement of Lexicography in this country: it has commanded admirers and supporters: and it has deterred competition (1835: 39).

Richardson takes issue with Johnson on the matter of etymology. As a self-confessed disciple of Horne Tooke ('the undoubted chief of philosophical grammarians'), Richardson believed that

> a word has one meaning, and one only; that from it all usages must spring and be derived; and that in the Etymology of each word must be found this single intrinsic meaning, and the cause of the application in those usages (1835: 41).

He thus finds Johnson wanting because, in Richardson's view, he imposes arbitrary distinctions of meaning which distract the reader from the 'one true meaning'. Discussing the example of *arrive* from Johnson's *Plan* cited above (p. 42), Richardson writes:

> It may seem harsh, but it is strictly true; – that a great variety of instances might, with very little trouble, be collected of distinctions, where no differences subsist; and where the quotation subjoined to one explanation might with equal propriety have occupied another position.
>
> To refer again to his own specimen – '*Arrive.*' What difference, in the meaning of the word, can be discerned in the expressions produced by Johnson: 'To *arrive* on the banks of the Nile:' and, 'To *arrive* on the verge of an estate.' And yet they *are* separated, as if different (1835: 39).

Richardson believed that the purpose of etymology was to reveal the 'root' of a word and hence its 'true' meaning: he was less interested in tracing the derivation of the word through 'the origin and formation of tongues, and the dialects of tongues'.

Moreover, his belief in 'one meaning, and one meaning only' led Richardson to group words together which he believed to be derived from the same 'root'. At times, he is mistaken in his derivations, and forces his definitions to 'fit' the supposed relationship between words. For example, he asserts that *abase* and *abash* are derived from the same root:

> The past tense and past part. of *Abase* was anciently written *abaisit*, *Abayschid*; whence the word *abash* appears to be formed: and is applied to –
> The *feelings* of those who are *abased*, depressed, disgraced, humbled.
> In Wicliff it is applied to –
> The feelings which overpowered, subdued, the witnesses of the miraculous restoration of the damsel by Christ.

Here, he is commenting on the use of the word in a quotation taken from Wycliff's translation of the Bible: 'And anoon the damysel roos and walkide: and sche was of twelve yeer, and thei weren *abayshid* with a great stoneying.'

Under *abase*, the second edition of the *OED*, by contrast, warns that this word 'must be distinguished from early and Northern forms of ABASH; of which *abayss*, *abaisse*, *abasse* became by phonetic change *abash* before *abesse* (by influence of base) became *abase*'. Thus Richardson starts from a false premise that *abase* and *abash* share the same 'single intrinsic meaning', and so is obliged to explain all uses of either word in terms of this.

In the case of *abase/abash* Richardson thus provides an explanation which turns out to be erroneous. Often, though, he leaves the reader to deduce the 'metaphorical' meanings of the word from a series of chronologically ordered literary quotations. Rowena Fowler points out that:

> Richardson, in spite of his extensive coverage of literature, feels under no obligation to account for every literary usage; he starts with the word and then selects a quotation to explain it. His Preface states that the quotations are 'produced for the purpose of exemplifying, confirming, and illustrating the explanations which precede them', but in practice he often dispenses with explanation altogether: 'For the application, see the quotation' is a typical formulation (Fowler, forthcoming).

Richardson's use of literary quotations both harks back to Johnson and foreshadows the *OED*. Whereas Johnson, as we have seen, concentrated on authors writing between 1560 and 1660, Richardson used a wider range. He divided his sources into four periods:

> The first, commencing with the Rhyming Chronicles of Robert of Gloucester and Robert of Brunne, and continuing through the reigns of Henry VIII and his two immediate successors; the second extending from the accession of Elizabeth to the return of the second Charles, or from Hooker and Spenser to Milton and Bp. Taylor: the third, from the Restoration to the establishment of the House of Hanover upon the throne; or from Waller and Barrow to Pope and Samuel Clarke: the fourth from the reign of George II to the beginning of the present century (1835: 51).

Within these periods, Richardson takes examples from a wider range of authors than Johnson did, such as Hakluyt, Drayton and Beaumont and Fletcher. His purpose is partly to alert his readers to these works, in the hopes that they will read more: 'Chaucer and Gower will stimulate their zeal to become masters of these older productions of their native tongue, which are collated in the pages of this Dictionary' (1835: 52). Richardson, like Johnson, avoided using examples from the works of living authors, but he does use the works of near contemporaries: as Fowler points out, 'Byron ... who died in 1824, immediately starts to be quoted in the Dictionary from the letter F onwards' (forthcoming: 6). He includes some recent innovations, such as *abolitionist*, 'a modern word, lately of frequent use', and *phrenology*, 'a compound term of modern formation, in very common use, but not very clearly explained by those who employ it'. As Fowler points out, these words were so topical at the time of Richardson's compilation that he assumed readers would understand the meaning. Richardson seems not to regard his work as intended for posterity, but for the contemporary reader. He does, however, have a very grand view of the extent of such a readership. In the last section of his preface, he 'congratulate[s] himself upon the enjoyment of a prospect, much more rich and spacious than could fall to the lot of the compiler of a similar work in any Language of the European Continent' (1835: 60). Here, Richardson is referring to the global spread of English as the language of the Empire:

> 'The treasures of our tongue' are spread over continents, scattered among islands in the Northern and the Southern Hemisphere, from the 'unformed occident, to the strange shores of unknowing nations in the East'. The sun, indeed, now never sets upon the Empire of Great Britain (1835: 61).

He concludes with a romantic, if self-important vision of the global reach of his dictionary:

> At the very moment, when I am concluding this final page, I have reason to believe that the early portions of these volumes have found a resting place upon the tables of an English Settler on the banks of La Plata: I am assured that they are admitted to relieve the languor of military inaction at the Mess of Abednuggar; and that they have already found employment for the acuteness of nearly a century of critics in the United States of America (1835: 61).

As we shall see in the next section, this sense of English as the 'world language' is also evident in the *OED*, albeit expressed in less triumphalist terms. In several ways, Richardson's dictionary acts as a link between Johnson and the *OED*.

Richardson's was, according to Zgusta (1989: 208) the only 'historical dictionary in the 19th cent. that would handle chronology in [a] mechanically objective way', and 'Richardson is the only lexicographer mentioned in the preface to the *OED*' (1989: 189). Although, as we shall see in Section 3.4, the *OED* moved away from the 'philosophical' approach to etymology inspired by Tooke, towards a more 'scientific' one informed by philology, the primacy of the 'root' meaning is still evident. Likewise, the *OED* represents a further refinement of Richardson's method with regard to quotations. As we have seen, Richardson expected his reader to deduce meanings from the quotations, whilst the *OED* provides definitions, and a historical order for the meanings. James Murray, the first compiler of the *OED*, acknowledges that Richardson's method could have worked, had a greater number of illustrative quotations been supplied, and that his dictionary provides 'a valuable repertory of illustrations' (1900: 45). This debt to Richardson continues to be acknowledged by Onions, who, in his introduction to the 1933 edition of the *OED*, refers to his dictionary as a 'natural storehouse'. As Fowler points out, 'Richardson ends where Murray in his Scriptorium began, with the raw materials of a dictionary on historical principles, from which the meanings still remained to be deduced' (forthcoming: 5). Dolezal makes this same point, illustrating it with Richardson's entry for the group of words related to *deflour*:

> For the collected headwords **DEFLOUR**, v.; **Deflourer.**; **Defloration.**; **Deflouring**, n.; **Deflourish.**; RICHARDSON enters these partial synonyms: 'to viciate, to defile, to pollute.' There is, of course, the literal meaning also (illustrated by example – the same example is also found in the OED), but it is in the quotations that the readers learn that the defiling and viciating is something inflicted upon virgins (along with other uses):
>
> Dany of Rothesay prince of the realme . . . was accused to his father of dyuers heinous crymes, and in especial of lasciuioius & dissolute lyuyng, as rauyshyng of wiues, *deflouring* of virgins, and *defouling* of maidens. *Hall. Hen iv an. 8.*
>
> As thoughe marriage were an entraunce into violent whoredome, and a filthy *deflourer* of virginitie, which rather sanctifieth it to increase God's honour, as in Abraham & Sara, Zachary and Helysabeth. *Bale. English Votaries. Pt ii.*
>
> If a man had defower'd a virgin . . . *Milton, Tetrachordon.* [This is a rather long quotation that also includes 'deflowerer'.]
>
> [and this usage of one of the other headwords]
> He is ever a thief and robber of his good name, a *deflourer* and *defiler* of his reputation, an assassine and murtherer of his honour. *Barrow. Vol.i.Ser.1* (2000: 133).

Richardson's dictionary deserves a place in the history of English lexicography. As Dolezal points out 'a NEW DICTIONARY OF THE ENGLISH LANGUAGE by CHARLES RICHARDSON, even with all of its flaws, helped set the agenda for subsequent historical dictionaries of English' (2000: 148).

It would be tempting at this point to move straight on to a consideration of the *OED* itself. However, Richardson's was not the only important English dictionary of the nineteenth century. This account has so far only considered dictionaries produced in Britain, but two important and influential dictionaries which appeared in America also made their mark: Webster's *Dictionary of the English Language* (1828) and *The Century Dictionary* (1889), which was the project of no less a figure than William Dwight Whitney.

Noah Webster is, of course, the first and perhaps the best-known figure in American English lexicography. His name is still used by Merriam–Webster, publishers of *Webster's Third New International Dictionary, Unabridged* (1993, online edition 1996) and the *Merriam–Webster New Collegiate Dictionary* (1997). Webster had published his *Compendious Dictionary* in 1806, in order to introduce lexical innovations not recorded in Johnson: the full title of this work is *Compendious Dictionary of the English Language, in which Five Thousand Words are added to the number found in the best English Compends*. In fact, Webster had taken Entick's (1764) spelling dictionary as a model, and added 5,000 new words, mostly Americanisms never before included in any dictionary. Webster had originally planned a small dictionary for schoolchildren, to complement his *American Spelling Book*, which was widely used in American schools. However, in order to maximize the potential readership, he decided to produce a dictionary aimed at adults as well as children. In 1800 he placed what was in effect a press release advertising the fact that he intended to produce three dictionaries: 'a small Dictionary for schools, one for the counting-house, and a large one for men of science'. Unger (1998: 247) suggests that he did this in order to persuade potential buyers to 'postpone buying other dictionaries until his came off the press'. This provoked a counterblast from Webster's enemies, ridiculing the very idea of introducing new words as well as the prospect of Webster conferring the authority of a dictionary on the spelling reforms advocated in his (1790) *Essays and Fugitiv Writings*. As we shall see, Webster was pragmatic enough to modify his spelling reforms in response to these criticisms, but did not compromise his plan to introduce Americanisms. Indeed, in the 'advertisement' to the *American Dictionary* (the 'large one for men of science?') Webster again emphasizes as a selling-point the sheer size of his dictionary compared with its predecessors:

> The *Dictionary* of WALKER has been found by actual enumeration, to contain, in round numbers, *thirty-eight* thousand words. Those of JOHNSON, SHERIDAN, JONES and PERRY, have not far from the same number. The American edition of TODD's *Johnson* contains *fifty-eight* thousand. In the work now submitted to the public, the number has been increased to *seventy* thousand (1832: iii).

In each case, Webster is promoting the idea that this is a new dictionary for a new nation: bigger and better than anything produced in England. In one sense, this really is an 'advertisement': as Simpson (1986: 53) points out, 'Webster was not blind to the possibility of turning a penny'. However, there is a clear political aspect to Webster's dictionaries, which represent a deliberate attempt to create a separate standard for American English. As early as 1789, Webster was advocating this separation:

> Customs, habits and *language*, as well as government should be national. America should have her *own* distinct from all the world. Such is the policy of other nations, and such must be *our* policy, before the states can be either independent or respectable. To copy foreign manners implicitly, is to reverse the order of things, and begin our political existence with the corruptions and vices which have marked the declining glories of other republics (1789: 179).

Even as he argues for the necessity of providing a dictionary that will deal with American words and senses, Webster's choice of examples is politically loaded, emphasizing the decadence of England and its language:

> From the changes in civil policy, manners, arts of life and other circumstances attending the settlement of English colonies in America: most of the language of heraldry, hawking, hunting, and especially that of the old feudal and hierarchical establishments of England, will become utterly extinct in this country – much of it already forms a part of the neglected rubbish of antiquity (1806: xxii).

This language is modified slightly in the preface to the *American Dictionary*: here, the emphasis is on different political systems requiring a different vocabulary, or different senses of the same words. The influence of Horne Tooke can also be detected in the correspondence between language and ideas:

> Language is the expression of ideas; and if the people of one country cannot preserve an identity of ideas, they cannot retain an identity of language. Now an identity of ideas depends materially upon a sameness of things or objects, with which the people of the two countries are conversant ... But the principal differences between the people of this country and of all others, arise from different forms of government, different laws, institutions and customs. Thus the practice of *hawking* and *hunting*, the institution of *heraldry* and the *feudal system* of England originated terms which formed, and some of which now form, a necessary part of that country; but, in the United States, many of these terms are no part of our present language, – and they cannot be, for the things which they express, do not exist in this country. They can be known to us only as obsolete or foreign words. On the other hand, the institutions of this country which are new and peculiar, give rise to new terms or to new applications of old terms, unknown to the people of England; which cannot be explained by them, and which will not be inserted in their Dictionaries, unless copied from ours. Thus the terms, *land-office; land-warrant; location of land; consociation* of churches; *regent* of a university; *intendant* of a city; *plantation, selectmen, senate, congress, court, assembly, escheat,* &c. are either words not belonging to the language of England, or they are applied to

> things in this country which do not exist in that ... With our present constitutions of government, *escheat* can never have its feudal sense in the United States (1832: vii).

This more moderate tone was probably prompted by the warm welcome which Webster had received when he visited England in 1825, in order to consult earlier dictionaries and other books in libraries there. Indeed, he completed the *American Dictionary* in his lodgings in Cambridge, England, and it was the endorsement of Cambridge scholars which paved the way for the dictionary's enthusiastic reception in America. Of course, Webster would also have realized in the interim that there was a market for his *American Dictionary* in Britain. Indeed, the quotation above is taken directly from a London reprint 'by E. H. Barker, Esq. of Thetford, Norfolk, from a copy communicated by the author', proving that there was a market for his dictionary in Britain, and that his more moderate stance was judicious. Even if Webster did have one eye on the international market, his patriotism cannot be doubted. At times, his vision is as grandiose as that of Richardson cited above (p. 48): 'our language, within two centuries, will be spoken by more people in this country than any other language on earth, except the Chinese, in Asia, and even that may not be an exception' (1832: viii). Grandiose though this sounds, history was to prove it an understatement: even Webster could not have foreseen the global dominance of American English in the late twentieth century. Webster's mission was to establish a model of American English equal, if not superior, to that of British English. To this end, like Johnson before him, he sets out 'to ascertain the true principles of the language ... to purify it from some palpable errors, and reduce the number of its anomalies' (1832: viii). Webster's dictionary thus has its prescriptive side, but it is for his innovations that Webster is chiefly known. In his *Compendious Dictionary* and *American Dictionary*, Webster authorized the moderately reformed spelling which is the distinguishing characteristic of written American English today. Webster's reforms, mainly involving the choice of different alternatives to those becoming established in Britain, such as Latin *-or* rather than French *-our* in *honor*, *labor*, etc., single rather than double consonants in participial forms in *traveled*, *traveling*, and loss of 'redundant' letters such as the *a* in *mediaeval*, were very moderate compared to those advocated by Benjamin Franklin and William Thornton in America, or indeed by James Elphinston or Thomas Spence in Britain (see Beal, 2002 for a fuller discussion of eighteenth-century ideas on spelling reform). Webster had moderated his reforms in response to the negative reaction to his original proposals: nevertheless, unlike the schemes of more radical reformers, Webster's succeeded. Above all, Webster's *American*

Dictionary succeeded in conferring authority on words which would be dismissed as 'Americanisms' by the British: *skunk, hickory* and *chowder* are examples. Webster also deliberately set out to include citations from American authors. Quoting Johnson's maxim that 'the chief glory of a nation arises from its authors', Webster writes:

I do not indeed expect to add celebrity to the names of FRANKLIN, WASHINGTON, ADAMS, JAY, MADISON, MARSHALL, RAMSAY, DWIGHT, SMITH, TRUMBULL, HAMILTON, BELKNAP, AMES, MASON, HARE, SILLMAN, CLEAVELAND, WALSH, IRVING, and many other Americans distinguished by their writings, or by their science; but it is with pride and satisfaction that I can place them, as authorities, on the same page with those of BOYLE, HOOKER, MILTON, DRYDEN, ADDISON, RAY, MILNER, COWPER, DAVY, THOMSON and JAMESON (1832: vii).

In terms of method, Webster's *American Dictionary* does not represent much of an advance on Johnson: Webster's system of numbering definitions, and his use of citations, is very similar to that of Johnson. Even Webster's etymologies are not noticeably different, despite his insistence that he has compared words in 20 languages 'to obtain a more correct knowledge of the primary sense of original words' (1832: vi). Apart from his importance in establishing a separate set of norms for American English, Webster's chief contribution to the history of English lexicography is in the lexical innovations that he records. In his 'advertisement' Webster conveys the sense of the 'wonderful century' referred to in Chapter 1:

Since the time of JOHNSON a complete revolution has taken place in almost every branch of physical science. New departments have been created, new principles developed, new modes of classification and description adopted. It is not surprising, therefore, that a great part of his definitions of terms in the *Arts* and *Sciences* are, at the present day, erroneous or defective ... Hence we find that, in that edition, the definition of *coral*, as 'a *plant* of a stony nature' of *water* as 'a very fluid *salt*', of *fermentation*, as 'a motion which subtilizes the soft and *sulphureous* particles', of *gas* as 'spirit not capable of being coagulated,' with hundreds of others founded on views of science long since exploded, are still retained in their original shape without comment or correction (1832: iv).

Webster's *American Dictionary* is thus a dictionary for the new scientific age, incorporating not only the lexical innovations, but also the more enlightened definitions, of the nineteenth century. It was to be a great success on both sides of the Atlantic: in America, it was adopted as the official standard by both Congress and the courts, whilst the *English Journal of Education* called Webster 'the greatest lexicographer that has ever lived' (Unger, 1998: 303). Unger goes on to write:

> Webster, the patriot, took his place at last among America's founding fathers, as the father of the American language. His name and dictionary – 'Webster's Dictionary' – entered the language, giving the phrase 'Look it up in Webster's' a cachet of authority matched only, perhaps, by 'The Bible says' (Unger, 1998: 303).

Although Unger's estimation of Webster's enduring fame as a household name in the USA is justified, his authority was not to go unchallenged amongst American linguists. Later in the nineteenth century, rival dictionaries were produced by, amongst others, Joseph Emerson Worcester. According to Drake, the publication of the quarto edition of Worcester's dictionary in 1860 'set off a rivalry between it and the Goodrich version of the *New Webster*, a rivalry in which nearly every literate person apparently took part' (1977: 19). Amongst Webster's detractors in this 'Great Dictionary War' (Andresen, 1990: 125) was George Marsh, who, in his *Lectures on the English Languages*, writes of 'a celebrated lexicographer' and 'ridicules him for suggesting that the etymology of *issue* coincides with Ethiopic *watsa*' (1860: 63; cited in Andresen, 1990: 125).

However, the American dictionary which was to provide the greatest challenge to Webster's did not appear until the end of the century, and was conceived by William Dwight Whitney, who had in turn been an editor of the 1864 edition of Webster's. We have already encountered *The Century Dictionary* in Chapter 2, when we saw that the 1909 *Supplement* was a major source of first citations in the *OED* online for that year. The preface to the *Century Dictionary* emphasizes the fact that this dictionary is more compendious than any that has gone before. Whitney writes here of 'a very large addition to the vocabulary of preceding dictionaries, about two hundred thousand words being here defined' (1889: v). He goes on to explain the inclusive policy of the *Century Dictionary*:

> The first duty of a comprehensive dictionary is collection, not selection. When a full account of the language is sought, every omission of a genuine English form, even when practically necessary, is so far a defect; and it is therefore better to err on the side of broad inclusiveness than of narrow exclusiveness (1889: v).

This policy marks a change in lexicographical practice: as we have seen in Section 3.2, Johnson's policy was to define very narrowly the period from which citations would be taken, and to exclude dialectal and technical words. Whitney's stance is exactly the opposite: the *Century Dictionary* is, he writes, 'designed to be a practically complete record of the main body of English speech, from the time of the mingling of the Old French and Anglo-Saxon to the present day' (Whitney, 1889: v). Whitney thus states his

intention to include obsolete words from Middle English, especially from
the works of Chaucer, and from the sixteenth and seventeenth centuries,
'the formative period of modern English'. Whitney argues that 'not to
include all of these terms, which from their etymological connections,
intrinsic literary value, or availability for modern use, are worthy of record,
is to make, not a dictionary of English, but merely a dictionary of modern
and selected English' (Whitney, 1889: v). He also argues that dialectal
words should be included where they 'appear to be an important part of the
history of the language' (1889: vi). To a much greater extent than any
dictionary before it, the *Century Dictionary* is, like the later *OED*, a
dictionary on historical principles, in which the discoveries of the new
discipline of philology are to the forefront. When Whitney writes of 'the
time of the mingling of the Old French and Anglo-Saxon' and of the
sixteenth and seventeenth centuries as 'the formative period of modern
English', he is referring to a narrative of the history of English which has
become commonplace today, but which would hardly have been known to
Johnson. Whitney acknowledges his debt to philology later in the preface,
when he outlines the principles behind his etymologies:

> They have been written anew, on a uniform plan, and in accordance with the
> established principles of comparative philology. The best works in English
> etymology, as well as in etymology and philology in general, have been
> regularly consulted, the most helpful being those of Prof. Skeat and Eduard
> Müller, and the 'New English Dictionary on Historical Principles,' edited by
> Dr. J. A. H. Murray (which, however, could be consulted in revising the proofs
> of A and part of B only); but the conclusions reached are independent (1889:
> vii).

Whitney was thus aware of the principles behind the *New English
Dictionary on Historical Principles* (later the *OED*), and followed these
in *The Century Dictionary*. In fact, despite Whitney's open acknowledgement of his debt to the *New English Dictionary*, a 'dictionary war' broke
out in the late 1880s and early 1890s. British reviewers, and indeed
Murray himself, accused Whitney of various faults, from poor scholarship
to outright plagiarism, such was the fear that the success of *The Century
Dictionary* might undermine the *New English Dictionary* project. As we
shall see in Section 3.4, the *New English Dictionary* had a very long
gestation, so Murray and his supporters would have feared that *The
Century Dictionary* might corner the market for a large, inclusive English
dictionary on historical principles. Any charge of plagiarism against
Whitney was unfounded: the principles behind *The Century Dictionary*
and the *New English Dictionary* were similar because the new science of
philology was flourishing in the USA as well as Europe, and informed the

thinking of both editors. *The Century Dictionary* also follows the same principle of inclusiveness as the *New English Dictionary*: apart from the introduction of historical and dialectal words omitted from earlier dictionaries, *The Century Dictionary*, like Webster's before it, introduced new technical terms and Americanisms. The latter, Whitney writes, 'have received the recognition naturally to be expected from an American dictionary, many being recorded for the first time' (1889: vi). However, it is the technical terms which account for the greatest number of innovations introduced in *The Century Dictionary*. Whitney writes that 'much space has been devoted to the special terms of the various sciences, fine arts, mechanical arts, professions, and trades, and much care has been bestowed upon their treatment' (1889: xii). He cites authorities in each specialized field who have acted as consultants, thus bestowing authenticity. The specificity of the fields named here bears testimony to the discoveries of the 'wonderful century', recorded and celebrated at its end:

> The definitions of that part of general biological science which in any way relates to animal life or structure, including systematic zoology, have been written by Dr. Elliott Coues, who has been assisted in ichthyology and conchology by Prof. Theodore N. Gill, in entomology by Mr. Leland O. Howard and Mr. Herbert L. Smith, and in human anatomy by Prof. James K. Thatcher (1889: xiii).

Thus the authority of *The Century Dictionary* comes not, in the Johnsonian sense, from the *ipse dixit* statements of its authors, but from the scientific and scholarly credentials of its advisers, and indeed its chief editor, Whitney, who was Professor of Comparative Philology and Sanskrit at Yale University. In this respect, it is very much a dictionary of its time, both in its emphasis on scientific innovation and authority and its philological basis. Jeffrey A. Triggs, who is producing an online edition of *The Century Dictionary*, describes it as 'the Titanic of dictionaries, fabled in its day as the largest, most comprehensive dictionary yet completed' (http://216.156.253.178/CENTURY/why.php). Although in size, at least, it has since been superseded by the *OED*, *The Century Dictionary*, like Webster's dictionaries, is also important, because, as Triggs points out, 'its American orientation (excellent American pronunciations, preference given to American spelling forms, attention to words of American origin) gives it a special relevance in our time. It is still an American treasure.' Whilst clearly influenced by European scholarship, *The Century Dictionary* stands as a monument to American scholarship at the end of the nineteenth century, and, in turn, its contribution to the *OED* foreshadows the emergence of American English as the most influential variety of English in the twentieth and twenty-first centuries.

3.4 The New English Dictionary on Historical Principles/Oxford English Dictionary

We have seen in the previous section that, both in Britain and the USA, English lexicography was far from dormant in the nineteenth century, with Webster, Richardson and Whitney all producing innovative dictionaries. However, at least in Britain, Johnson was to remain the household name for most of the century. R.G. Latham, Professor of English at University College, London, produced a revised edition of Johnson's dictionary for Longman as late as 1866, and put his own name to *A Dictionary of the English Language* 'founded on that of Dr Samuel Johnson, as edited by the Rev. H. J. Todd, M.A.' in 1882 and J. M. Dent and Sons published a revised version of the pocket edition in London as late as 1891. Whilst Todd's edition had 'numerous emendations and additions', as well as a preface by Latham in addition to Johnson's, it is notable that Longman still saw Johnson's name as an important selling-point as late as the end of the nineteenth century. What caused Johnson's dictionary to become regarded as a historical work of scholarship rather than a dictionary for everyday use was the emergence of that giant of twentieth-, and indeed twenty-first-century lexicography, the *OED*.

The Philological Society, which had been founded in 1842, set up its Unregistered Words Committee in 1857, in the first instance to produce a supplementary lexicon of 'words and idioms hitherto unregistered'. This committee consisted of Richard Chenevix Trench, author of *On the Study of Words* (1851) and *English Past and Present* (1855); the scholar and editor Frederick James Furnivall; and Herbert Coleridge, the grandson of the poet Samuel Coleridge. However, the need for a new dictionary based on different principles to those of its predecessors was set out by Trench in two papers delivered to the Philological Society in November 1857, published as *On Some Deficiencies in Our English Dictionaries* (1857, 2nd edn 1860). Trench's arguments led to the Philological Society producing a *Proposal for the Publication of a New Dictionary* in 1859, and Trench, along with Furnivall and Coleridge, was subsequently appointed to the Literary and Historical Committee set up to advise on editorial policy. Coleridge was appointed first editor of the *New English Dictionary* but died in 1861, at which point Furnivall took over. Coleridge had written in 1860: 'in about two years we shall be able to give our first number to the world' (1860: 77). He had massively underestimated the size of the task: the first fascicle, A–ANT, was not published until 1884, and the *New English Dictionary* was not completed in its entirety until 1928, when it was published in twelve volumes. The complete dictionary amounted to 15,487 pages containing 414,825 entries (Johnson had 39,000). Nevertheless, by the time the full *New English Dictionary* appeared, there was already an apparent need for a supplement to include words coined in the 44 years since the first fascicles were published: this appeared in 1933, under the editorship of William Craigie and Charles Onions. Whilst we shall only consider the *New English Dictionary* and its 1933 *Supplement* here, it should be noted that the *OED* is in a constant state of revision, its most recent manifestation being the *OED* online (www.oed.com).

From the very beginning, those involved with the *New English Dictionary* project set out to produce an English dictionary unlike any of its predecessors: 'an entirely new Dictionary; no patch upon old garments, but a new garment throughout' (Trench, 1860: 1). Above all, the new dictionary was to abandon the prescriptive stance of earlier dictionaries such as Johnson's, and set out 'to collect and arrange all the words, whether good or bad, whether they do or do not commend themselves to judgement' (Trench, 1860: 5). Trench goes on to state his opposition to prescriptivism in terms which directly contradict those used by Chesterfield about Johnson (cited above p. 44):

> I cannot understand how any writer with the smallest confidence in himself, the least measure of that vigour and vitality which would justify him in addressing his country men in written or spoken discourse at all, should consent in this matter to let one self-made dictator, or forty, determine for him what words he should use, and what he should forbear from using (1860: 5).

This descriptive, empirical approach was, of course, entirely in keeping with the principles of philology. Just as all languages and dialects were now seen as equally rule-based, and therefore equally valid, so all words used by speakers (or rather, writers) of English were to be seen as equally worthy of being recorded in the *New English Dictionary*. This principle was restated in the *Proposal for the Publication of a New Dictionary*:

> The first requirement of every lexicon is, that it should contain *every word occurring in the literature of the language it professes to illustrate*. We entirely repudiate the theory, which converts the lexicographer into an arbiter of style, and leaves it in his discretion to accept or reject words according to his private notions of their comparative elegance or inelegance (Philological Society, 1859: 2–3).

Murray, in the preface to the first volume of the *New English Dictionary*, states this again, appealing to the idea of the organic nature of 'natural language':

A literary language, with its more accessible store of words already in use and sufficient for all ordinary requirements, its more permanent memories and traditions, its constant appeal to authoritative precedent – 'Where did you find that word? Can you cite it from any of the masters of English Prose? Is it in the Dictionary? Is it English at all?' – is hostile to word creation. The new word is apt to die almost as soon as it is born, ashamed of its own newness, ashamed of the italics or inverted commas which apologize for its very existence, or question its legitimacy. But such is not the case with natural language (Murray 1888: viii).

The *New English Dictionary* was to be based on a corpus of English writing from which no word would be excluded. However, the very definition of the corpus involved selectivity, and therefore the favouring of certain varieties and registers of English over others. Above all, it was to be a record of Standard English. Coleridge states in the *Proposal* that 'as soon as a standard language has been formed, which in England was the case after the Reformation, the lexicographer is bound to deal with that alone' (1859: 3). Thus regional dialect is excluded, not, in this case, because the editors considered dialects as inferior to Standard English, but because they considered them outside the 'common core' of English which was to be their concern. The Philological Society instead supported a parallel project for an *English Dialect Dictionary* under the editorship of Joseph Wright (1905). (We shall discuss Wright's project in Chapter 8.) Some dialect words were included, notably those which had appeared in literature and/or in earlier dictionaries such as Ray's *Collection of English Words not Generally Used* (1674). An example of this is *clem*, 'to pinch as hunger or fasting does; to waste with hunger, starve', cited from Ray but also from Ben Jonson and the dialect writer John Collier ('Tim Bobbin'). Nevertheless, the professed inclusiveness of the *New English Dictionary* was limited by a view that an 'English Dictionary' should only deal with Standard English, thus excluding the usage of a large part of the population.

Another area in which the inclusiveness of the *New English Dictionary* must be called into question is in its treatment of scientific and technical vocabulary. In the original conception of the dictionary, the main volume was to include such scientific words as had 'passed out of their peculiar province and into general use' (Trench et al., 1860: 4). Technical vocabulary was to be dealt with in a supplementary volume. However, as Hoare and Salmon (2000) point out, Murray was interested in and knowledgeable about science, and tried to include scientific treatises such as those of Darwin and Faraday in the lists of works to be consulted. In his presidential address to the Philological Society of 1880, he urged readers to 'devote themselves to the examination of scientific and technical books' (1881: 263, cited in Hoare and Salmon, 2000: 161). Murray thus wished to include scientific vocabulary as far as possible, but, as we saw in the previous chapter (p. 23), Trench had warned against the use of technical words, which were mere 'signs' like algebraic formulae. Murray's policy on the inclusion of words from outside the 'core' vocabulary is set out in the preface to the *New English Dictionary*. The diagram shows that:

> the circle of the English language has a well-defined centre but no discernible circumference. Yet practical utility has some bounds, and a Dictionary has definite limits: the lexicographer must, like the naturalist, 'draw the line some-where', in each diverging direction. He must include all the 'Common Words' of literature and conversation, and such of the scientific, technical, slang, dialectal, and foreign words as are passing into common use, and approach the position or standing of 'common words', well knowing that the line which he draws will not satisfy all his critics (1888: xvii).

Determining which scientific words were 'passing into common use' was not an easy matter. Although the more popular scientific periodicals such as *Nature* and *Scientific American* would provide some evidence, there would still be an element of guesswork involved in deciding which coinages would 'catch on'. Murray put the problem to the audience at his presidential address:

> Do we take a series of animals: *Horse ... Amoeba, Agama*; or a series of plants: *Rose, Anemone ... Geranium, Pelargonium* ... where do the general words end, and the technical begin? ... Shall we insert *Gold*, and omit *Aluminium*, or insert *Aluminium* ... but omit *Tellurium* and *Rubidium*? (1880: 133–4).

Murray concludes that it is best to err on the side of inclusiveness, because 'for one person that will turn to the dictionary to learn the meaning of *Camel*, ten will turn to learn what an *Agama* is' (1880: 134). However, as Hoare and Salmon (2000) point out, there are some omissions from the *New English Dictionary* which, at least with the benefit of hindsight, are surprising: amongst these are *appendicitis* (first cited 1886), *chromosome* and *radium* (both 1889). Hoare and Salmon suggest that newly coined scientific terms were less likely to be included in the *New English Dictionary* than other specialised lexis.

> Why, to take just one example, was there such unquestioning and compre-hensive inclusion of heraldic terms (*bordure, bendlet, frett, fitchee*, and so on, and most of them barely naturalized at that) in the *OED* when scientific words far more likely to gain everyday importance were summarily ruled out? No doubt a similar crop of legal and theological obscurities could be cited.

Clearly 'passing into common use' was never a sufficient or a necessary condition for inclusion; scientific words simply faced a prejudice based on little more than their perceived lack of the right pedigree and literary flavour (2000: 169).

Of course, the heraldic terms were included because they were ancient: *bordure* has a first citation from 1460 and *bendlet* from 1575, but it is certainly the case that Craigie and Onions, in the 1933 supplement, needed to pay much more attention to the scientific vocabulary that had been omitted from the *New English Dictionary*. Craigie points out in his preface to the 1933 edition that this 'embraces not only the standard language of literature and conversation, whether current at the moment, or obsolete, or archaic, but also the main technical vocabulary, and a large measure of dialect usage and slang' (1933: v). The subsequent history of the *OED* has been one of increasing inclusiveness, to the chagrin of those who expect a dictionary to fulfil the dictatorial role envisaged by Chesterfield. The annual publication of the *OED*'s list of newly included words provides a gift for journalists becalmed in the August 'silly season': lists of slang words 'allowed in' to the dictionary will be fulminated against in tabloid and broadsheet alike. A recent discussion in the *Guardian* of 21 August 2003 of neologisms such as *blamestorming*, 'the practice of holding a meeting in order to decide who to blame when something goes wrong', was incorporated in a discussion of the increasing misuse of hyphens and apostrophes. There is, however, nothing new in this: as Mugglestone (2000a: 194–5) points out, Murray himself had to defend his inclusion of the word *advertisemental* to a reader who objected.

The inclusiveness of the *New English Dictionary* was, above all, restricted by the range of material consulted by the volunteer readers who provided Murray with citations. In the Philological Society's *Proposal for the Publication of a New English Dictionary*, it was stated: 'We admit as authorities all English books, except such as are devoted to purely scientific subjects, as treatises on electricity, mathematics, &c., and works written subsequently to the Reformation for the purpose of illustrating provincial dialects' (1859: 2–3). However, as Brewer (2000) points out, the works from which large numbers of citations are taken tend to be canonical, and certain authors receive far more thorough treatment than others. Schäfer (1980, 1989) found that, whilst almost every word used in Shakespeare's texts can be found in the *OED*, several of his contemporaries, such as Nashe and Wyatt, received much more patchy treatment. Thus the use of *mirror* as a verb is given a first citation of 1800, from Keats' *Lamia*, but had been used by Nashe 227 years earlier. Brewer points out similar biases in the treatment of nineteenth-century authors:

The usage of Dickens (about 8,550 quotations), Browning (3,070 quotations), Tennyson (6,970 quotations), Carlyle (6,620 quotations), or Ruskin (3,315 quotations), sometimes highly idiosyncratic, is minutely attended to . . . while that of Wilkie Collins (something under 30 quotations), Christina Rossetti (134 quotations), or Blake (112 quotations) is, by contrast, minimally quoted (2000: 56).

These omissions and biases are being rectified in the *OED* online, but it would appear that the vocabulary of the *New English Dictionary* was, to a certain extent, determined by the preference of its readers for canonical texts by major authors. Willinsky suggests that this undermines the *OED*'s claim to historical objectivity, for it 'defines the scope of the English Language ... it establishes the possibility of fixed points of meaning, definite senses, located in the publishing activity of a number of writers' (1994: 7).

Although the *New English Dictionary* was intended to be a descriptive account of the language derived from a corpus, it could thus be argued that the biases apparent in this corpus brought in prescriptivism by the back door. However, signs of more overt prescriptivism can also be detected. As Mugglestone (2000a) points out, the kind of 'branding' exercised by the likes of Johnson also occasionally finds its way into the pages of the *New English Dictionary*. Mugglestone draws our attention to the 'armoury of status labels used throughout the dictionary. *Darling* ("sweetly pretty and charming") is labelled *affected*, *ambilogy* is "needless" ... *forfex* is pedantic, if *humourously* so ("*Humourously pedantic*. A pair of scissors"), editorial judgement in each case attempting to convey some sense of the stylistic overtones of particular usages' (2000a: 199). She also points out that, whilst Murray often resisted attempts by contributors to prescribe or proscribe certain usages, he occasionally succumbs to the temptation himself, especially where semantic change was involved. Thus she notes that under *avocation*:

Sense 3 ('That which has the effect of calling away or withdrawing one from an occupation. *Hence*, A minor or less important occupation, a by-work') is unmarked, and supported by citations from Fuller, Johnson, Godwin as well as Furnivall. Sense 4 ('Ordinary employment, usual occupation, vocation, calling') in contrast displays a striking resistance to the semantic extension, which it attests: 'But as, in many cases, the business which called away was of equal or greater importance (see quot. In a., where *avocation* is rightly used), the new meaning was improperly foisted upon the word' (2000a: 197).

Thus Trench's original vision of a dictionary that would include all the words in the language 'whether they do or do not commend themselves to judgement' was compromised to a certain extent by the time the *New English Dictionary* appeared in print. Whilst certain biases and instances of prescriptivism can be detected, though, we must not allow our critique to become a witch-hunt. Every corpus involves a process of selection, and it is all too easy for one man or woman's selectivity to be seen as another's discrimination. The *New English Dictionary* was, above all, a Victorian project, and reflects the preoccupations of its age. Along with other monumental publications of this period, the *Encyclopaedia Britannica* (the ninth edition of which was published in 1880) and the *Dictionary of National Biography* (the first edition of which appeared in 1885), the scale of the project suggests great national confidence and a sense that all knowledge had been achieved and could be codified. The fact that Murray was able to command such a large army of volunteers indicates that the dictionary project tapped into the Victorian Zeitgeist. Murray's address to the Philological Society in 1880 appeals to the 'civilizing mission' of the British Empire and evokes the spirit of exploration and discovery of that age:

> The language of a civilized nation, the individuals of which are constantly growing in their knowledge of the objects, actions, and customs of other climes and other times, which objects, actions, and customs are constantly becoming the subject matter of new *ideas*, and the theme of new discourse, is constantly adding to the sound-combinations, or *words*, by which it expresses these new ideas, and which are, indeed, the *only* means in existence for expressing them (1880: 132).

Both Crowley (2003) and Willinsky (1994) present a critique of the *New English Dictionary* as both a product and a tool of British imperialism. Willinsky argues:

> The dictionary contributed to Rule Britannia by equipping the conquering language with a coherent history that ran back through the nation's best writers ... As readers assembled the citations for the dictionary, Great Britain and other European nations were parceling up the African subcontinent ... The OED was but one of many vehicles that formalized aspects of English culture in preparation for advancing the Anglicizing mission (1994: 202).

Crowley suggests that the 'history of the language' presented in the *New English Dictionary*, far from being an objective account, presents the language as an organic entity, evolving towards a more 'civilized' state in the late nineteenth century. In this respect, it is very much of its time, given the influence of Darwinian thinking on philology. As we saw in Chapter 2, words introduced into English from the far reaches of the Empire are described as coming from 'native languages', whilst those with Indo-

European etymologies are provided with a full set of cognates, demonstrating their place in the 'family tree', their pedigree. For example, whilst *Aardvark* has the etymology: 'Adopted from the Dutch colonists in South Africa, who have so named it from Dutch *aarde*, in comp, *aard-* earth + *vark* = OE *fearh*, OHG *farh*, L. *porc-us* pig', for *Abaca* we simply find 'the native name of the palm (*Musa textilis*) which furnishes what is commonly known as Manilla Hemp', without even the identification of the fact that the donor language was Tagalog. Of course, it could be argued that there was less knowledge of the 'native languages' and their genealogical relationships (though this was certainly not the case at the time with the Austronesian languages, to which Tagalog belongs), but the contrasting treatment of words such as these would have reinforced the readers' sense of the superiority of European languages (note that *aardvark* is described as Dutch).

Of course, this critique of the *New English Dictionary* is one that could only have been carried out in 'post-modern times'. At the time of its compilation and well after its publication, the view of linguistic history put forward here would have been accepted as scientific and objective. The *New English Dictionary*, for all its flaws, was the most comprehensive and inclusive dictionary of English that had ever been produced and came closest to the descriptive ideals of its founders. If it smacks of imperialism to twenty-first-century readers, this should come as no surprise, since it was conceived at the high point of the British Empire. Subsequent editions of, and supplements to, the *OED* have brought the dictionary closer to the inclusiveness envisaged by Trench: technical, slang and dialect words are now included, and the gaps in the historical record are being filled. Whilst other dictionaries of the twentieth century, notably those produced by Collins and Longman, are more likely to be found in the average home, the *Oxford English Dictionary* has become an institution, and, indeed, an object of study in its own right. As well as the works already cited in this chapter (Mugglestone, 2000b; Schäfer, 1980, 1989; Willinsky, 1994), there has been Katherine Elisabeth Murray's (1977) biography of her grandfather, D. R. Raymond's (1987) account of prefaces to the *OED*, and numerous articles and chapters in journals and histories of lexicography. Only Johnson's and Webster's dictionaries have received a similar amount of scholarly attention.

This account of dictionaries in the later modern period is not intended to be exhaustive: there are many interesting dictionaries which have not been discussed here, and a whole genre of works which were used and intended as dictionaries, the pronouncing dictionaries, will be discussed in Chapter 7. What I have tried to show here is that whilst, on the one hand, the history of English lexicography can be seen as a progression from the 'hard word' lists of the seventeenth century to the inclusive record of the whole language which the *OED* strives to be, it is also clear that each dictionary is a product of its time, and is informed by the political, philosophical and linguistic preoccupations of its compilers.

4

Syntactic change in Later Modern English

4.1   Introduction

Until very recently, the topic of syntactic change in the later modern period attracted little interest from scholars. Indeed, Denison, introducing his (1993) work on English historical syntax, admits that 'the majority [of topics covered] concern Old and Middle English data since it is during Middle English that syntax changes most' (1993: x). The most comprehensive survey of Later Modern English syntax to date is Denison's chapter in volume IV of *The Cambridge History of the English Language*, which he introduces with a note of caution:

> Compared with the towers of published syntactic research which the Syntax chapters of volumes I–III in this series have been launched from, this chapter has had to rely rather more on its own bootstraps. All research surveys are by definition provisional, this one especially so (1998: 92).

A few topics have received, and continue to receive, a good deal of scholarly attention, most notably the increase throughout the period in both the frequency of use and the functions of what we shall call *be* + *-ing* forms. These constructions, which will be discussed in Section 4.3, have probably dominated research in this area because they constitute one of the few areas of categorical innovation: in 1700 constructions such as *The house is being built* were ungrammatical, but by 1900 they were normal. In other areas of syntax, 'older' constructions which varied with 'newer' alternatives during the early modern period were falling out of use or becoming marked as non-standard by the end of the eighteenth century. As we shall see in Section 4.2.2, the 'regulation' of variants such as *I loved/I did love; I do not love you/I love you not; Does she love him?/Loves she him?*, which has been investigated by scholars of Early Modern English (e.g. Ellegård, 1953;

Hope, 1990) was well on the way to completion by 1700, at least in Standard English.

Readers encounter little in the works of Swift or Austen or Dickens that they would consider ungrammatical, though many constructions might strike them as 'old-fashioned', or in some way 'marked'. Whilst 200 lines of Shakespeare would be enough to provide a sample for commentary, an equivalent extract from a published author of the eighteenth or nineteenth centuries would yield very little. Research on Later Modern English syntax has only flourished since the later twentieth century, when the availability of large corpora of both printed works and private correspondence has made it possible to trace variation and change across thousands of words. Indeed, pioneers in the study of later modern syntax, such as Dennis (1940) and Strang (1982), foreshadowed this approach by searching large bodies of text 'by hand', recording examples on index cards, and calculating the distribution of variants in percentages. Denison notes:

> Since relatively few categorical losses or innovations have occurred in the last two centuries, syntactic change has more often been statistical in nature, with a given construction occurring throughout the period and either becoming more or less common generally or in particular registers. The overall, rather elusive effect can seem more a matter of stylistic than syntactic change (1998: 93).

Visser's (1963–73) volumes on historical syntax concentrate largely on the verb phrase, but provide a vast number of examples from all periods right up to the mid twentieth century. He thus provides valuable evidence for the appearance and disappearance of constructions, rather like a syntactic equivalent of the *OED*. His work is still the most obvious starting-point for anyone wishing to carry out further research on the history of a particular verbal construction. However, any scholar wishing to make an original contribution to research in this area must now make use of, or even build, a corpus. Examples of corpora of Later Modern English usage include the *Corpus of Nineteenth-Century English (CONCE)* (Kytö, Rudanko and Smitterberg, 2000); the *Corpus of Public and Private Writing (PPW)* (Oldireva, 2001); and the *Network of Eighteenth-Century English Texts (NEET)* (Fitzmaurice, 1998; forthcoming). These corpora include texts from a range of genres, including less formal and private forms of writing, such as letters and journals, thus providing a cross-section of writers similar to the samples of speakers selected for synchronic socio-linguistic studies. Before such corpora were available, accounts of syntactic change in the later modern period tended to rely heavily on the pronouncements of eighteenth- and nineteenth-century grammarians, just as synchronic studies rely on 'native speaker intuition'. An example of this is McKnight's pronouncement on second-person pronoun usage:

> That in this period the singular form *thou* of the personal pronoun had been in general superseded by *you* appears from Greenwood's statement: 'And it is counted ungentile and rude to say, *Thou dost so and so*' (1928, reprinted 1968: 335).

With regard to other features of eighteenth-century grammar, such as the distribution of *who* and *whom*, McKnight does attempt to compare prescription with actual usage, albeit from a very narrow range of literary texts, but he has nothing more to say about *thou* and *you*. The assumption is that Greenwood was simply stating a fact. Later accounts, such as those of Strang (1970: 139–40) and Görlach (2001: 131–2), do not necessarily contradict this statement, but provide much more in the way of evidence from eighteenth-century texts. I shall include insights both from grammars and from corpus studies at appropriate points in this chapter, but, as new work in this field is emerging every year, like Denison (quoted above), I have to make a disclaimer that much of this chapter is provisional. I shall not follow Strang (1970) or Denison (1998) in strictly dividing this chapter into sections dealing with the noun phrase and the verb phrase. Instead, I shall deal with developments in an order which is primarily chronological, and secondarily thematic. Thus we shall begin with developments that mark the regulation, or 'tidying up', of variation resulting from changes in Early Modern English, and end with changes initiated in the early twentieth century, after dealing with changes that follow a steady trajectory through the later modern period.

4.2   Regulation of variants resulting from changes in Early Modern English

It is a commonplace amongst historians of English that the flexibility and variability which characterize Shakespeare's language were to be subjected to regulation by the grammarians of the eighteenth century. Thus McKnight writes:

> The general impression gained from a survey of the grammar of Shakespeare is that of an intermediate stage in a course of development, of a language little governed as yet by rules, but on account of its very irregularity, flexible, and, therefore, adaptable to the expression of varied meaning (1928, reprinted 1968: 204).

McKnight goes on to describe how seventeenth- and eighteenth-century revisions of Shakespeare regulate the language. Davenant's version of

Hamlet (1676), for instance, changes (adverbial) *prodigall* to *prodigally*; *more richer* to *richer*; and *he which hath* to *he who hath*, in each case bringing the text into conformity with the prescriptions of the later modern age. Whilst McKnight's statement suggests an evolutionary view of language, if not a rather condescending attitude, there is more than an element of truth in the suggestion that sixteenth-century variants had, by the end of the eighteenth century, often been relegated to non-standard usage, or to special registers. In this section, I shall consider three such areas of variation: *thou* versus *you* forms of the second-person singular pronoun; relative clauses; and uses of the auxiliary *do*.

4.2.1   Regulation of second-person pronouns

In Early Middle English, the use of second-person pronouns in English was determined by number and case. Thus, in the singular *thou* was used as subject, and *thee* in other cases, whilst in the plural *ye* and *you* were used respectively. However, from the thirteenth century onwards, probably under the influence of French, it became fashionable amongst the higher classes to use *ye/you* as polite forms of address to a single interlocutor. By the sixteenth century, the use of *thou/thee* versus *ye/you* was socially and pragmatically constrained, and authors such as Shakespeare could use this variation to reflect the shifting moods and relationships of his characters. The inappropriate use of *thee/thou* was considered such an insult that a verb *to thou* (c.f. French *tutoyer*) had been coined. In *Twelfth Night*, Sir Toby, advising Sir Andrew how to taunt Malvolio, suggests 'if thou thou'st him some thrice, it shall not be amiss' (Act III, Scene 2, 42–3). The sociolinguistic, pragmatic and stylistic implications of this variation have been the subject of a number of studies, including Barber (1981), Brown and Gilman (1960, 1989) and Mulholland (1967). However, in English, unlike most other modern European languages, this subtly constrained variability was to be considerably reduced, and eventually to disappear from standard usage in the course of the later modern period. Strang writes:

> During most of II [1570–1770] *thou* could be used between intimates or between superior and inferior, but by 1770 it survived only in dialects, among Quakers, in literary styles as a device of heightening ... and in its present religious function (1970: 140).

The alternation between *thou/thee* and *ye/you* in English was never as strictly hierarchical as in other European languages: *ye/you*, originally reserved for upper-class usage and reference, became the normal or 'unmarked' term (if in doubt, avoid giving offence). *Thou/thee* became increasingly 'marked' as a term of intimacy, contempt, heightened emotion, or special reference, e.g. addressing God and other supernatural beings (see Lass, 1999: 148–55, for a summary of these developments). There is some evidence of this system lingering into the early eighteenth century: Denison points out that 'in Sheridan's comedy *A Trip to Scarborough* (1777), *thou* forms are intermittently used, mainly in anger or in patronizing intimacy, and never to a social superior' (1998: 106). Richardson likewise had his upper-class male characters use *thou*, but seems to have been reflecting the usage of an earlier period here. Tieken points out that one of his readers criticized Richardson for this usage, suggesting that, 'in *Sir Charles Grandison* (1753–4) *thou* should be changed to *you*!' (1998: 413). Throughout the eighteenth, nineteenth and early twentieth centuries, *thou* continued to be used in increasingly restricted contexts, at least in Standard English. Apart from the usage of Quakers, who had defied convention in the seventeenth century by refusing to give mere mortals the honour due only to God, thus using *thou/thee* to their social superiors, the use of *thou/thee* was mainly confined to religious and poetic usage. Even this was to fall away in the later twentieth century, when the modernist movement in literature, and modernization of the church, disfavoured the archaic *thou/thee* forms in these contexts. A comparison of twentieth century translations of the Bible shows this final loss of *thou/thee*: in the *Revised Standard Version* (1946–52), God the Father addresses Christ thus: 'Thou art my beloved Son; with thee I am well pleased.' In the *Revised English Bible* (1989) this has become 'You are my beloved Son; in you I take delight' (Mark I: 11). By the end of the twentieth century, then, *thee/thou* had disappeared from Standard English, except in the liturgical usage of very conservative Christians.

The loss of *thee/thou* as unmarked forms of the second-person singular left Standard English with no means of marking the singular/plural distinction when addressing one or more people. In the early eighteenth century, this was marked by using *you was* for the singular and *you were* in the plural, but this solution was condemned by most eighteenth-century grammarians. Lowth describes it as 'an enormous solecism' (1762: 48), but goes on to quote 'authors of the first rank' who have used it. These include Swift, Addison and Pope, all, as we shall see in the next chapter, frequent targets of Lowth's criticism. Whilst both Buchanan (1762) and Webster (1789) accept *you was* as good usage, the latter describes it as colloquial:

> In books *you* is commonly used with the plural of the verb *be*, *you were*; in conversation it is generally followed by the singular, *you was* . . . This practice is not merely vulgar; it is general among men of education who do not affect to be fettered by the rules of grammarians, and some late writers have indulged it in their publications (1789: 233–4).

It seems that the 'rules of grammarians' won the day in this case, though, for *you was* is now considered non-standard usage on both sides of the Atlantic. Pragmatic solutions to the potential of misunderstandings caused by the lack of number marking include paraphrases such as *you three, you lot, you guys*, etc. In non-standard dialects, either *thou/thee* persists, or new plural formations have been coined. These include *yous*, which is first cited in the *English Dialect Dictionary* (Wright 1898–1905) as occurring in Ireland, the USA and Australia, but not in England or Scotland. By the end of the twentieth century, this usage had spread to a number of English and Scottish cities, all with a high proportion of inhabitants of Irish ancestry: Glasgow, Liverpool, Newcastle and Manchester. In the USA, *yous* is found in some north-eastern cities (notably New York), but the alternative plural form *you all* is used in the southern states. According to Lass, '*you-all* has become regionally standard in the southern US, and in some varieties, is well enough integrated to have developed its own genitive, *you-all's*' (1999: 155). A third plural form, *yins*, is confined to Pittsburgh, where stereo-typical dialect speakers are referred to as *yinsers*. (The *OED* has first citations for *you all* from 1824, and for *yous* from 1893.) In more traditional English dialects, *thou/thee* are still used, and even retain some of the social and pragmatic constraints of sixteenth-century standard usage. Cave (2001) conducted an ethnographic study of the language of the former mining community in Barnsley, South Yorkshire. He found that use of *thou/thee* forms was confined to men in the corpus he collected, but that the wives of the former miners admitted to using these forms to their husbands in the home. In nearby Sheffield, *thee-ing and tha-ing* is a term used by the more sophisticated urbanites to denigrate the dialect of their small-town neighbours, as well as to suggest an inappropriate use of the less respectful form of address. A woman interviewed in 1981 for the *Survey of Sheffield Usage*, on being asked about use of *thou/thee* replied *Thee the-and-tha thyself and see how thou likes it!* Shorrocks also found *thou/thee* forms used for the second-person singular in Bolton, and some evidence that singular *you* is still used as a polite form: 'there are still sons in the Bolton area who appear to use only the *you* form when addressing their fathers' (1999: 74). Thus the variation that was typical of the early modern period had all but disappeared from Standard English by the end of the eighteenth century, but non-standard dialects either retain vestiges of the old pattern, or have created new patterns to restore the number marking of Early Middle English. The increasing acceptability of *you all* in the southern USA, and the spread of *yous* in Britain (see Cheshire, Edwards and Whittle, 1993), suggests that, in future, the singular–plural distinction may even be restored to Standard English.

4.2.2   Regulation of the uses of *do*

The auxiliary *do*, along with other auxiliary verbs including the modals *can, could, may, might, must, will, shall, should*, is characterized in present-day English by what have become known as the NICE properties. These are:

- Use in Negative sentences, e.g. *She did not eat the bread.*
- Inversion of auxiliary and subject in Interrogative sentences, e.g. *Did she eat the bread?*
- Code usage, to avoid repetition of a lexical verb, e.g. *She ate the bread and so did he.*
- Emphatic usage, e.g. *She **did** eat the bread!*

Use of *do* in any other context (except, of course, as a lexical verb), is described as non-standard. Early studies of the development of auxiliary *do* such as Engblom (1938) and Ellegård (1953), as well as many standard histories of English (e.g. Barber, 1976; Baugh and Cable, 1978), suggest that the NICE properties emerged in the course of the middle and early modern periods and regulation of *do* was more or less complete by the beginning of the eighteenth century. However, more recent studies, notably Tieken (1987) and Nevalainen and Rissanen (1985), demonstrate that the change from 'unregulated' to 'regulated' usage had not been completed by 1700, and that, to some extent, variation is still present today.

For poets and playwrights of the early modern period, optional use of *do* in affirmative sentences provided flexibility: the addition of *do* provides an extra syllable where necessary, without altering the meaning. Thus a line such as 'What we do determine, oft we break' (*Hamlet*, Act III, scene 2, 186) is a perfect iambic pentameter, with *do* periphrasis on the first verb, but not the second. Indeed, this use of *do* in affirmative declarative sentences seems to have been first attested in poetry, becoming common in prose only from the fifteenth century. However, by the early modern period, it had become common in prose too, with this usage reaching its peak in the middle of the sixteenth century: Ellegård (1953: 162) shows a gradual decline in the percentage of *do* forms in affirmative declarative sentences from the mid-sixteenth century to the early eighteenth century, when it comes close to zero. Contemporary grammarians bear testimony to this change, suggesting that *do* in this context is regarded as an acceptable variant in the mid-fifteenth century, but stigmatized 200 years later. Thus Palsgrave's comment, '*I do* is a verb moche comenly used in our tonge to be put before other verbs, as it is all one to say "I do speake", and suche lyke, and "I speake" (1530: 523), contrasts with Johnson's 'Do is sometimes used superfluously, as I do love, I did love; simply for I love or I loved: but this is considered as a vitious mode of speech' (1755: Sig. B2v).

This would suggest that *do* periphrasis in this context had disappeared from educated usage by the mid-eighteenth century. Teiken (1987) found that, in her corpus of 948,700 words of eighteenth-century prose, this construction was still in use, albeit rarely. She found 14 instances of this construction, of which 13 occurred before 1760. Thus the construction is on its way out, at least in the genres represented in Tieken's corpus (informative prose, epistolary prose and direct speech in plays, novels and biography). Examples from Tieken's corpus include:

> I told him, least the Servant should have neglected it, that I did call to pay my Respects to Mr. And Mrs. A[lle]n (Richardson, in Carroll, 1964: 226–7).

> As for that fellow of a curate, if I do catch him . . . (1751, Smollett, *Peregrine Pickle*).

Although Tieken's corpus includes representations of direct speech, it is, of necessity, a corpus of written usage. Nevalainen and Rissanen (1985) found that *do* periphrasis was still being used in unemphatic contexts in the London–Lund and Lancaster–Oslo/Bergen corpora of late twentieth-century educated spoken English. They suggest that this usage is 'connected with discourse processing' (1985: 43) and hence more likely to be found in spoken than in written usage. Rissanen (1999) goes so far as to suggest that the origin of *do* periphrasis may well lie in colloquial spoken usage rather than in the poetic contexts first identified in the written record. It is certainly much more common in certain non-standard dialects, where it has a habitual function. These dialects include those of the south-west of England, Irish English and Welsh English.

The use of *do* periphrasis in poetry also lingered beyond the mid-eighteenth century, despite being stigmatized: presumably the semantically empty syllable as a line filler was too convenient to resist. Thus Duncan's (1789) translation of Boethius' *Consolation of Philosophy*, contains the lines:

> I who of late did sing in chearful strain,
> Must now, alas! In doleful notes complain.
> (cited in Görlach, 2001: 340)

Wordsworth was to make use of this device as late as 1827:

> The hapless creature which did dwell
> Erewhile within the dancing shell.
> (*The Blind Highland Boy*, 193–4)

By the mid-twentieth century, the regular metre and rhyme which made *do* periphrasis an attractive option for poets were out of vogue, so that its use is now confined to the discourse contexts identified by Nevalainen and Rissanen (1985), to legal usage, and to non-standard dialects.

The introduction of *do* in negative and interrogative sentences was an innovation of the early modern period. Ellegård's much-cited graph (1953: 162) shows the percentage of *do* forms in affirmative interrogatives rising from zero in 1400 to over 90 per cent by 1700, whilst the use in negative interrogatives goes from zero to 100 per cent in the same period. Negative declaratives lag behind a little, rising from zero to over 80 per cent, but not showing a steep rise until the second half of the seventeenth century. Early studies suggest that the residue of negatives without *do* can be accounted for largely by the tendency for certain verbs to be negated without *do*. Söderlind's (1951) study of Dryden's prose revealed that 23 verbs tended not to take *do* in the negative. These are *believe, care, change, deny, derive, desire, die, do, fear, give, go, insist, leave, mistake, perform, plead, pretend, proceed, prove, stand, stay, suffer* and *value*. Engblom (1938: 27) found *say, boot, trow, wot, care, doubt* and *know* patterned in this way, whilst Ellegård (1953: 199) added *fear, skill* and *list* to Engblom's list. Tieken (1987) found an average of 24 per cent of negative sentences without *do* in her corpus, a figure fairly consistent with Ellegård's diagram, but suggesting that the decline of this construction was gradual through the eighteenth century. She also found that the verbs *know* and *doubt* resist *do* in the negative more than any others, perhaps because *I doubt not* and *I know not* had become fixed expressions. In the second half of the eighteenth century, in informative prose, *do*-less negation becomes increasingly restricted to sentences with *know*. In the twentieth century, this construction is confined to imperative use in idioms such as *forget-me-not*, and *waste not, want not*, although *I jest not* and *I kid you not* are still used as humorous archaisms in British English. Tieken also notes that the decline in *do*-less negative and interrogative sentences is a change in progress throughout the eighteenth century, and that the extent of an author's use of the constructions with or without *do* correlates with their education and with the genre of writing. Use of *do* is associated with more educated authors, and with the genre of essays. Given that use of *do* in negative and interrogative sentences is prescribed by the grammarians of the eighteenth century, this would appear to be a classic case of what Labov (1972) describes as 'change from above'. Tieken's analysis does not contradict the findings of Ellegård (1953): indeed her average figures of approximately 24 per cent and 5 per cent for *do*-less constructions in negative and interrogative sentences, respectively, are remarkably similar to those at the end-point of Ellegård's graph. However, she does demonstrate that the regulation of *do* had not been completed by 1700, and that a socio-historical approach to the study of syntactic change in Later Modern English can yield interesting and useful results.

4.2.3 Regulation of relativizers

As was the case with auxiliary *do*, the patterns of relativization found in present-day Standard English were introduced during the early modern period, and subjected to regulation in the eighteenth century. Likewise, the distribution in non-standard dialects, and in colloquial spoken Standard English, differs from that of formal, written Standard English. Table 4.1 shows the patterns of relativization available from 1100 to 1600. The use of *that* as a relativizer is possible throughout this period, as is the use of a 'zero' or 'contact' relative (e.g. *The book Ø you read last night*). From about 1400, a new type of relativizer is introduced, the so-called *wh*-relatives. These are introduced gradually, with oblique and prepositional forms appearing first, and the use of *who* to mark relatives with animate antecedents in subject position coming last. The position in 1600 appears to be one of maximal variability, with *that*, zero and all *wh*- relatives available. Romaine carried out a socio-historical study of the introduction of *wh*-relativizers into Scots. She concludes:

> It appears that WH-marked relative clauses entered the language and spread from more formal to less formal styles and from less frequently relativized syntactic positions (e.g. genitive) to more frequently relativized ones (e.g. subject) gradually displacing *that* as a relative clause marker. While the modern written language shows WH-forms in nearly all styles and all syntactic positions, there remains a significant residue of *that* forms in the spoken language (1982: 60).

Table 4.1 The expansion of relative markers in the history of English: a reconstruction (after Romaine, 1982; 53ff.)

Strategy	*c.* 1100	*c.* 1400	*c.* 1500	*c.* 1600
th-	that	that	that	that
wh-		of which to which	of which to which	of which to which
	the	whose whom	which whose whom	which whose whom who
Ø-	Ø	Ø	Ø	Ø

She goes on to assert that 'infiltration of WH into the relative system . . . has not really affected the spoken language' (1982: 212).

In present-day standard English, *wh-*, *that* and zero relativizers are all used, but are subject to restriction. *That* is not used in unrestricted relative clauses (i.e. where the usage is parenthetical), e.g. *We're having spaghetti, which I hate* as opposed to *It's spaghetti bolognese that I hate most*, and is less favoured when the antecedent is human. The use of *who* and *which* is differentiated by the animacy of the antecedent, with *who* confined to human and some animal antecedents. These restrictions were introduced during the eighteenth century, and were the subject of overt prescription by grammarians. Lowth (a clergyman) explicitly condemns the use of *Our Father, which art in Heaven* in the King James Bible (1611) and notes '*That* is used indifferently both of persons and things: but perhaps would be more properly confined to the latter' (1762: 134). Thus the use of *which* with a human (or, in this case, divine) antecedent, is more robustly condemned than *that*. Other eighteenth-century authors are more explicit in their condemnation of *that* as a relativizer, notably Addison, whose *Humble Petition of Who and Which* (1711) satirizes excessive use of *that*, and who corrected instances of *that* with human antecedents to *who* in his own work. *That* is condemned because it is used in so many different contexts, as relativizer, determiner and demonstrative. As we shall see in Chapter 5, the eighteenth-century grammarians' love of order and 'analogy' meant that they favoured forms which were maximally distinctive and minimally ambiguous, so *that* was bound to be disfavoured. In colloquial and non-standard usage, *that* is still used today, particularly (though not exclusively) in restrictive relative clauses. However, in a study of variation and change in Tyneside English over the second half of the twentieth century, Beal and Corrigan (2000; forthcoming) found that, *contra* Romaine, the use of *wh-* relativizers had increased, probably due to the influence of Standard English.

In present-day Standard English, the zero relative is only used where the antecedent is the object of the clause, or in existential or cleft sentences, such as *It's spaghetti bolognese I hate most, There's some spaghetti here needs draining, It was the spaghetti needed draining*. These last three types of sentence would be confined to more informal registers and styles. This restriction, like those constraining the use of *which* and *that*, was introduced in the eighteenth century. Visser writes:

> In the course of the eighteenth and the nineteenth centuries a remarkable decline in the currency of the zero-construction becomes perceptible. Only writers whose style is natural and easy . . . go on freely using it, whereas many others, such as Johnson (who called the omission of the relative 'a colloquial barbarism') . . . consciously avoid it (1963–73: 540).

This would indicate that the regulation of the use of zero relatives is a 'change from above', introduced by grammarians and those who followed their rules. However, Raybould (1998: 191) notes that 'Swift, Gray and Walpole constantly omit the relative and Johnson and Gray go so far as to leave it out even in the nominative'. It would appear that, whilst grammarians of the eighteenth and nineteenth centuries condemned the omission of the relative, those same grammarians used the zero construction in informal writing. Johnson uses it in *The Idler,* Sheridan uses it in his plays (Denison, 1998: 281, gives examples from *School for Scandal* and *A Trip to Scarborough*) and, according to Phillips (1970: 171–2), Jane Austen uses it as a marker of social class, with 'the most acceptable people' avoiding this construction. Denison (1998: 281) notes that 'during the twentieth century, the construction has largely regained its place in literary language'. It would appear that the zero construction has always been used in colloquial and/or lower-class usage, but that its acceptability in literary English has fluctuated, waning and waxing in an inverse ratio to the influence of prescriptive grammarians.

In non-standard varieties of English, a number of alternative relative markers are used. The *Survey of English Dialects*, for which fieldwork was conducted in the 1950s, shows little use of *wh-* relativizers in traditional dialects. Where a relative construction is not avoided by periphrasis (e.g. *That's the chap thou knows, his uncle drowned hissen*: Orton and Halliday, 1963: 1086), *as, at, that, what* and zero are used in various locations, with *what* more common in the south and *as/at* in the north. Cheshire, Edwards and Little (1993) found that, in a survey conducted in schools throughout Britain, *what* was reported 'far more frequently than any of the other non-standard relative pronoun forms' and 'was reported just as frequently in the North of England as in the South'. However, this is not borne out by Beal and Corrigan's (forthcoming) comparison of corpus-based material from Newcastle and Sheffield, in which *what* was frequent in the Sheffield corpus, although only one instance was found in the Newcastle one.

4.3 Innovations of the later modern period

The changes discussed in Section 4.2 involved regulation of variants which resulted from innovations introduced in the early modern period. In each case, variants which had once been used in Standard, or rather literary, English did not disappear from the language, but continue to be found in non-standard, dialectal or colloquial usage. The prescriptive grammarians of the eighteenth and nineteenth centuries both influenced and reflected these regulatory changes. We shall discuss the grammarians further in

Chapter 5, but will now turn to changes which were either initiated or gathered momentum in the later modern period, despite the resistance of grammarians.

4.3.1   The *be + -ing* construction

Possibly the most spectacular change in English syntax during the later modern period is the increase in both the frequency and range of uses of what has variously been termed the 'progressive', the 'expanded form', or, simply, the *be + -ing* form of verbs. This construction was not new, but it is noticeable that in Early Modern English it is not always used where it would be today. Thus in *Hamlet*, Polonius's *What do you read my Lord?* (Act II, scene 2, 190) would today be replaced by *What are you reading?* The form without *-ing* would now be understood as referring to habitual actions, and the expected answer would be something like *Science fiction, and the occasional thriller*. When the focus is on a particular moment after the beginning but before the end of an action, what Visser (1963–73) calls 'the post-inception phase', the *be + -ing* form becomes more and more frequent as the later modern period progresses. Leah Dennis concludes from her early corpus-based study that:

> our day uses five to ten times as many progressive forms as did 1600, and ten to twenty times as many as did 1500, or – more rashly perhaps – that the use has approximately doubled in each successive century throughout Modern English (1940: 860).

In fact, this increase slows down in the eighteenth century, and accelerates in the nineteenth: Arnaud in a study of private letters noted a 300 per cent increase in the use of this form during the nineteenth century (1983: 84). Strang's study of literary narrative prose reveals that this increase continues in the twentieth century, but that, whilst the construction is largely confined to subordinate clauses during the first half of the eighteenth century, from 1750 onwards 'the figures rise overall, but proportionately most in non-subordinate clauses' (1982: 442). Strang goes on to state that, in the nineteenth and twentieth centuries, the overall usage of *be + -ing* forms doubles, but the use in non-subordinate clauses almost quadruples.

The increase is partly accounted for by the fact that, as the later modern period progresses, the *be + -ing* form is used in more and more constructions, and with more and more verbs. With verbs which denote 'instant' actions, i.e. actions whose beginning and end coincide and which logically do not have what Visser calls a 'post-inception phase', the *be + -ing* form is rarely used before the nineteenth century. An early example is from

Jane Austen: *a water-party; and by some accident she was falling overboard* (*Emma*, 1816). Strang (1982) suggests that Austen used the progressive experimentally in her novels. In this example, the effect is to involve the reader in watching the action as it happens, almost as an 'action replay'. Today, the construction is perfectly acceptable, but in Austen's time it flouted received views on grammar and logic. Even today, the so-called 'stative' verbs are defined by their avoidance of the *be + -ing* construction, but they can be used in this way to denote a state or behaviour which is not permanent: thus *I am living in London* suggests that the speaker expects to move, and *I'm loving every minute of this* focuses on the speaker's immediate feelings. Visser has no examples of this usage before the twentieth century, but Denison (1998: 146) gives the following nineteenth century examples:

> The tars *are wishing* for a lick, as they call it, at the Spanish galleons (1803, *Naval Chron.* X.258 [OED]).

> Do not live as if I *was not existing* – Do not forget me (1820, Keats, *Letters.*).

The use of *be + -ing* with nominal and adjectival complements was likewise rare before the nineteenth century. Once again, Keats provides an early example:

> You will be glad to hear ... *how diligent* I have been and *am being* (1819, *Letters*, cited in Denison, 1998: 146).

The earliest example with a noun complement found by Denison is from 1834:

> I really think this illness *is being* a good thing for me (1838, R. H. Froude, cited in Denison, 1998: 147).

The introduction of *be + -ing* with adjectival complements in the nineteenth century is, as Denison suggests, linked with the development of the progressive passive. The two constructions are both roundly condemned by the American grammarian Richard Grant White:

> Could there be a more absurd affectation than, instead of, the tea has been drawing five minutes, to say, The tea has been being drawn five minutes? *Been being* – is that sense, or English? – except to children, who say that they have been being naughty, thereby saying only that they have been naughty' (1871: *Words* xi. 362).

White is objecting to the combination of *have + been +-ing*, which was rare before the twentieth century, but even the combination of *be + -ing* and the passive met a good deal of resistance. This combination was used as early as the fifteenth century in informal writing: Curme and Kurath (1931: 443) point out the following example from a letter of John Shillingford, *c.* 1447:

> Wyne is being *y-put* to sale (italics in Curme).

However, such examples are rare before the later modern period. If the speaker or writer wished to convey the idea that an action was both passive and incomplete, the following strategies were available:

a) The passive only is marked. Examples are:

> I went to see if any play *was acted* (1662, Pepys, *Diary*).

> He found that the coach had sunk greatly on one side, though it *was* still *dragged* forward by the horses (1838–9, Dickens, *Nicholas Nickleby*).

b) The *be + -ing* form is used with the prefix *a-*:

> Then to Rochester and there saw the Cathedrall, which is now fitting for use, and the Organ then *a-tuning* (1660, Pepys).

c) The *be + -ing* form only is marked:

> before whom I was examined for Deacon's orders . . . I *was* quite half an hour *examining* (1763, Woodeforde, *Diary*).

In the course of the eighteenth century (c) takes over from (b). Dr Johnson (1755) writes:

> The grammar is now printing, brass is forging . . . in my opinion a vitious expression probably corrupted from a phrase more pure but now somewhat obsolete: a printing, a forging.

In the first half of the eighteenth century, non-passival examples of (b) can be found in literature, but a century later such constructions are confined to the representation of non-standard speech:

> This girl is always *a-scribbling* (Richardson, *Pamela*, 1740).

> I hope, sir, you're not *a-thinking* as I bear you any ill-will . . . I'm not *a-defending* him (1860, George Eliot, *The Mill on the Floss*).

It would seem that the passival use of *a- + -ing* becomes disfavoured along with the non-passival. The passival use of *be +-ing*, as in (c), becomes increasingly popular through the eighteenth and nineteenth centuries, with criticisms such as Johnson's fading away as the attention of grammarians turned to the more objectionable progressive passive. From the second half of the nineteenth century, the use of the passival decreases, though instances can still be found with verbs of cooking, printing, preparing and others. Familiar examples, which native speakers do not think of as passive until this is pointed out to them, include *Now showing at a cinema near you; The kettle is boiling; The play is rehearsing*. The progressive passive is not used until the last quarter of the eighteenth century. Visser's earliest example is from Southey:

> you, like a fellow whose uttermost upper grinder is being torn out by the roots by a mutton-fisted barber . . . will grin and endure it (1795, Southey, *Life*).

However, Denison (1998: 152) provides the following earlier examples:

> I have received the speech and address of the House of Lords; probably, that of the House of Commons was being debated when the post went out (1772, Harris, *Letters*).

> The inhabitants of Plymouth are under arms, and everything is being done that can be (1779, Mrs Harris, *Letters*).

It is worth noting that all three of these early examples come from letters, the most informal of written mediums. Grammarians continue to protest about this construction well into the nineteenth century. Marsh writes of the passival (form (c) above):

> Upon the whole, then, we may say, that the construction 'the house is building' is sustained by the authority of usage, and by many analogies in the English and cognate languages. Nor is it objectionable as an equivocal phrase, because it is very seldom used when the subject is of such a nature that it can be the agent, and always with a context, or under circumstances which show that the participle must be taken in a passive sense. To reject it therefore, is to violate the laws of the language by an arbitrary change; and, in this particular case, the proposed substitute [is being built] is at war with the genius of the English Language (1870: 465, cited in Visser, 1963–73: 2016).

Arnaud (1998) suggests that the increase in use of the progressive generally in the eighteenth and nineteenth centuries is a 'change from below', both in the sense of 'below the level of consciousness', and of 'from a lower social group'. Certainly, in the case of the progressive passive, the eventual acceptance of the newer construction is achieved in the face of considerable opposition from grammarians. Even as late as 1931, Curme's acceptance of this construction is somewhat grudging:

> From 1825 on ... the form with *being* + perfect participle began to lead all others in this competition, so that in spite of considerable opposition the clumsy *is being built* became more common than *is building* in the usual passive meaning, i.e., where it was desired to represent a person or thing as affected by an agent working under resistance vigorously and consciously to a definite end: 'The house *is being built*.' 'My auto *is being repaired*' (Curme and Kurath, 1931: 444).

The extension of the passive progressive to longer verb groups with modals and/or perfect *have* took longer. In the late nineteenth century, such constructions appear only as artificially constructed examples in grammars. Marsh continues his defence of the passival, cited above, by presenting what he sees as a ridiculous alternative:

> They must say therefore ... the great Victoria bridge *has been being built* more than two years; when I reach London, the ship Leviathan *will be being* built; if my orders had been followed, the coat *would have been being made* yesterday; if the house had then *been being built*, the mortar would *have been being* mixed (1860: 654).

Less than 60 years later, such constructions were being used by literary authors. Two of the earliest examples (cited in Denison 1998: 158) are:

> She doesn't trust us. I *shall* always *be being pushed* away from him by her (1915, Galworthy, *Freelands*).

> There's no wedding. Who *could be being* married? (1918, Barrie, *Barbara's Wedding*).

Curme and Kurath, however, assert that 'in the compound tenses the construction with the present participle is still ... employed in the usual passive meaning' and that 'the accumulation of auxiliary forms would be intolerable' (1931: 445). Curme was writing in the USA, so it is possible that the use of *be* + *-ing* in longer constructions was resisted for longer on that side of the Atlantic. That they were being used by American authors is proved by the following example from Ford Madox Ford:

> By 1.30 I *must have been being introduced* (1923, *Marsden Case*, cited in Denison, 1998: 158).

Although such constructions are rare even today, this is because the occasions for using them are rare. As Denison points out 'no formal grammar which admits the progressive passive is likely to rule out these longer but analogous verbal groups. Though clumsy, they are occasionally needed and used' (1998: 158).

4.3.2 Group-verbs

The term 'group-verb' is used by Denison to denote 'a multi-word lexical item with verbal function' (1998: 221). Under this heading, he discusses four major categories: intransitive phrasal verbs, such as *eat out, wise up*; transitive phrasal verbs, such as *clean (object) out; mess (object) up*; prepositional verbs, such as *insist on (object), deal with (object)*; and phrasal-prepositional verbs, such as *hang up on (object), get away with (object)*. Although, as Denison admits, the histories of individual group-verbs are of lexical rather than syntactic interest, the increase in verbs of this type in Later Modern English does lead to comments by grammarians, particularly when preposition-stranding leaves the preposition at the end of a sentence.

Strang points out that what she calls 'verb–particle combinations' were 'virtually unknown' in Old English, but begin to appear from the twelfth century, when there was a sharp rise in the number of prepositions in English. Although these verbs were introduced in small numbers during the Early Middle English period, as Strang points out, 'by the mid-12c verb–particle combinations already have so specialised a lexical sense (*give up* = 'surrender, 1154) that we must suppose the type to have become deeply entrenched even before' (1970: 275). Strang has little more to say about this matter, except that phrasal verbs are 'hugely productive' in the period 1370–1570 and that the trend towards the formation of these structures is 'said to be accelerating' in the mid-twentieth century (1970: 193, 59). By the eighteenth century, the number of group-verbs in the language was sufficient to attract the attention of grammarians and lexicographers. Johnson gave separate entries to group-verbs such as *set out, set up* and *take up*, and makes the following remarks in his *Preface* (1755):

> There is another kind of composition more frequent in our language than perhaps in any other, from which arises to foreigners the greatest difficulty. We modify the signification of many verbs by a particle subjoined; as to *come off*, to escape by a fetch; to *fall on*, to attack; to *fall off*, to apostatize; to *break off*, to stop abruptly; to *bear out*, to justify; to *fall in*, to comply; to *give over*, to cease; to *set off*, to embellish; to *set in*, to begin a continual tenour; to *set out*, to begin a course or journey; to *take off*, to copy; with innumerable expressions of the same kind, of which some appear wildly irregular, being so far distant from the sense of the simple words that no sagacity will be able to trace the steps by which they arrived at the present use. These I have noted with great care; and though I cannot flatter myself that the collection is complete, I have perhaps so far assisted the students of our language, that this kind of phraseology will be no longer impenetrable.

Johnson here appears to accept these constructions, albeit grudgingly. The group-verbs which he uses as examples here all belong to the first three of

Denison's categories: the intransitive phrasal (*give over, set out*), the transitive phrasal (*take off, bear out*) and the prepositional (*fall on, set off*). This suggests that extensive use of the phrasal-prepositional type is more recent: for instance *put up with* has a first citation of 1755 in the *OED*, but is not included in Johnson's *Dictionary* until the 1765 edition, where it is defined as 'to suffer without resentment'. Denison suggests that phrasal-prepositional verbs begin to take over from transitive phrasal verbs in Later Modern English. He suggests that this 'one effect is to lessen the transitivity of the group-verb; thus, for example, BEAT *up on* need not signify actual physical attack, whereas BEAT *up* almost always does' (1998: 223). He goes on to provide examples of transitive phrasal verbs and their more recent phrasal-prepositional equivalents. Amongst these are *get away* (first cited 1375)/*get away with* (1878); and *cut down* (1857)/*cut down on* (1939). The dates here suggest . . . not so much that phrasal-prepositional verbs as a class are taking over, as that once a transitive phrasal verb is established, it can be supplemented, and perhaps eventually replaced, by a phrasal-prepostitional one. However, it does appear that phrasal-prepositional verbs only become common from the mid-eighteenth century.

The extract from Johnson's *Preface* cited above suggests that he was more concerned with identifying and defining such group-verbs as had been lexicalized than with condemning them as 'vitious' or inelegant. Other seventeenth- and eighteenth-century commentators were less tolerant, not so much of group-verbs per se as of the preposition-stranding which occurs when these verbs appear with relative clauses. Dryden was the first to notice this in his own writing but the eighteenth-century grammarians propagated the shibboleth, which still raises its head today. Lowth, who, as we shall see in Chapter 5, was one of the most influential eighteenth-century grammarians, writes thus:

> The Preposition is often separated from the Relative which it governs, and joined to the Verb at the end of the Sentence, or some Member of it: as 'Horace is an author, *whom* I am much delighted *with*' . . . This is an idiom, which our language is strongly inclined to: it prevails in common conversation, and suits very well with the familiar style in writing: but the placing of the Preposition before the Relative is more graceful, as well as more perspicuous; and agrees much better with the solemn and elevated style (1762: 127).

Here, Lowth does not condemn preposition-stranding outright: indeed, he (perhaps ironically) uses the construction himself (*an idiom, which our language is strongly inclined to*). Rather, he suggests that such constructions are inevitable in 'common conversation' and informal written usage, but not elegant enough for a 'solemn and elevated style'. As we shall see in

Chapter 5, this is one of many instances in which Lowth proves less prescriptive than many twentieth-century scholars have judged him to be. Although the more descriptive grammarians of the twentieth century simply analyse this construction as an informal one more common with zero relatives, the shibboleth persists. Thus, whilst Curme writes that 'for many centuries the position of a preposition at or near the end of a proposition has been one of the outstanding features of our language' (Curme and Kurath, 1931: 568), as late as 2003 this usage is still being condemned in style guides. Strang points out that a different type of 'group-verb', of the type *have a try, take a look*, 'develops rapidly from about 1800' (1970: 101). In these constructions, the verb carries little lexical meaning, with most of the semantic information carried by the noun phrase. She goes on to state that another type, in which the verb carries more information, such as *laugh one's thanks, grope one's way*, are first recorded at about the same time. However, although the *OED* has the first citation of *have a try* from 1832, that for *grope thy way* is from 1724, and *take a look* appears in Sterne's *Tristram Shandy* (1761), so, in some cases, the usage is a little older than Strang indicates. Nevertheless, it would appear that usage both in terms of types and tokens of all kinds of 'group-verb' increases throughout the later modern period, to become an important feature of present-day English (Olsen, 1961).

4.3.3 Decline of the subjunctive

The constructions discussed in Sections 4.3.1 and 4.3.2 are both innovations, or at least increase in usage during the later modern period. In both cases, grammarians of the time condemned these innovations, but in vain. In this section, we shall consider a construction which is used less as the period progresses, and has virtually disappeared today: the inflectional subjunctive.

The subjunctive mood, in English as in other Indo-European languages, is used to express 'unreal' conditions such as wishes, doubts, etc. It is strongly associated with certain prepositions which likewise mark conditionality, most notably *if*. Thus, even in present-day English, it is possible to say *if I were you*, although the indicative *was* is an alternative (indeed, as I write this, the US grammar check programme has underlined *were* and suggested I substitute *was*). From Middle English, if not earlier, loss of inflections had considerably reduced the distinctions between indicative and subjunctive forms of most verbs. By 1700, the distinction was only maintained in the third-person singular of lexical verbs (*If she go/she goes*) and that only in the present tense. The verb *be* maintained the indicative/subjunctive distinction in all persons of the present tense, and in the singular of the past. In fact, the indicative/subjunctive distinctions in the paradigm of *be* were actually increased in the early modern period, when *are* replaced *be* in the plural forms of the present indicative (older usage of indicative *be* is fossilized in the phrase *the powers that be*). The contrasting forms are (indicative/subjunctive): in the present tense, *I am/be; thou art/be; s/he is/be; we/you/they are/be;* and in the past tense *I was/were; s/he was/were.* Strang writes that from the fifteenth century onwards the subjunctive was 'largely a function of *be*' and that, from this point on, there has been 'a decline in the sense of where the subjunctive should appropriately be used, a decline that has continued to this day, reversed sporadically only by the tendency to hypercorrection in 18c and later teachers and writers' (1970: 209). More recent evidence from corpus-based studies (Denison, 1998) shows that the chronology provided by Strang is correct, but that use of the inflectional subjunctive in the eighteenth and nineteenth centuries is not entirely confined to the verb *be*. Denison (1998: 300) demonstrates that *if*-less conditional clauses such as *I would do it, feared I not my father*, in which the subjunctive is signalled by inversion of the verb and subject, maintain a relatively high frequency of usage until 1800, after which there is a sharp decline to virtual disappearance by the mid-twentieth century. Görlach (2001: 123) suggests that this construction is 'a hallmark of formal eighteenth-century style', citing Murray (1795: 130) as ascribing to it 'a particular neatness'. The further decline of subjunctive usage in the twentieth century is indicated by the fact that, to a speaker of British English in the twenty-first century, examples cited by Curme and Kurath (1931: 427) as typical of 'loose colloquial speech' would be acceptable in any style or register, whilst their alternatives seem stilted and dated. Curme and Kurath's examples are: '"If it *was* (instead of *were*) not so cold, he would be allowed to go out", and "What appears more real than the sky? We think of it and speak of it as if it *was* as positive and tangible a fact as the earth" (Burroughs, *The Light of Day,* Ch. XIV, VIII)'. Although both *was* and *were* are grammatical in these contexts both in 1931 and in 2004, to Curme and Kurath, *was* is marked in these examples, but to the twenty-first-century reader, *were* is the marked case.

4.3.4   Other changes

Whilst the preceding paragraphs have outlined the major grammatical changes in Later Modern English ('major' in the sense of having been subjected to a reasonable degree of scholarly attention), a number of others have been noted. Strang notes the development of what she calls, after

Sweet, 'the prop-word', i.e. the use of *one* to replace a noun which would otherwise be repeated, as in *two green balloons and a red one*. Strang points out that, whilst 'prop uses of *one* have been developing for perhaps a thousand years', the use of this prop-word after determiners seems to have occurred from about 1800 onwards. Citing examples from Jespersen (1909–49: II, 256–63), Strang (1970: 96–7) produces a chronology in which examples with post-modification (*the one preferred*) are found from Jane Austen onwards, but other usages, such as *this/that one, those ones; the one*, meaning 'the right one'; and *one* after possessives, e.g. *her one*, are more recent. Of the latter construction, Jespersen writes that it was 'beginning to be used', but Strang in 1970 considered it 'perfectly normal'. The only restriction on the use of the 'prop-word' *one* today is that, according to Strang '*a one* is depreciatory'. This restriction certainly applies in present-day Standard English, but in some non-standard dialects, notably those of Tyneside and Northumberland, even this restriction has been lifted. Thus the answer to *Would you like a drink?* could be *Thanks, I'll have a one*. As Jespersen describes some of his more 'recent' examples as found in conversation or colloquial speech, perhaps the integration of the 'prop-word' *one* has been a 'change from below' which is more advanced in non-standard dialects. Further investigation of these constructions in corpora of Later Modern English could prove interesting, especially since, as Strang points out, this is 'one of the most unusual features of English nominal usage' (1970: 98).

Use of the passive seems to have declined in the course of the later modern period. Biber (2000) demonstrates that it was more common in all registers in the eighteenth century than in the twentieth, by which time it had become mainly restricted to informational registers such as scientific writing. Seoane-Posse (2002) shows that use of the passive in scientific writing declines in the second half of the twentieth century in both British and American English, but more sharply in the latter. Indeed, in the USA, use of the passive is explicitly proscribed in style guides, whilst in British English it is allowed, even if more 'reader-friendly' constructions are sometimes favoured. The US grammar check in Word never fails to suggest the active voice as a preferred alternative.

Other changes which have been noted include an increase in the use of *more, most* + adjective/adverb, as against adjective/adverb + *-er, est*; (Barber, 1964; Strang, 1970: 58) and a shift towards use of noun + *-'s* rather than *of* + noun for the genetive (Barber, 1964; Strang, 1970: 58). Citing these as examples of 'changes within living memory', Strang laments that 'we lack figures to confirm these trends'. However, as the discussion above has demonstrated, the increasing availability of corpora of Later Modern

English means that such 'figures' will soon become available, and a more complete account of morpho-syntactic change in this period will be possible.

Throughout this chapter, it has been evident that, more than in any other period, changes in the morphology and syntax of Later Modern English are the subject of overt comment. The grammarians of the period, in some cases, if not directly responsible for the changes 'from above', at least contribute to the codification of such changes, whilst, in other cases, their protests against changes 'from below', may, in Johnson's words, 'retard what [they] cannot repel'. Other changes, which have not been discussed in this chapter, affect only Standard English, and can perhaps be more clearly attributed to the influence of grammarians: examples of these would be the decline of multiple negation, 'double' comparatives and superlatives, and the proscription of the 'split infinitive'. These will be considered in the next chapter, which concentrates on the nature and influence of grammars and grammarians in the later modern period.

5
Grammars and Grammarians

5.1 The 'doctrine of correctness'

5.1.1 Introduction

In many general histories of English, such as Baugh and Cable (1978), Bourcier (1981) and Freeborn (1992), the main or even the only issue discussed in chapters devoted to the eighteenth century is the emergence of prescriptive grammars. Bourcier, for instance, devotes only five pages (204–8) to this period, under the heading 'Post-Restoration social and intellectual attitudes'. Here, certain key words reveal Bourcier's view that this is a single-issue century: 'order and discipline . . . codification . . . a regulatory body . . . prescriptive grammar'. Bryant likewise defines the eighteenth century in these terms:

> As progress was made towards a uniform standard in the English language, freedom decreased. Rules began to be formulated, efforts began to be made to fix the language, to determine what was right and what was wrong, to prescribe the goal to be attained. This attitude reached its height in the eighteenth century, the age in which reason and logic were uppermost (1962: 89–90).

All of these works take their lead from what was for a long time the most influential work on eighteenth-century grammars and attitudes to language, S. A. Leonard's (1929) *The Doctrine of Correctness in English Usage 1700–1800*. Whilst, as we shall see, Leonard's work was seminal and still commands serious attention, the iconicity of the phrase 'doctrine of correctness' was to prove damaging to eighteenth-century studies. In an age when 'prescriptive' had become a term of abuse amongst linguists, the eighteenth century was seen as a period fit only to be trawled for instances of malpractice. Even after Alston's (1967–70) microfiche series made access to original texts much easier, statements made about eighteenth-century grammars often relied on secondary sources. As Pullum (1974: 63) points out, twentieth-century linguists mention Lowth's grammar frequently, but rarely show any indication of having read it. Only very recently have a number of scholars, including Crowley (1991), Rodriguez-Gil (2002) and Tieken (2000), challenged this monolithic view of eighteenth-century grammars, turning to the original texts and viewing them and their authors in the social and intellectual context of their time. What emerges from these studies is that eighteenth-century grammarians had a range of motives for writing their grammars, and that these and later grammars, far from being uniformly 'prescriptive', would be better described as occupying different points on a prescriptive–descriptive continuum.

That said, it cannot be denied that the eighteenth century, and in particular the second half of that century, sees an unprecedented number of grammars published. Only a handful of extant English grammars were published before 1700, and about 50 between 1700 and 1750, but over 200 appear in the second half of the eighteenth century. Whilst many of these were published in London, other centres were important: more grammars were published in Newcastle than any other Anglophone city outside the English capital, but Boston, Dublin and Edinburgh followed close behind, and many smaller provincial towns such as Sunderland and Warrington could boast at least one grammar. Clearly, there was a market and a readership for English grammars in the second half of the eighteenth century, and that market was being supplied by a large number of printers and authors. Before examining some of these grammars in detail, I shall consider why the demand for grammars of English arose at this time.

5.1.2   Standardization and codification

One reason for the increase in both supply of and demand for grammars in the later eighteenth century can be found in the history of Standard English. Haugen (1971) states that there are four main processes involved in the standardization of languages, and that these may happen either in stages or simultaneously. They are:

1. *Selection* of an existing language or variety as the basis of the standard. This is usually that of the most powerful or influential group.
2. *Codification*, involving the reduction of variability within the selected language or variety and the establishment of norms.
3. *Elaboration*, which ensures that the standard can be used for a wide range of functions.
4. *Implementation*, whereby use of the standard is encouraged by making texts available in it, discouraging the use of alternative varieties, and fostering loyalty to, and pride in the standard.

By 1700, the first process had been completed as far as the written language was concerned and, as we shall see in Chapter 7, was well under way for the spoken variety as well. By the beginning of the early modern period, a Standard English had emerged as the only acceptable variety for use in published texts in England, and by 1700 this variety had also supplanted Scots as the written standard for Scotland. Elaboration had also taken place in the sixteenth and early seventeenth centuries when, as we saw in Chapter 2, a massive influx of learned words, largely adapted from Latin, supplied the vocabulary necessary for English to be used as a medium of scholarly discourse. However, the codification and implementation of the standard were yet to be realized. At the beginning of the eighteenth century, several authoritative figures made explicit demands for the codification of English. Foremost among these is Swift, who, in *A Proposal for Correcting, Improving and Ascertaining the English Tongue*, addressed the Lord High Treasurer as follows:

> My LORD; I do here, in the Name of all the Learned and Polite Persons of the Nation, complain to Your LORDSHIP, as *First Minister*, that our Language is extremely imperfect; that its daily Improvements are by no means in proportion to its daily Corruptions; that the Pretenders to polish and refine it, have chiefly multiplied Abuses and Absurdities; and, that in many Instances, it offends against every Part of Grammar (1712: 8).

Notice here that Swift's idea of 'grammar' is very different to that taught in university departments of linguistics in the twenty-first century. Today's linguist would consider it impossible for the language produced by a native speaker to 'offend against every Part of Grammar' or for a language to be either corrupted or improved, but that is exactly what Swift and his readers believed. The key word in Swift's proposal, repeated by other eighteenth-century authorities such as Johnson (1747), is *ascertaining*: 'What I have most at Heart is, that some Method should be thought on for *ascertaining* and *fixing* our Language for ever, after such Alterations are made in it as shall be thought requisite' (1712: 31). To *ascertain* at this time meant to make certain, or to fix: in other words, to codify. Swift advocated setting up a committee similar to the Académie Française, which had been established in 1634. He suggested that 'a free judicious Choice should be made of such Persons, as are generally allowed to be qualified for such a Work' and that they 'should assemble at some appointed Time and Place, and fix on Rules by which they design to proceed' (1712: 30). McKnight points out that Swift's plan almost succeeded. In a dedication to Lord Chesterfield in 1747, David Mallet wrote that the plan 'was agreed to by the late Treasurer Oxford: and a certain annual sum, for the support of it, was certainly promised' (cited in McKnight [1928] 1968: 322). However, by the time Mallett attempted to interest Chesterfield in the revival of the scheme, it had already been rendered unnecessary by the emergence of several grammars, including those of Gildon and Brightland (1711) and Greenwood (1711). Moreover, Johnson was soon to be hailed by Chesterfield as the one-man academy to whose 'dictatorship' he was willing to surrender all his 'rights and privileges in the English Language' (1754, cited above, p. 44). Nevertheless, half a century after Swift published his proposal, his words were still being used as arguments for the codification and implementation of Standard English. Thus Lowth, one of the most successful and influential grammarians of the eighteenth century, prefaced his *Short Introduction to English Grammar* with the following:

> It is now about fifty years since Doctor Swift made a public remonstrance, addressed to the Earl of Oxford, then Lord Treasurer, of the imperfect State of our Language; alledging in particular, 'that in many instances it offended against every part of Grammar'. Swift must be allowed to have been a good judge of this matter. He was himself very attentive to this part, both in his own writings, and in his remarks upon those of his friends: he is one of our most correct, and perhaps our very best prose writer. Indeed the justness of his complaint, as far as I can find, hath never been questioned; and yet no effectual method hath hitherto been taken to redress the grievance of which he complains.
>
> But let us consider, how, and in what extent, we are to understand this charge brought against the English Language. Does it mean, that the English Language as it is spoken by the politest part of the nation, and as it stands in the writings of our most approved authors, oftentimes offends against every part of Grammar? Thus far, I am afraid, the charge is true (1762: iii).

As we shall see, Lowth proves his point by citing 'the writings of our most approved authors' as examples of bad practice throughout his grammar. To a great extent, the repetition of Swift's complaint acts as a justification for Lowth's work: if the language had already been codified, there would be no need for a new grammar. Even in the nineteenth century, when readers had access to a number of authoritative and influential grammars, including Lowth's, the complaint tradition continues. H. H. Breen writes that 'the most striking characteristic of English literature in the nineteenth century, is the loose and ungrammatical diction that disfigures every species of prose composition' (1857: 3, cited in Bailey, 1996: 215). In a similar vein, Bailey cites a writer in *Blackwood's Magazine* who complains that 'with the exception of Wordsworth, there is not one celebrated author of this day who has written two pages consecutively without some flagrant impropriety in the language (Bailey, 1996). Like the authors of self-help books today, grammarians of the eighteenth and nineteenth centuries had to establish that there was a problem in order to sell their solutions to readers anxious to avoid being censured for grammatical solecisms. Some of these grammars were very successful: for instance, Lindley Murray's was first published in 1795, and went into 65 editions, the last of which appeared in 1871. The market for grammars of English was a very competitive one, and authors appealed to the anxieties of their potential readers by suggesting that even 'celebrated' or 'most approved authors' were incapable of writing correctly without recourse to whichever grammar was being advertised in this way. To understand why grammars of English became such a marketable commodity in the eighteenth century, we first need to look at changes in society during this period.

5.1.3   Social mobility and linguistic insecurity

As we saw in Chapter 1 (p. 5), the later modern period was a time of social change and social mobility in Britain. As the economy shifted from being land-based to money-based, and as the Industrial Revolution proceeded, it became possible for a person born into a lower social class to rise to a higher position in society. Swift notes this shift in the *Examiner* (1710): '*Power*, which according to an old maxim was used to follow *Land*, is now gone over to *Money*' (cited in Corfield, 1991: 106). However, the standard form of English which, to use Haugen's terminology, had been selected and elaborated in the fifteenth and sixteenth centuries, and which was being codified in the eighteenth, was based on the usage of the court, of 'men civill and graciously behavoured and bred' (Puttenham, 1589). As British society became more meritocratic, and indeed plutocratic, people of relatively humble origins could acquire many of the trappings of gentility: fashionable clothes, prestigious houses and land. Yet their new position in society would bring them into contact with 'old money': the representatives of the landed gentry, whose place in society was a matter of birthright. This clash of cultures is a well-rehearsed theme in plays and novels of the late eighteenth and nineteenth centuries. In Steele's play *The Conscious Lovers*, the merchant Sealand stakes a claim for his class being 'as honourable, and almost as useful, as you landed Folks, that have always thought yourself so much above us' (cited in Corfield, 1991: 107). As Phillips points out, the social aspirations of those 'in trade' were viewed with alarm by the upper classes. He cites the following extract from Mrs Gaskell's *North and South* (1854):

> Are those the Gormans who made their fortunes at Southampton? Oh! I'm glad we don't visit them. I don't like shoppy people. I think we are far better off, knowing only cottagers and labourers and people without pretence (cited in Phillips, 1984: 93).

The socio-linguistic consequence of this social mobility was the creation of what Labov has termed the 'linguistic insecurity' typically associated with the middle class, or, in Labov's words, the 'second-highest status group'. Members of this social class are aware that some linguistic variants are 'better' or more prestigious than others, but that they themselves do not always use these. Labov found that this led to the use of 'hypercorrect' forms in more formal speech styles such as formal interviews, reading out word lists, etc. In the eighteenth century, this same insecurity would create a demand for prescriptive guides to 'correct' usage. Indeed, a number of grammarians deliberately play on these anxieties. Withers notes that 'purity and politeness of Expression ... is the only external Distinction which remains between a Gentleman and a Valet, a Lady and a Mantua-maker' (1788: 161). He pitched his grammar both at the gentlemen and ladies who would wish to avoid being confused with their social inferiors, and at those who aspired to attain such 'purity and politeness of expression' in order to achieve the veneer of gentility necessary for conducting business:

> The importance of a correct Mode of Expression in *Business* is sufficiently obvious. SHOPMEN, CLERKS, APPRENTICES, and all who are engaged in the Transactions of commercial Life, may be assured that the acquisition will procure them Respect, and be highly conducive to their Advancement in Life (1788: 30).

Buchanan advertised his *Complete English Scholar* as intended for boys 'who are to be put to Trades' (1753: xii). Ash likewise advocated the teaching of English grammar to 'young Gentlemen designed merely for trade' (1763: iii) and Lowth claimed that his *Short Introduction to English Grammar* (also 1762) would be useful to readers from 'all classes'. Grammarians such as Spence (1775) and Cobbett (1823) were exceptional in aiming their works at the lower classes, referred to by Spence as 'the laborious part of the people', and by Cobbett as 'Soldiers, Sailors, Apprentices and Plough-boys'. Spence and Cobbett were both Radicals, for whom the education of the lower classes was a means to their liberation and eventual enfranchisement. However, they were not alone in having a political motivation for producing their grammars.

5.1.4   'No enemy so formidable as the pen': language and politics

Smith (1984) and Crowley (1989, 1991) have both emphasized the importance of the link between linguistic and political ideologies in the eighteenth and nineteenth centuries. Crowley goes so far as to suggest a new

approach to 'the history of the language' in which texts such as Swift's
Proposal are seen 'as belonging not to a continuous tradition, but as
interventions in debates and historical conjunctures designed to bring about
certain effects' (1991: 3). Crowley argues, as shall I, that 'prescriptivism . . .
takes a multiplicity of forms, practices and purposes' (1991: 3). Whilst it is
perfectly valid to see eighteenth- and nineteenth-century grammars both as
the necessary agents of codification and as self-help guides for the aspiring
middle classes, it cannot be denied that many of the authors of these works
were politically and/or ideologically motivated.

The conventional view of the early eighteenth century, the 'Augustan
Age', is of a period of relative political stability after the upheavals of the
seventeenth. Grammarians of this period are seen as wanting to 'fix' the
English language in order to achieve the stability in language that they
hoped to retain in government and in society. As Crowley points out, Swift's
Proposal explicitly connects the health of the English language at various
periods in its history to that of the nation. He looks back to 'the Period
wherein the *English* Tongue received most Improvement' as that beginning
with the accession of Elizabeth I, and ending with 'the great Rebellion in
Forty-Two' (1712: 17). Periods of social and political upheaval are
explicitly connected with the 'corruption' of the language:

> From the Civil War to this present Time, I am apt to doubt whether the
> Corruptions in our Language have not at least equalled the Refinements of it;
> and these Corruptions very few of the best Authors in our Age have wholly
> escaped. During the Usurpation, such an Infusion of Enthusiastick Jargon
> prevailed in every Writing, as was not shook off in many Years after. To this
> succeeded that Licentiousness which entered with the *Restoration*, and from
> infecting our Religion and Morals, fell to corrupt our Language (1712: 18).

As Milroy and Milroy point out (1999: 8), this view of language is still
espoused by some twentieth-century writers, who believe that 'it is moral
deficiency that leads to failure to use the "best" English'. In recent years,
such views have tended to be held by those on the political right, and Swift,
as a Tory, sought to stabilize the language in order to bring credit to Queen
Anne. He wished to ensure that her reign would 'be recorded in Words more
durable than Brass, and such as our Posterity may read a thousand Years
hence' (1712: 37). In other words, by *ascertaining* and *fixing* the language,
Swift's intention was that 'the values to be handed down from the present
were to be encased in a language which would ensure their effective trans-
mission to the future' (Crowley 1991: 30). Swift's motivation was thus
conservatism in every sense of the word: as a political conservative, or Tory,
he wished to support the monarchy against any repetition of the

'Usurpation', and to protect society from the excesses of both religious 'enthusiasm' and 'licentiousness'. At the same time, he saw linguistic conservatism as an important force for maintaining the values which he held so dear.

The beginning of the eighteenth century (1707, to be exact) saw the unification of the English and Scottish parliaments and the creation of the 'United Kingdom of Great Britain'. Although Standard English had replaced Scots as the language of publishing in Scotland soon after the Union of Crowns in 1603, the private writing of educated Scots retained a number of 'Scotticisms' which became a matter of concern in the eighteenth century. In this period, the words 'Britain' and 'British' become politically loaded, making explicit reference to the recent Union. Thus Buchanan's *British Grammar* (1762), along with his *Linguae Britannicae Vera Pronuntiatio* (1757) and *Essay Towards Establishing a Standard for an Elegant and Uniform Pronunciation of the English Language, Throughout the British Dominions* (1766), all invoke the name of Britain. Buchanan set out to impose a common standard in order to bind together Scots and English as citizens of the new Union who will 'speak the same language'. As Cohen points out:

> For Buchanan, such standardized language teaching contributes to social and political ends and, more specifically, to English goals as represented by Whig policies at mid-century: a regularly taught language will lead to the reconciliation between England and Scotland and to the suppression of 'provincial dialect, so unbecoming gentlemen' (p. x) (1977: 82).

As Buchanan was mainly concerned with facilitating the acquisition of a standard pronunciation by his fellow 'North Britons', I shall discuss his work further in Chapter 7. However, he was not alone in aiming to expunge Scotticisms. David Hume, first in 1752 and then in the *Scots Magazine* of 1760, set out a list of Scotticisms to be avoided. In a letter to Gilbert Elliot in 1757, Hulme states that he and his fellow Scots 'speak a very corrupt Dialect of the Tongue which we make use of' (Greig, 1932: II, 154). Hume's list in the *Scots Magazine* begins with an account of the 'correct', i.e. English, rules for the use of *shall* and *will*, *would* and *should* and *these* and *those*, but gives no indication of the ways in which Scots usage deviated from these norms. He also cites various preterite and past participle forms: *proven, improven, approven* for *proved,* etc. and *drunk, run* for *drank, ran* (the Scots form is given first in each case here). Hume also notes that *to be angry at* should be *angry with*, and *hinder to do* should be *hinder from doing*. This list of Scotticisms was to be repeated and expanded in the works of Sinclair (1782), Beattie (1787) and Mitchell (1799). Sinclair (1782: 72) notes that 'there is nothing that the inhabitants of Scotland are so apt to err in, as in the use they make of *shall* and *will*, *should* and *would*, *these* and *those*'. The use of *shall* and *will* was to become a shibboleth of Scots speech in the eighteenth and nineteenth centuries. Sinclair, Beattie and Mitchell all give as an example of a Scotticism *I will be drowned* for *I shall be drowned*, but only Sinclair elaborates on this by relating what was to become a common joke at the expense of both the Scots and the Irish in eighteenth- and nineteenth-century grammars of English:

> As an instance of the different manner in which the Scots and English use *shall* and *will* in the first person singular, a story is told of a Scotchman, who having fallen into a river in England, had almost perished in it, in consequence of his calling out, *I will* for *I shall be drowned*, the spectators having for some time hesitated, whether they should venture their own lives for the safety of one, who, as they were led to imagine, was determined to make away with himself (1782: 73–4).

As Leonard (1929: 178–9) points out, 'no discussion of the *shall* and *will* matter in the latter part of the eighteenth century or later, could get under way without condemnation of the Scotch and Irish for their misuses'. After 1707, the political imperative on both sides of the border was to impose the norms of Standard English usage in order to bolster up the Union.

Swift was a Tory, and Cohen associates Buchanan with 'Whig policies', so it is clear that the 'doctrine of correctness' was not the preserve of any one political party. Towards the end of the eighteenth century, English Radicals, inspired by the American (1775–83) and French (1789) revolutions turned their thoughts to issues of language and power. Perhaps the most politically radical writer of this period was Thomas Spence, whose *Grand Repository of the English Language* will be discussed in Chapter 7, as it is primarily a pronouncing dictionary. However, as I have indicated above, Spence's work stands out from the majority of eighteenth-century writings on language, in that it was written by and for representatives of 'the laborious part of the people'. Spence was an advocate of common ownership of the land, and is regarded by political historians as the 'missing link' between the diggers and levellers of the seventeenth century and the chartists and socialists of the nineteenth. Born into a dissenting artisan family in Newcastle, he firmly believed that the only way to liberate the poor from the oppression of landlords was to teach them to read. Once literate, they would be able to read political tracts such as his lecture to the Newcastle Philosophical Society (for which he was expelled) and would become politicized. To this end, Spence devised a system of phonetic spelling which he used to indicate the 'most proper and agreeable pronunciation' in his *Grand Repository of the English Language* (1775). Although Spence's main preoccupation was with spelling reform and pronunciation, the *Grand Repository* does contain a short grammar, which is an abridged version of Ann Fisher's *A New Grammar* (1754). Whilst Fisher's was by no means the most prescriptive of grammars in this period, the inclusion of a grammar in Spence's most important linguistic work indicates that the acquisition of 'correct' grammar was an important part of his plan for the education and hence liberation of the labouring classes. This link between grammar and the emancipation of the lower orders is made much more explicit by William Cobbett, whose *Grammar of the English Language, in a Series of Letters* was intended 'for the Use of Schools and of Young Persons in general; but more especially for the Use of Soldiers, Sailors, Apprentices, and Plough-boys' (1823: title page). Like Spence, Cobbett was self-educated and from relatively humble origins. His father was a farmer, and Cobbett spent some time in the army, so plough-boys and soldiers were particularly close to his heart, but his reasons for addressing a grammar to young people from the lower classes were more political than personal. Cobbett, like Spence, was active in the cause of social and parliamentary reform in the turbulent years at the beginning of the nineteenth century. Whilst Spence was imprisoned several times, Cobbett spent time in America, but returned to become an MP after the passing of the Reform Act in 1832. What concerned Cobbett was that those who had most to gain from parliamentary reform were unable to state their case because their language was considered 'vulgar' and therefore not fit to express an intelligent argument. The author of *The Art of Speaking* referred to 'the depraved Language of common People' (Anon, 1708: 41), and a century later petitions calling for reform were dismissed by parliament, on the basis that the language in which they were written was thus 'depraved', and so the ideas expressed could not be worthy of consideration. Smith (1984: 30–4) cites examples of petitions that were rejected by parliament on the grounds that the language in which they were written was not sufficiently 'decent and respectful'. It is to such events that Cobbett refers in the following extract from his newspaper *The Political Register*:

> The present project ... is to communicate to all uneducated Reformers, *a knowledge of Grammar*. The people, you know, were accused of presenting petitions *not grammatically correct*. And those petitions were *rejected*, the petitioners being '*ignorant*': though some of them were afterwards *put into prison*, for being 'better informed' ...
>   There was only one thing in which any of you were deficient, and that was in the mere art of so arranging the words in your Resolutions and Petitions as to make these compositions what is called *grammatically correct*. Hence, men

of a hundredth part of the mind of some of the authors of the Petitions were
enabled to cavil at them on this account, and to infer from this incorrectness
that the Petitioners were a set of *poor ignorant creatures*, who knew nothing
of what they were talking; a set of the '*Lower Classes*', who ought never to
raise their reading above that of children's books, Christmas Carrols, and the
like.

For my part, I have always held a mere knowledge of the rules of grammar
very cheap. It is a study, which demands hardly any powers of mind (29
November 1817).

Here, Cobbett vehemently denies the parliamentarians' assumed link
between 'correct' grammar and intelligence, suggesting that it is very easy to
learn grammar, as he himself did by reading Lowth. However, rather than
advocate tolerance for 'incorrect' grammar, he suggests that intelligent
members of the 'lower classes' beat their opponents at their own game by
learning grammar. Cobbett's grammar is no less prescriptive than most of its
competitors, but he subverts the 'doctrine of correctness', turning grammar
into the deadliest weapon of the class war. In the introduction to his
Grammar of the English Language, which was written in the form of letters
to his son, Cobbett states this motive quite explicitly:

> To the acquiring of this branch of knowledge, my dear son, there is one
> motive, which, though it ought, at all times, to be strongly felt, ought, at the
> present time, to be so felt in an extraordinary degree: I mean that desire which
> every man, and especially every young man, should entertain to be able to
> assert with effect the rights and liberties of his country ... you will find that
> tyranny has no enemy so formidable as the pen ([1823] 1984: 4).

Cobbett's subversiveness emerges in many aspects of his grammar: where
Lowth uses examples from the Bible and respected authors, Cobbett cites
the inferior usage of members of parliament. In the third edition, Cobbett
added 'Six Lessons, intended to prevent Statesmen from using false
grammar, and from writing in an awkward manner' (1823: title page).
Lesson V is a set of 'remarks on a Note presented by Lord Castlereagh to
the Ambassadors of the Allies, at Paris, in July 1815, relative to the Slave
Trade'. After citing the note in full, Cobbett writes:

> **Now, I put this question to you:** *Do you understand what this great Statesman
> means?* Read the Note three times over, and then say whether you *understand
> what he wants?* You may *guess;* but you can go little further. Here is a whole
> mass of grammatical errors; but it is the obscurity, the unintelligibleness of the
> Note, that I think constitutes its greatest fault ([1823] 1984: 127).

Here, Cobbett presses home the point made in *The Political Register* that
they had no right to condemn the petitioners on the grounds of language or

intellect. Elsewhere, he uses exemplification to score political points, as in the second edition of his *Grammar*:

> A verb is called active when it expresses an *action*, which is produced by the nominative of the sentence: as, 'Sidmouth *imprisoned* Benbow'. It is passive, when it expresses an action, which is received, or endured, by the person or thing which is the nominative of the sentence, as, 'Benbow is *imprisoned*'. It is neuter, when it expresses simply the state of being, or of existence, of a person or thing: as 'Benbow *lies* in irons' (1819: 46).

By presenting the horror of Benbow's situation in this context, Cobbett both finds a clever way to escape censorship and challenges the idea that grammar can be politically neutral. As Smith points out, 'to use political material to explain the language implies, as Cobbett intended to, that political conflict is the very essence of language' (1984: 246). Cobbett also introduces topicality into his *Grammar*: by the 1823 edition, the examples above have been changed to 'Pitt *restrained* the Bank' and 'The Bank is *restrained*' respectively ([1823] 1984: 33).

Grammar continues to be invoked for political reasons throughout the later modern period. The fallacy, which Cobbett tried to dismiss, that 'incorrect' language is a product of an inferior mind, simply does not go away. Henry Alford advocated the use of 'the Queen's English' as a patriotic duty:

> The language of a people is not a trifle. The national mind is reflected in the national speech. If the way in which men express their thoughts is slipshod and mean, it will be very difficult for their thoughts themselves to escape being the same ... That nation must be (and it has ever been so in history) not far from rapid decline, and from being degraded from its former glory. Every important feature in a people's language is reflected in its character and history (1864: 5–6).

This led to resistance to and complaints against 'foreign' words and 'colonial' expressions, especially Americanisms. Alford refers to the 'deterioration which our Queen's English has undergone at the hands of the Americans':

> Look at those phrases which so amuse us in their speech and books; at their reckless exaggeration, and contempt for congruity; and then compare the character and history of the nation – its blunted sense of moral obligation and duty to man; its open disregard of conventional right where aggrandizement is to be obtained; and, I may now say, its reckless and fruitless maintenance of the most cruel and unprincipled war in the history of the world (1864: 6).

In the previous century, Webster in his *Grammatical Institutes* had taken the opportunity of criticizing the English for their adherence to grammars based on Latin (see Section 5.2.2 for further discussion of this). He expresses his surprise

> That the English nation at large have, till very lately, entertained the idea that our language was incapable of being reduced to a system of rules; and that even now many men of much classical learning warmly contend that the only way of acquiring, a grammatical knowledge of the *English Tongue*, is first to learn a *Latin Grammar*. That such a stupid opinion should ever have prevailed in the English nation – that it should still have advocates – nay that it should still be carried into practice, can be resolved into no cause but the amazing influence of habit upon the human mind (1784: 3).

The 'doctrine of correctness' was thus invoked by writers of all political persuasions, so it would be a mistake to argue that any set of political circumstances created the market for grammars in the eighteenth and nineteenth centuries. It might be wiser to agree with Crowley that 'language becomes a crucial focus of tension and debate at critical historical moments, serving as the site upon which political positions are contested' (2003: 217). Thus, the emergence of these grammars and the accompanying discussions about language and power are symptomatic of the turbulent times in which they were written.

5.1.5   Grammars and the teaching of English

Perhaps the most pressing and practical reason for the production of grammars in the eighteenth century was the need created by an increasing emphasis on the teaching of English in schools. Jones (1953) has demonstrated how a dramatic shift in attitude in the last quarter of the sixteenth century saw English 'triumph' over Latin to become accepted as a suitable language for learned discourse. However, grammar schools still promoted a classical curriculum to the extent that students were not allowed to use English to communicate with each other, even in the playground (Nelson, 1952: 131–2). Such books as dealt with English in this period were mainly concerned with transferring classical precepts of rhetoric in order to facilitate the attainment of a suitably eloquent style by writers. In the seventeenth century, some authors advocated the teaching of English grammar as a means of helping students to learn Latin. An example of such a text is Poole's *The English Accidence; or, a Short, Plaine and Easy Way, for the more speedy attaining to the Latin tongue, by the help of the English* (1646). Poole, in his preface, writes:

> My drift and scope therefore is, to have a childe so well verst in his Mother tongue, before he meddle with Latine, that when he comes to the construing

of a Latine Author, he shall from the signification of his words in construing, be in some good measure able to tell distinctly what part of Speech every word is ... And when he is put to translation, or making of Latine, he shall know from his English, both what part of Speech every word is, and what Syntaxis, or ordering it should have in Latin (cited in Rodrigues-Gil, 2002: 38).

It was not until the second half of the seventeenth century that the teaching of English came to be viewed as an end in itself. Wharton justifies his (1654) *The English Grammar; or, the Institution of Letters, Syllables, and Words in the English-Tongue* by emphasizing the greater practicality of English. He argues 'our mother-tongue is likely in practice to bee most useful, and is capable of any Scholar-like expressions, as any whatsoever' (1654: A4r). He goes on to point out that for every grammar-school pupil who progresses to university, or to a profession, 'a hundred are taken away before'. These would very soon 'forget their Latine; so that if they bee not bettered in the knowledge of their Native Language, their labour and cost is to little or no purpose' (1654: A4v). Wharton's plea for a more practical, English-based curriculum for the majority of students was to be echoed by one of the most influential thinkers of the seventeenth century, John Locke:

> Can there be anything more ridiculous, than that a father should waste his own money, and his son's time, in setting him to learn the Roman language when, at the same time, he designs him for a trade ...? Could it be believed, unless we had every where amongst us examples of it, that a child should be forced to learn the rudiments of a language, which he is never to use in the course of a life that he is designed to, and neglect all the while writing a good hand, and casting accounts, which are of great advantage in all conditions of life, and to most trades indispensably necessary? But though these qualifica-tions, requisite to trade and commerce and the business of the world, are seldom or never to be had at grammar schools; yet thither not only gentlemen send their younger sons intended for trades, but even tradesmen and farmers fail not to send their children, though they have neither intention nor ability to make them scholars ([1690] 1823: 152–3).

Locke's ideas on language and philosophy were to be highly influential throughout the eighteenth century, but it is probably the social imperative discussed in Section 5.1.3 that created the greatest impetus towards the teaching of English. Buchanan takes up Locke's point concerning the lack of any alternative to the grammar schools, telling his readers that 'a certain Alderman of a Country corporation took it highly ill that some Mechanics sent their sons to a Latin School, before they put them to trades; for what else, says he, can we, Gentlemen, do for our sons?' (1769: xvii). He goes on to make an explicit plea for the establishment of English as a subject in all schools:

> We have Latin Grammar schools in most incorporate towns; but we have not a professed English Grammar school in all Britain; notwithstanding, that take the youths of the United Kingdom in general, hardly one of a hundred requires a Latin education; though those of all ranks require an English one. English Grammar ought to be taught in every Latin school: And there ought to be a Master for the English language in each of those seminaries of Westminster, Eaton, etc. (1769: xxiii).

Buchanan here echoes Wharton's estimation that only one pupil in a hundred will actually need Latin in his future career. Whilst a classical education continued to be seen as the mark of a 'gentleman' for many years, the teaching of English was advocated as part of a more practical curriculum, particularly, though not exclusively, for those who would never be part of this elite 1 per cent. Dissenters were barred from the universities on religious grounds, and the academies set up for their education were at the forefront in introducing this new curriculum. Priestley, who wrote his *Rudiments of English Grammar* whilst teaching at the Warrington Academy, writes in the preface to this work:

> The propriety of introducing the *English Language* into *English Schools*, cannot be disputed; a competent knowledge of our own language being both useful and ornamental in every profession, and a critical knowledge of it absolutely necessary to all persons of a liberal education (1761: viii).

Faced with the problem of devising lessons in English for the Academy, Priestley wrote his own grammar, as did many other eighteenth-century teachers of English: schoolteachers made up the vast majority of authors of English grammars in this period. Apart from the dissenting academies, private schools were being opened to provide an education for those who had neither the time nor the money to attend the grammar schools, and these too promoted the more practical curriculum in which English, rather than Latin grammar, would be taught. Girls of all classes were denied entry to grammar schools and universities, and several prominent grammarians advocated the teaching of English to the 'Fair Sex'. Ash pointed out the importance of an 'English Education . . . not only for Ladies, but for young Gentlemen designed merely for trade' (1763: iii), and Buchanan made a very full and explicit case for the education of girls:

> It is greatly to be lamented that the Fair Sex have been in general so shamefully neglected with regard to a proper English Education. Many of them, by the unthinking Part of the Males, are considered and treated rather as Dolls, than as intelligent social Beings. And though in Point of Genius they are not inferior to the other Sex, yet due Care is not always taken to cultivate their Understandings, to impress their Minds with solid Principles, and replenish them with useful Knowledge.

> Is a Lady of Birth or Fortune to be cruelly deprived of the animating and
> lasting Pleasure, resulting from a Capacity of expressing herself with Fluency
> and Accuracy in speaking or writing her Mother Tongue? A Qualification
> which would so eminently distinguish, add a Lustre to, and place in every
> Point of View all her other Accomplishments? (1762: xxix–xxx).

Buchanan goes on to suggest that 'in every Boarding-School where there are
young Ladies of Rank, proper Masters should attend at least three Days in
the Week; in order to teach them not only to read with an accurate
Pronunciation ... but to write their own Language grammatically' (1762).
He also advocates for these 'young ladies' a liberal curriculum, including
geography, natural history and philosophy. We must be careful not to put
too feminist an interpretation on Buchanan's remarks: although he pays
lip-service to the equality of the sexes, the education which he advocates for
women is limited, and intended, above all, to add to their attractiveness as
companions for men. 'Correctness' in speech and writing, as defined by
grammarians, was a mark of ladylike status: as Crowley points out, 'women
had to swallow their master's tongue in order to qualify for entrance into
polite society' (1996: 90). Just as early dictionaries were designed for 'ladies
and other unskillful persons', so the teaching of English grammar in the
eighteenth century was mainly advocated for those who were deemed not to
need a classical education: women, dissenters and the middle classes. As
Crowley points out, one of the earliest grammars of the century,
Brightland's (1711) *Grammar of the English Tongue*, was designed for
'Children, Women, or the ignorant of both sexes'. Later in the century,
Ussher recommends his *Elements of English Grammar* as an easy and
practical textbook suitable for use in 'Ladies Boarding Schools':

> As a grammatical knowledge of English is become essentially necessary in the
> education of Ladies, it is certainly a desirable object to render that study as
> easy and useful to them as possible. For this reason, in a treatise of grammar
> intended for their use, all abstract terms that could be dispensed with, should
> be rejected (1785: vi–vii, cited in Crowley, 1996: 91).

Crowley suggests here that Ussher is 'writing down' to his readership.
Whilst this may be the case, one effect of this emphasis on an English-based
curriculum for girls, and for those boys destined to a life in trade or more
practical pursuits, was that some of the grammars produced for use in the
classroom were innovative, rejecting the classical models and introducing
new pedagogical techniques. As we shall see in Section 5.2.2, one of the
most innovative and influential grammarians of this period was Ann Fisher,
who opened a school for 'young ladies who chuse to learn the English
Grammar' in Newcastle in 1750 (Rodriguez-Gil, 2002: 145). Thus the

opening up of an English-based education to 'ladies, gentlewomen and other unskillful persons' stimulated the production of grammars in the eighteenth century, as a demand for suitable textbooks was created. Robinson suggests that grammars and other textbooks printed in the eighteenth century were aimed at a wide readership: 'even more advanced works on English, such as Fisher's Tutor, were almost all between nine pence and one shilling and six pence; this price was still within the means of most artisans' (1972: 341). Robinson goes on to suggest that, since these texts were advertised in local newspapers around Christmas, they were bought by parents as well as by the schools. One answer to the question why so many grammars were produced in the second half of the eighteenth century is that there is a healthy market for them, created largely by the ambitions of middle-class parents for the education of their children of both sexes.

5.2 Models and theories of grammar

5.2.1 Prescriptive or descriptive grammars

As I pointed out in Section 5.1.1, the eighteenth century has been defined in most histories of English as an age of prescriptivism, when the 'doctrine of correctness' held sway. A typical evaluation of eighteenth-century grammars is that provided by Rydén:

> Grammar came to be viewed essentially as the selection of 'proper' forms, or, as Dr Johnson (1755) has it, 'the art of using words properly'. These prescriptive grammarians (for example Lowth and Murray), whose rules were largely a mixture of Latin grammar, 'logic', 'reason' and prejudice, were ignorant of or unwilling to accept the processes of linguistic change and unaware of the fact that usage is essentially a matter of social convention (1981: 513–14).

Rydén's language here is extremely judgemental: terms such as *ignorant*, *unwilling* and *unaware* betray a very negative view of eighteenth-century grammars, which is typical of most twentieth-century linguists. As Cameron points out, 'the very first thing any student of linguistics learns is that linguistics is "descriptive not prescriptive" ... Prescriptivism thus represents the threatening Other, the forbidden; it is a spectre that haunts linguistics and a difference that defines linguistics' (1995: 5). Cameron here suggests that prescriptivism is a sort of taboo to twentieth-century linguists, who have set up a binary opposition between what they see as the arbitrary and subjective pronouncements of earlier grammarians and the scientific, objective statements of their own more enlightened age. Often, eighteenth-century grammarians are condemned without either a full examination of their works, or due consideration of the historical context in which they were writing. As Tieken (2000) points out, this has led to erroneous statements being made. Aitchison, using language as value-laden as Rydén's, writes:

> Lowth's influence was profound and pernicious because so many of his strictures were based on his own preconceived notions. In retrospect, it is quite astonishing that he should have felt so confident about his prescriptions. Did he believe that, as a bishop, he was divinely inspired? It is also curious that his dogmatic statements were so widely accepted among educated Englishmen. It seems that, as a prominent religious leader, no one questioned his authority (1991: 12).

Tieken notes that, since Lowth 'did not become a bishop until several years after the grammar was first published', Aitchison's waspish comments are somewhat misinformed. Tieken demonstrates that Lowth was not a grammarian by calling, but produced his *Short Introduction* because he was commissioned to do so by the bookseller Robert Dodsley. She also argues that the success of Lowth's grammar was due to Dodsley's entrepreneurial skills, rather than Lowth's authority as a 'religious leader'. Perhaps the most important point Tieken makes is to challenge the received view of Lowth as a prescriptivist whose pronouncements on grammar were arbitrary and subjective. She demonstrates that his grammar was based on usage, albeit not his own, but that of the aristocracy, or at least what he believed to be the language of the aristocracy. Whilst Lowth's grammar is certainly normative, it is also descriptive. Lowth the authoritarian clergyman and Priestley the empirical, descriptive man of science have been presented as binary opposites in, for example, Leonard (1929), but, as Rodriguez-Gil points out, their statements on the matter of *shall* and *will* are remarkably similar:

> Use hath, of late, varied, and, as it were, interchanged the sense of them: for when we simply *foretell*, we use *shall* in the first person, and *will* in the rest; as *I shall* or *he will write*: but when we *promise, threaten* or *engage*, we use *will* in the first person, and *shall* in the rest; as *I will*, or *he shall* write (Priestley, 1761: 22).

> *Will* in the first Person singular and plural promises or threatens; in the second and third Persons only foretells: *shall* on the contrary, in the first Person simply foretells; in the second and third Persons commands or threatens (Lowth, 1762: 59).

> This distinction was not observed formerly as to the word *shall*, which was used in the Second and Third Persons to express simply the event. So likewise *should* was used, where we now make use of *would* (Lowth, 1762: 59).

Although statements concerning the use of *shall* and *will* can ultimately be traced back to Wallis (1653), it would appear that Priestley, Lowth and other eighteenth-century grammarians were here describing patterns of usage rather than prescribing arbitrary rules. Hulbert (1947) and Taglicht (1970) both demonstrate from seventeenth- and eighteenth-century corpora that these 'rules' were, in fact, accurate statements of usage. It is also worth pointing out that both Priestley and Lowth here acknowledge the existence of linguistic change: Priestley writes 'use hath, of late varied', whilst Lowth notes 'this distinction was not observed formerly'. Neither of these eighteenth-century grammarians can justly be accused of being, in Rydén's words, 'ignorant of or unwilling to accept the processes of linguistic change'. Whilst, as we saw in Section 5.1.1, these grammarians were normative in the sense that they deliberately set out to codify, or 'ascertain', the language, this does not necessarily mean that the basis of their rules was always arbitrary or subjective. In the following sections, I shall examine a number of eighteenth-century grammars to determine whether they were, as Rydén suggests, based on 'Latin grammar, "logic", "reason" and prejudice'.

5.2.2   The influence of Latin

We have seen in Section 5.1.5 that, at least until the end of the seventeenth century, education at all but the most elementary level was based on a classical curriculum, in which 'grammar' was understood to be Latin grammar. This meant that the categories and definitions used in the teaching of grammar were those inherited from the classical tradition. Michael points out that 'linguistic study was confined to two languages, structurally similar; Greek, from which the first categories had been drawn, and Latin, from which they had been finally systematized. Broadly speaking, the classical languages ... *were* Language; and their grammar *was* Grammar' (1970: 9–10). Indeed, so dominant was Latin that 'its grammar was not just one grammar out of many; it *was* grammar ... If Latin "had" a grammar it was not for English to have anything different. It could only have the same, and less of it' (1970: 492). Michael goes on to demonstrate that this adherence to the model of Latin sometimes led to distortions of English. Lyly (1567) translates the Latin pluperfect into English as *to had loved, might had loved*, and these structures are repeated in nine English grammars in the eighteenth century. More commonly, the dependence on Latin models leads to grammarians describing English as having the same declensions or tenses as Latin, even though nouns in Modern English are not inflected for any case except the genitive, and the future is expressed, not by tense, but by the use of auxiliaries. The influence of Latin is also evident in the naming of 'parts of speech'. Michael shows that the most popular system used in eighteenth-century grammars was one which can be traced back to the earliest extant grammar in the west, that of Dionysius Thrax, produced in the second century BC. Dionysius classified words as: nouns, verbs, participles, articles, pronouns, prepositions and adverbs. This eightfold division, along with the names and definitions, was to be taken up by Lyly in 1527 and was to be the most popular system in English grammars right through to the middle of the eighteenth century. That this was, in the first place, due to the established practice of teaching Latin, is clear from a number of comments in early grammars of English. Michael (1970: 215) cites Brown (1700, 3rd edn 1707), who writes, 'note, that I divided the Parts thus, on account of the Method used in teaching Latin', whilst the author of the *English Scholar Compleat* (1706) asserts that 'in English, as in Latin, there are eight parts of speech'. However, just as we saw in Section 5.1.5 that the move towards teaching English rather than Latin stimulated the production of grammars, so a number of grammarians in the eighteenth century deliberately attempted to devise models of grammar more suited to the description of English. Michael identifies a total of 25 grammars making up what he calls a 'movement of reform' in the eighteenth century. Grammars belonging to this movement can be identified by their use of a 'reduced', fourfold system of parts of speech, and an attempt to use English-based terminology rather than the classical *noun, adjective*, etc. Examples of reforming grammarians are Dyche and Pardon (1735), and Fisher (1750, 1754). Dyche tells his readers 'neither shall I divide the Language into eight Parts or Distinctions, as is generally done; but into four only, that being sufficient for my present Purpose, which is only to give a generall Hint how Grammar may be as effectually applied to the English Tongue as to any others' (1735: sig. A4, cited in Michael, 1970: 257–8). Fisher likewise presents a fourfold system, avoiding Latin terminology:

> Q. *Into how many Parts of Speech are the Words in the* English *Tongue divided?*
> A. Four: I. NAMES; which express *Things* or *Substances*.
> 2. QUALITIES; which express the *Manners, Properties*, or *Affections of Things*.
> 3. VERBS; expressing the *Actions, Passions*, or *Beings of Things*.
> 4. PARTICLES; shewing the *Manner* or *Quality* of *Actions, Passions*, or *Beings*, &c. (1754: 61).

The terminology used by Fisher can ultimately be traced back to Gildon and Brightland (1711), who, in the preface to *A Grammar of the English Tongue*, accuse Ben Jonson of having 'extended and tortur'd our Tongue to confess the Latin Declensions, Conjugations, and ev'n Construction, whereas there is nothing so different'. These 'reforming' grammars amount to less than 10 per cent of the 273 grammars listed by Michael, but he notes a peak in the years 1734–61, when 60 per cent of new grammars used a 'reduced' system of parts of speech. Michael suggests that the English-based system did not prevail because three highly influential grammars produced in the 1760s used Latin-based systems: these were Priestley's *Rudiments of English Grammar* (1761), Lowth's *Short Introduction to English Grammar* (1762) and Buchanan's *British Grammar* (1762). From this point on, the most popular system was an extended version of the Latin one, with ten parts of speech. Indeed, this system is used in descriptive (as opposed to theoretical) grammars today: such a model is used in Quirk, Greenbaum, Leech and Svartvik (1985: 44). Michael suggests that the reason for the popularity of the tenfold system was that it was considered easier to learn. He cites Bullen's justification for his use of such a system:

> If any Grammarian should feel disconcerted at hearing that there are ten parts of speech, let him remember that I write for children, not for critics. Properly speaking, perhaps, there are but three, the Substantive, the Adjective and the Verb; but if we exclude all the other names, what account are we to give of them which would be intelligible to young minds? It is therefore thought preferable to multiply terms a little than to take advantage of a simplicity which would be altogether obscure (1797: 115, cited in Michael, 1970: 224–5).

However, several of the reforming grammarians were likewise motivated by pedagogical concerns: Percy (1994: 123) points out that Fisher and other female grammarians in the early eighteenth century were 'associated with a repudiation of Latin', presumably because their intended (female) readers would not know Latin. Michael suggests that the reason why the Latin-based system has prevailed is simply because, apart from a few years in the mid-eighteenth century, it was always used in the majority of grammars and had the weight of tradition behind it. He concludes:

> Such stability, such a uniform (if monotonous) façade, has given authority to our grammatical tradition, and teachers have respectfully preserved the façade from the decay which should have destroyed it. Our respect has been misplaced: it should have been given to those ill-informed, dissatisfied, protesting, and sometimes perceptive schoolmasters [sic], who were making the first attempts to give English a grammar of its own, and to teach English children how to control the English language (1970: 518).

Since most eighteenth-century (and later) grammars of English were influenced by Latin grammar, at least in terms of the models and terminology used to describe the grammar, is Rydén justified in his comment that the rules for 'correct' usage in these grammars were likewise influenced by Latin? Before considering specific prescriptions, I should point out that not all grammarians who adopted a classical model for parts of speech were blind to the differences between Latin and English. Priestley, for instance, writes:

> We have no more business with a future tense in our language, than we have with the whole system of Latin moods and tenses; because we have no modification of our verbs to correspond to it; and if we had never heard of a future tense in some other language, we should no more have given a particular name to the combination of the verb with the auxiliary *shall* or *will*, than to those . . . with the auxiliaries *do, have, can, must* or any other (1768).

Nevertheless, it must be admitted that some of the shibboleths propagated by eighteenth-century grammarians have their basis in Latin. One example of this is the proscription against ending a sentence with a preposition. Although no grammarian explicitly states this, it would appear that the main reason for this rule is that the Latin-derived name for this part of speech suggests that it should be placed in front of, rather than after, another word. Definitions of the term reflect this:

> The PREPOSITION, put before nouns and pronouns chiefly, to connect them with other words, and to shew their relation to them (Lowth, 1762: 8)
>
> PREPOSITIONS, so called because they are commonly put *before* the words to which they are applied (1762: 91).
>
> The Prepositions are, *in, to, for, from, of, by, with, into, against, at,* and several others. They are called *Prepositions* from two Latin words, meaning *before* and *place*; and this name is given them because they are in most cases *placed before* Nouns and Pronouns: as, 'Indian corn is sown *in* May' (Cobbett [1823] 1984: 16).

The proscription against ending a sentence with a preposition seems to have been first noted, perhaps even invented, by Dryden, who criticizes Ben Jonson's *The bodies that those souls were frightened from* on the grounds of 'the preposition in the end of the sentence; a common fault with him, and which I have but lately observ'd in my own writings' (1672, cited in Bolton, 1966: 60). Dryden is known to have tested the purity of his English prose by translating it into Latin, so it is highly likely that the contrast between the English preposition-stranding and the position before the noun in Latin brought this 'fault' to Dryden's attention. This has been a shibboleth ever since, and still occurs in the letters of complaint made by readers of newspapers and listeners to the BBC. Lowth, in particular, has been blamed by twentieth-century linguists such as Aitchison (1981), for propagating this 'rule', yet, when we examine Lowth's own words on the matter, we find them far from dogmatic on the subject:

The Preposition is often separated from the Relative which it governs, and joined to the Verb at the end of the Sentence, or of some member of it: as 'Horace is an author *whom* I am much delighted *with*.' 'The world is too well bred to shock authors with a truth, *which* generally their booksellers are the first that inform them *of*.' This is an idiom which our language is strongly inclined to; it prevails in common conversation, and suits very well with the more familiar style in writing; but the placing of the Preposition before the Relative is more graceful, as well as more perspicuous; and agrees much better with the solemn and elevated Style (1762: 127–8).

Lowth is not condemning preposition-stranding outright here: rather, he suggests that it is more suitable for informal usage. Tieken (2000) points out that Lowth used stranded prepositions in his informal letters, and that his use of the construction in the above passage ('an idiom which our language is strongly inclined to') is intended as a joke. Lowth's demonization is even more surprising when we compare his statement above with that of Priestley, who has been beatified by linguists from Leonard (1929) onwards as the supreme descriptivist of his age:

It is often really diverting to see with what extreme caution words of such frequent occurrence as *of* and *to* are prevented from fixing themselves in the close of a sentence; though that be a situation they naturally incline to, where they favour the easy fall of the voice, in a familiar cadence; and from which nothing but the solemnity of an address from the pulpit ought to dislodge them; as in any other place they often give too great a stiffness and formality to a sentence (1761: 50–1).

These two grammarians were writing within a year of each other, so any norms of usage to which they refer must have been the same. Although both used a classical system of parts of speech, neither is influenced by Latin here: they both describe preposition-stranding as a naturally occurring feature of English, more suited to informal usage. The difference between Lowth and Priestley is one of emphasis only, far from the prescriptive–descriptive polarization which we have been led to expect.

Another shibboleth which has been attributed to the influence of Latin is the 'split infinitive'. As Burchfield explains, 'in Latin such a construction could not arise because an infinitive (*amare* 'to love', *crescere* 'to grow') is indivisible and is not preceded by a grammatical particle' (1996: 736). A myth has grown up that this, like other prescriptive rules relating to English grammar, was a product of the eighteenth century. One web encyclopedia goes so far as to blame the usual suspect, Robert Lowth, without citing one word of evidence:

Lowth set out to develop a system of grammar that elevated English to the level of <u>Latin</u>, and attempted to regulate English usage within the rules of

Latin grammar. His most famous (or infamous) contribution to the study of grammar was his prescription that forbade the use of the <u>split infinitive</u>, a rule that has been a subject of dispute for grammarians ever since (http://en2.wikipedia.org/wiki/Robert_Lowth, accessed 6/01/04).

However, the proscription of the split infinitive first occurs in 1834. In an article in the *New England Magazine*, 'P' notes:

> The practice of separating the prefix of the infinitive mode from the verb, by the insertion of an adverb, is not unfrequent among uneducated persons . . . I am not conscious, that any rule has been heretofore given in relation to this point: no treatise on grammar or rhetoric, within my knowledge, alludes to it. The practice, however, of not separating the particle from its verb, is so general and uniform among good authors, and the exceptions to it are so rare, that the rule which I am about to propose will, I believe, prove to be as accurate as most rules, and may be found beneficial to inexperienced writers. It is this:– *The particle* To, which comes before the verb in the infinitive mode, must not be separated from it by the intervention of an adverb, or any other word or phrase; but the adverb should immediately precede the particle, or immediately follow the verb (1834: 469, cited in Bailey, 1996: 248).

The split infinitive was to become such a shibboleth in the nineteenth century that, when British diplomats were negotiating the Alabama Claims in 1871, the government stated in a telegraph message that 'in the treaty, they would not endure adverbs between "to" [the sign of the infinitive] and the verb. The purity of the English language they nobly and courageously defended' (Lang, 1890, quoted in Bailey, 1996: 249–50). What is striking about both these proscriptions, against preposition-stranding and the split infinitive, is that they continue to be the target of critics precisely because the proscribed constructions are difficult to avoid in all but the most formal written English. The 'rules' devised are not natural rules of English, because they are based on the structure of Latin. However, when we examine eighteenth-century grammars carefully, we see that the most prominent grammarians presented preposition-stranding as acceptable in informal usage, and had not even noticed the split infinitive. It is therefore rather misleading to suggest that grammarians such as Lowth were overly influenced by Latin.

5.2.3   The application of logic to grammar

The discussion in Section 5.2.2 casts considerable doubt on Rydén's accusation that eighteenth-century grammarians based their rules on Latin, but what of 'logic' and 'reason'? The eighteenth century is often referred to as the 'Age of Reason', and logical principles are certainly invoked by grammarians of this period. Finegan points out that Priestley, who, as we have seen in Section 5.2.2, is generally viewed as the least prescriptive of eighteenth-century grammarians, 'allowed the practice of "good authors" only a limited role where different authors exhibited different practices' (1998: 547). In Priestley's own words 'since good authors have adopted different forms of speech, and in a case that admits of no standard but that of *custom*, one authority may be of as much weight as another; the *analogy of language* is the only thing to which he can have recourse, to adjust these differences' (1761: vi, cited in Finegan, 1998) By *analogy*, eighteenth-century grammarians meant conformity to or regularity within some pattern or paradigm. Thus analogy would favour alternatives which allowed for full paradigms, such as distinct preterite and past participle forms. For instance, Lowth comments on the recommended paradigm *sit*, *sat*, *sitten*: 'frequent mistakes are made in the formation of the Participle of this Verb. The analogy plainly requires *sitten*; which was formerly in use' (1762: 75). Lowth follows this with a series of quotes from earlier authors such as Raleigh and Hobbes, to prove that *sitten* was 'formerly in use'. The preference for a fully differentiated paradigm would also favour the *wh-* relatives *who, whom, whose, which* over invariable *that*, but here the analogy with Latin *qui, quae, quod*, etc., could also be a factor in their favour. However, despite the fame of Addison's *Humble Petition of Who and Which* (1711), grammarians are less dogmatic on this point than we might expect. Lowth's only prescription with regard to *that* is that it 'is used indifferently both of persons and things: but perhaps would be more properly confined to the latter' (1762: 134). This statement is remarkably similar to that made by Burchfield in his revision of Fowler's *Modern English Usage*, which claims to be descriptive: 'normally use *who* as the relative pronoun following a human antecedent and *that* (or *which*) following an inanimate antecedent' (1996: 773). Buchanan includes *that* in his list of relative pronouns – 'He, that, who, whom without a question, are called Relatives' (1762: 99) – but omits it from his table of pronouns. However, Buchanan does not explicitly proscribe *that*. We can conclude that, whilst eighteenth-century grammarians' preference for *wh-* pronouns was influenced by analogy, this did not lead to the prescription of unnatural rules.

The influence of 'logic' on eighteenth-century grammarians can be detected in rules concerning multiple negation and comparison. The 'double negative' was common in earlier English, but was first overtly condemned by Greenwood, who stated that 'two *Negatives*, or two *Adverbs* of Denying, do in *English* affirm' (1711: 160). This mathematical principle that 'two negatives make a positive' was later asserted by Fisher:

A Negative in *English*, cannot be expressed by two Negatives; as *it was not good for Nothing; I cannot eat none*, &c. such Expressions are Solecisms, which, instead of Negatives, make Affirmatives and signify as much; as *It was good for something; I can eat some* (1754: 120).

Lowth likewise states in the second edition of his grammar that 'two Negatives in English destroy one another, or are equivalent to an Affirmative' (1763: 139). (Tieken (forthcoming) points out that this, and other additions introduced by Lowth in his second edition, were the result of suggestions sent in by readers of the first edition.) Although eighteenth-century grammarians thus regularly invoke mathematical logic in justifying this proscription, it would appear that multiple negation was already becoming socially stigmatized. Burchfield points out that 'at some point between the 16c. and the 18c., for reasons no longer discoverable, double negatives became socially unacceptable in standard English. Playwrights placed them in the conversation of vulgar speakers' (1996: 227). Tieken (1982) and Austin (1984) demonstrate that double negation was used in informal and lower-class writing and speech throughout the eighteenth century, so, whilst the grammarians cited here appear to base their rules on 'logic', they are not out of line with usage in formal, Standard English.

Double comparatives were likewise condemned by Fisher as illogical:

Q. *Is it good* English *to say* more fairer *or* most fairest?
A. No: you ought to say, *fairer* or *more fair*; *fairest* or *most fair*; for *more fairer* would signify as much as *more more fair*, and *most fairest* as much as *most most fair* (1754: 79).

Yet, as with double negatives, this construction seems already to have been disappearing from standard usage (Rodriguez-Gil, 2002: 402). In both these cases, eighteenth-century grammarians were undoubtedly influenced by 'logic', but their proscriptions would only serve to endorse changes which were already under way at least in Standard English.

It is fair to say that some eighteenth-century grammarians were driven by their veneration for 'logic' to a kind of witch-hunt for 'concealed errors' which would not otherwise have been noticed, and which therefore persist in all but the most formal written English. Campbell objects to several constructions in which a deleted element appears elsewhere in the sentence, but in a different form. Examples are *He has never gone and never will* and *Any book that has, is, or shall be published*. However, in most cases where the application of 'logic' or 'analogy' seems to have influenced the judgement of eighteenth-century grammarians, other factors, such as social and/or stylistic differentiation in actual usage, must be taken into account.

5.2.4 'Prejudice' and *ipse dixit* statements

The final charge which Rydén lays against eighteenth-century grammarians is that their rules and remarks simply reflect personal prejudice. However, as we have seen in Sections 5.2.2 and 5.2.3 above, in many cases the constructions proscribed by grammarians such as Lowth were falling out of use, at least in the written language of the educated upper-class speakers whose usage formed the model of 'correct' English. Tieken suggests that 'the linguistic norm which lies at the basis of his grammar was not intended to reflect the language of eighteenth-century gentlemen, as Leonard suggested, but what Lowth, being a member of the middle classes himself, perceived to be the language of the social class above him' (forthcoming). If Lowth can be accused of 'prejudice', it can only be the general prejudice of the time in favour of educated Standard English usage. Most eighteenth-century grammarians refer to 'custom' and 'usage' at various points, and Lowth is no exception. I have already noted above (p. 107) that with regard to the 'rules' for *shall* and *will*, Lowth shows awareness not only of current usage, but of language change ('this distinction was not observed formerly'). He defines grammar as 'the Art of rightly defining our thoughts by Words' but goes on to state that any language 'applies those common principles to that particular language, according to the established usage and custom of it' (1762: 1). Thus, as Rodriguez-Gil (2002) points out, his grammar is prescriptive, but in the sense that it is based on usage, it is also descriptive. Leonard (1929) used the term *ipse dixit* (meaning 'he himself said') to describe what he saw as the arbitrary pronouncements of eighteenth-century grammarians. In fact, unsupported statements of 'correct' versus 'incorrect' usage were rare in this century, and, even where an appeal is made to the structure of Latin, or to 'analogy', the prescriptions and proscriptions are usually in line with usage, if only that of a very restricted set of speakers. As we shall see in the next section, *ipse dixit* statements are much more common in the nineteenth century.

5.3 English grammars of the nineteenth century

As we saw in Chapter 3, the rise of the new discipline of philology in the nineteenth century led to a more scientific approach to the study of language. Towards the end of the century, descriptive and historical grammars such as Sweet's *A New English Grammar, Logical and Historical* (1891–8), appeared. At the same time, as we shall see in Chapter 8, under the influence of the Neogrammarians in Germany, English scholars such as Joseph Wright were asserting that regional dialects had their own grammars, equally worthy of serious study. It seems paradoxical then that, as Bailey points out, 'attitudes toward grammar during the century hardened into ideology' (1996: 215). Alongside these scholarly grammars, there appeared works such as Alford's *The Queen's English* (1864), already cited above (p. 100); handbooks of 'errors', such as Hodgson's *Errors in the Use of English* (1882); and manuals advising on 'correct' behaviour in all aspects of daily life, such as *Enquire Within upon Everything* (1878). In addition to these, the more popular eighteenth-century grammars continued to be published: Lowth was published in many editions up to 1838, whilst the most influential grammar until the last quarter of the century was Lindley Murray's *English Grammar, Adapted to the Different Classes of Learner*.

McKnight tells us that 'in the course of 11 years [Murray's] larger *English Grammar* ran through 20 editions in England and twice that many in America and the *Abridgement* through 20 editions in England, 30 in America' ([1928] 1968: 498) The reason for this continued proliferation of prescriptive grammars in the nineteenth century is exactly the same reason that, in the twenty-first century, newspaper advertisements still appear offering help to those 'shamed' by their English, and the best-selling non-fiction book of Christmas 2003 in Britain was a handbook on 'correct' punctuation (Truss, 2003). To put it bluntly, these books continue to be produced because there is still a market for them. In the nineteenth century, both in Britain and in the USA, the development of a service economy led to the rise of a lower middle class with aspirations to propriety in speech, manners and dress, whilst the expansion of education created an even greater demand for schoolbooks. As we shall see when we discuss popular guides to pronunciation in Chapter 7, the lower middle classes could not afford either the time or the money for large, theoretical volumes. They needed accessible guides to help them avoid social embarrassment, hence the proliferation of titles advising what *not* to do, the starkest of which is *Don't*, subtitled 'A Little Book dealing Frankly with Mistakes & Improprieties more or less Common to All' (1888). In these books, the explanations and justifications provided by the likes of Lowth and Priestley give way to *ipse dixit* pronouncements. As Finegan points out:

> They propagated pronouncements made with authority no better than the writer's say-so ... With no manifest inclination to justify many of their prescripts, these masters of dogma broadcast their linguistic condemnations and their prescriptions for linguistic correctness in magazine pieces and handbooks that the educated public eagerly embraced (1998: 572).

These handbooks typically deal with 'mistakes' of pronunciation and usage of words as well as of grammar, so I shall return to them in Chapter 7. A few examples here should suffice to demonstrate the nature of the advice provided: as Finegan states, it is 'characteristically absolute, often unsubstantiated, and typically baseless' (1998: 573).

Enquire Within upon Everything (1878) is clearly directed mainly at women, as the title page boasts 'to which is added *Enquire Within upon Fancy Needlework*', and the editor promises help with any activity that 'has relation to the necessities of domestic life'. Along with sections on 'Bird-keeping, bee-keeping, poultry-keeping' and 'Destruction of vermin, noxious animals', it includes a section on 'Correct speaking, hints on writing'. This section contains 256 'rules', including the following:

31. Do not use double superlatives, such as *most straightest, most highest, most finest* (1873: 55).
97. Instead of 'We travel *slow*,' say 'We travel slowly' (1873: 57).
241. Instead of '*There's* fifty,' say 'There are fifty' (1873: 61).

This assumes that the reader will simply accept the editor's authority on these matters just as on bee-keeping and pest control.

Of course, alongside these manuals and handbooks, new grammars were published throughout the nineteenth century on both sides of the Atlantic. McKnight tells us that this century was particularly prolific as far as the production of American grammars was concerned:

> The number of grammars written by Americans and printed in America before 1800 is estimated at about 30, of which 18 were produced between 1790 and 1800. In the following decades the production was continuous; 14 between 1800 and 1810, 41 between 1811 and 1820, 81 between 1821 and 1830, 63 between 1831 and 1840, 66 between 1841 and 1850 ([1928] 1968: 498).

McKnight lists Greenleaf (1821), Brown (1823), Smith (1824) and Kirkham (1825) as the most popular American grammars of the first half of the nineteenth century. Kirkham's, in particular, 'passed through 94 editions between 1829 and 1851' ([1928] 1968: 499). He goes on to discuss the publication in 1851 of Brown's *The Grammar of English Grammars*, an encyclopedic work of over 1,100 pages, including comments on a wide range of earlier grammars. McKnight observes that, like the eighteenth-century British grammarians discussed in Section 5.2.3 above, Brown adopts reason as 'the principle basis for judgement in language' and so was 'in a position to find fault with the language of English writers early and late' ([1928] 1968: 499–500). In a striking example of 'knocking copy', he also points out errors in the works of other grammarians, including Murray and Kirkham, for which he provides corrected forms. The 'doctrine of correctness' was thus flourishing in nineteenth-century America. Indeed, as we have seen (above, p. 112), this period produced at least one new shibboleth in the 'split infinitive'.

In the second half of the nineteenth century, as Finegan points out, 'the empirical findings of comparative philology were coming to be well understood on both sides of the Atlantic' (1998: 574). Whilst prescriptive grammars and manuals continued to be published, some objecting voices were raised, notably that of Fitzedward Hall, who, in his *Recent Exemplifications of False Philology* (1872) and *Modern English* (1873) criticized the ignorance of his predecessors and some of his contemporaries. Other works of this period steer a middle path between prescription and description. We have already noted (above p. 100) the nationalist ideology of Alford's *The Queen's English*, and his prejudice against America in particular. This is reflected in his objection to 'omitting the "u" in words in -our':

> The first remark that I have to make shall be on the trick now so universal across the Atlantic, and becoming in some quarters common among us in England, of leaving out the '*u*' in the termination '-*our;*' writing *honor, favor, neighbor, Savior,* &c. Now the objection to this is, not that it makes very ugly words, totally unlike anything in the English language before ... but that it is part of a movement to reduce our spelling to uniform rule as opposed to usage, and to help forward the obliteration of all trace of the derivation and history of words (1864: 10).

Alford continues in this vein for another four pages, ignorant of the fact that spellings such as *honor* were used by English writers in the eighteenth century (Percy, 1999). Elsewhere, though, he shows awareness of current usage, and accepts 'new' constructions. We have seen in Section 4.3.1 that Marsh (1860) and White (1871) both objected to uses of the progressive passive. Alford, however, writing six and seven years earlier than these two respectively, accepts the usage:

> I am now going to speak of a combination of words which is so completely naturalised, that it would be vain to protest against it, or even to attempt to disuse it one's self. I mean, the joining together of a present and a past participle, as we do when we say '*The letter was being written,*' '*The dinner is being cooked.*' Such combinations were, I believe, not used by our best and most careful writers, until a comparatively recent date. The old and correct way of expressing what is meant by these phrases was, '*The letter was in writing,*' or '*was writing;*' '*The dinner was cooking:*' the verbs being used in a neuter sense. The objection to '*being written*' for '*in the process of writing,*' is this, – that '*written*' is a past participle, indicating a finished act. When I say

'*I have written a letter*,' I mean, I have by me, or have as my act accomplished, a letter written. So that '*being written*' properly means, existing in a state of completion. '*My letter being written, I put it in the post.*' And, strictly speaking, we cannot use the combination to signify an *incomplete* action. Still, as I have said, the inaccuracy has crept into the language, and is now found everywhere, in speech and in writing. The only thing we can do in such a case is to avoid it, where it can be avoided without violation of idiom, or giving harshness to the sentence (1864: 153–4).

Here, Alford rehearses the arguments of 'analogy', but grudgingly accepts the rule of usage. His is a more subtle prescriptivism, which, rather than making *ipse dixit* statements about errors, recommends what he considers the better usage. In this respect, Alford foreshadows the more prescriptive texts of the twentieth century, such as Fowler's *Modern English Usage* (first published in 1926).

Grammars in the nineteenth century, in both Britain and America, thus vary considerably from highly prescriptive handbooks of usage to scholarly, historically based works. On the one hand, advances in philology were leading scholars to an awareness of the validity of non-standard dialects as systems in their own right, and of the nature of linguistic change. On the other hand, the social forces at work in the eighteenth century continued to create a market amongst the aspiring middle classes for handy guides to 'correct' usage. The different types of 'grammar' were catering for different markets, one academic, the other popular. However, it would be a mistake to over-emphasize this polarity: one of the most influential works of this period, Alford's *The Queen's English*, combines aspects of both types. It is essentially aimed at middle Britain, the better-educated, who would know something about the history of English, but would still be more concerned with knowing that their usage was correct than with the academic study of the language. Alford is by no means ill-informed, as the citation above concerning the progressive passive demonstrates, but he is certainly normative and prone to caprice and prejudice.

5.4 Grammars in the early twentieth century

The early years of the twentieth century see a continuation of the trends noted in the previous section. It is in this period that most of the 'historical' English grammars are written by scholars whose names are written in the linguists' hall of fame. Among these are Jespersen's *A Modern English Grammar on Historical Principles* (1909–49); Poutsma's *A Grammar of Late Modern English* (1926); Kruisinga's *Handbook of Present-Day English* (1932); and Curme and Kurath's *A Grammar of the English*

Language (1931). These are all scholarly, historical grammars which have stood the test of time, and are still consulted by linguists today. For instance, Jespersen is cited in the chapters on syntax in both volumes III and IV of the *Cambridge History of the English Language* (Rissanen, 1999; Denison, 1998), whilst Poutsma is cited in volume III. There is little trace of the eighteenth-century prescriptions here. Curme and Kurath, for instance, introduce their section on prepositions with words that echo the statements of Lowth and Cobbett cited above (p. 110): 'As a preposition usually stands *before* the dependent word it is called a preposition (Latin "prae" *before* and "positio" *position*), (1931: 561). However, there is no sense here that a preposition must always precede its dependent word: on the contary, Curme and Kurath go on to state: 'in English, however, we often detach the preposition from the noun or pronoun and place it at the end of the proposition or clause' (1931: 561). Indeed, they devote an entire section to this phenomenon, providing an explanation of pied-piping in relative clauses which would be familiar to linguists today, and concluding:

> Thus for many centuries the position of a preposition at or near the end of a proposition has been one of the outstanding features of our language. It is so natural to put the preposition at the end that we have extended this usage beyond its original boundaries (1931: 568).

Whilst these historical grammars of the early twentieth century are thus descriptive, this does not mean that they are entirely objective in the sense of being free from ideology. Curme and Kurath, like the founders of the *OED* (above p. 63), take the view that the history of English is one of progress towards the 'better' state it is in by the twentieth century.

> The purpose of this volume is to present a systematic and rather full outline of English syntax based upon actual usage ... Everywhere attention has been called to the loose structure of the English sentence at that time [= Early Modern English] and to the subsequent development of our simple, terse, differentiated forms of expression – an eloquent testimony to the growing intellectual life of the English-speaking people (1931: v).

The authors here believe that their account is simply factual 'based upon actual usage', but they fail to be objective in their judgement of Early Modern English. Here, their association of linguistic usage and intellectual development echoes Alford's view that language reflects character: the only difference is that Curme and Kurath are contrasting historical periods rather than nations, and the Elizabethans have no right of reply. The lesson to be learnt here is that all grammars, however scholarly, are products of their time, and reflect the prevailing ideologies. I have argued in Section 5.2

that we should not condemn the prescriptivism of eighteenth-century grammarians out of hand without considering the historical context in which their works were written. Equally, we should recognize that grammars written in more recent periods, which appear more enlightened to us, still have a historical context, and should be read in this light.

In the early twentieth century, as in the nineteenth, prescriptive works on grammar and usage continued to be published alongside the scholarly works discussed above. If anything, the introduction of universal, compulsory primary education in 1870, and subsequent reforms in the early twentieth century, meant that prescriptive notions of 'correct' usage were being introduced to children of all classes. As we shall see in Chapter 7, the tone of reports by H.M. Inspectors of Schools in this period is highly normative. Handbooks first published in the nineteenth century continued to be popular: I have a copy of *Don't* which is undated, but has 1950 written in pencil on the fly-leaf. The addition of sections giving advice on correct behaviour 'In the Air' and 'At the Cinema' would suggest that this is an early to mid-twentieth-century publication. However, the most influential handbook of this period is one which, like Alford (1864), combines an awareness of the history of English with a subtle prescriptivism: H. W. Fowler's *Modern English Usage* (1930). H. W. Fowler and his brother F. G. Fowler had previously published *The King's English* (1906), a book whose title as well as its content has echoes of Alford. Both works were to be reprinted throughout the twentieth century. In his preface to the third edition of *The King's English*, H. W. Fowler writes that sales had 'maintained a yearly average of nearly two thousand copies '(1930: v) since 1906. Burchfield, in the preface to his revised third edition of *Modern English Usage*, ponders the continuing popularity of this work:

> The mystery remains: why has this schoolmasterly, quixotic, idiosyncratic and somewhat vulnerable book, in a form only lightly revised once, in 1965 by Ernest Gowers, retained its hold on the imagination of all but professional linguistic scholars for just on seventy years? It sold very well on publication, and has remained in print ever since. People of all kinds continue to tell me that they 'use it all the time', and that 'it never lets them down.' In the space of three weeks a judge, a colonel, and a retired curator of Greek and Roman antiquities at the British Museum told me on separate occasions that they have the book close at hand at all times (1996: ix).

Of course, a judge, a colonel and a retired museum curator hardly constitute 'all kinds of people': all would be educated, but not experts in linguistics, precisely the type of person most concerned with 'correct' usage in the twentieth century. That Fowler had his sights on a slightly lower stratum of society, the same 'middle Britain' that I have suggested (p. 119) made up

Alford's target readership, is confirmed in a letter written by H. W. Fowler to his publishers in 1911. Here, he writes 'we have our eyes ... on the half-educated Englishman of literary proclivities who wants to know Can I say so-&-so?' (cited in Burchfield, 1996: vii). A few examples from Fowler's works will illustrate the combination of descriptive and prescriptive tendencies that Burchfield describes as 'quixotic'. On the matter of ending sentences with prepositions, H. W. Fowler adds a note in the third edition of *The King's English*:

> Mention has been made here and there of the 'superstition' against ending clause or sentence with a preposition; but in 1906 it had not occurred to us to examine seriously the validity of what, superstition or no, is a widespread belief. It was indeed *spretae injuria formae* that brought home to us the need for such examination, a reviewer having condemned our book out of hand on the ground that the first paragraph of its preface ended in a preposition. I may perhaps be allowed to refer readers, for the result of our inquiry, to the article PREPOSITION AT END in *Modern English Usage* (1930: 179).

In *Modern English Usage*, Fowler cites examples of prepositions ending sentences from Ruskin's *Seven Lamps of Architecture*, but concludes that 'you cannot put a preposition (roughly speaking) later than its word in Latin, and therefore you must not do so in English' (cited in Burchfield, 1996: 618). On the one hand, Fowler rejects the absolute shibboleth, but then goes on to prescribe complicated rules for when it is or is not acceptable to end a sentence or clause with a preposition. The entry on the use of *like* as a conjunction in *Modern English Usage* treads a fine line between prescription and description, as Finegan (1998: 577) points out. Fowler writes: 'Every illiterate person uses this construction daily; it is the established way of putting the thing among all who have not been taught to avoid it' (cited in Burchfield, 1996: 458). Fowler goes on to cite the *OED*'s comment that the usage is 'now generally condemned as vulgar or slovenly, though examples may be found in many recent writers of standing'. Fowler thus has his cake and eats it: he acknowledges current usage, but makes his own distaste for it clear. Without actually going so far as to proscribe conjunctional *like*, he leaves the reader in no doubt as to what constitutes 'good' usage.

5.5   Conclusion

In this chapter, as in Chapter 3, I have attempted to demonstrate that grammars, like dictionaries, are each a product of the times in which they were written, and reflect the prevailing ideologies. I have challenged the binary opposition of prescriptive/descriptive, showing that eighteenth-century grammarians such as Lowth, who have been demonized by twentieth-century linguists, do not prescribe artificial usage, but base their rules as much on the perceived practice of the educated upper classes as on 'reason', 'logic' and the rules of Latin. On the other hand, nineteenth- and early twentieth-century grammars are not ideologically neutral, but reflect the prevailing historicism of their time. What is striking about these later periods is the continuity with our own: then, as now, we see a division between 'scientific' grammars, based on historical or contemporary corpora, and prescriptive handbooks. Just as Alford and Fowler were successful and popular in their day, so a number of works appear in today's best-seller list whose titles proclaim them to be semi-humorous, but seriously prescriptive: *Eats, Shoots and Leaves: A Zero-Tolerance Guide to Punctuation* (Truss, 2003); *Between You and I: A Little Book of Bad English* (Cochrane and Humphreys, 2003); and *The Grouchy Grammarian: A How-Not-To Guide to the 47 most Common Mistakes in English Made by Journalists, Broadcasters, and Others Who Should Know Better* (Parrish, 2002). It would appear that the efforts of grammarians from the eighteenth-century onwards have done little to 'fix' the language, but they have left us a legacy of 'linguistic insecurity', which still creates a market for the titles above.

6

Phonological change in Later Modern English

6.1 Introduction

In my book on the pronunciation of English in the eighteenth century, I point out that, of all the areas of historical linguistic study, it is the phonology of Later Modern English that, until very recently, has suffered most from the neglect of scholars. After reviewing a range of general histories of English, I conclude that 'where interest is shown in the eighteenth century, phonology is neglected, and where interest is shown in the history of English phonology, the eighteenth century is neglected' (Beal, 1999: 13). Charles Jones, himself a pioneer in the study of Later Modern English phonology, explains this neglect as follows:

> There has always been a suggestion ... especially among those scholars writing in the first half of the twentieth century, that phonological and syntactic change is only properly observable at a great distance and that somehow the eighteenth, and especially the nineteenth centuries, are 'too close' chronologically for any meaningful observations concerning language change to be made (1989: 279).

The approach of the twenty-first century seems to have provided the necessary 'distance', for, as well as Jones's chapter cited above, there are substantial chapters on the phonology of this period in volumes III and IV of the *Cambridge History of the English Language*, respectively dealing with the period up to 1776 (Lass, 1999) and after 1776 (MacMahon, 1998). The latter highlights another reason why the phonology of Later Modern English had hitherto been neglected. He points out that 'super-ficially, the period under consideration might appear to contain little of phonetic and phonological interest, compared with, for example, earlier changes such as the transition from Old to Middle English, and the Great

Vowel Shift' (1998: 373). However, MacMahon goes on to point out that 'there is other evidence to show that the pronunciation of English more than 150 years ago was *noticeably* different, for reasons mainly of phonotactics (structure and lexical incidence), from what it is today' (1998: 374). In distinguishing the 'big' systemic changes such as the Great Vowel Shift, from the phonotactically motivated changes of more recent years, MacMahon echoes Strang's remarks on the subject:

> Some short histories of English give the impression that changes in pro-nunciation stopped dead in the 18c, a development which would be quite inexplicable for a language in everyday use. It is true that the sweeping systematic changes we can detect in earlier periods are missing, but the amount of change is no less. Rather, its location has changed: in the past two hundred years changes in pronunciation are predominantly due, not, as in the past, to evolution of the system, but to what, in a very broad sense, we may call the interplay of different varieties, and to the complex analogical relationship between different parts of the language (Strang, 1970: 78–9).

Here, Strang comes close to refuting the 'uniformitarian principle', by suggesting that sound change in Later Modern English is of a different nature to that of earlier periods, a view contested by Jones (1989), who sets out 'to show how the eighteenth and nineteenth centuries manifest the same types of phonological processes we have met at earlier historical "moments"' (1989: 281). I would argue that the opposition set out by Strang between 'sweeping systematic changes' and what appear to be externally motivated changes is an illusion created by the different types of evidence available for the earlier and later periods. It is a matter of perspective: at a distance, a forest appears as a monolithic block, but, the closer you come to the forest, the more you notice the variation between individual trees. James Milroy makes this point with reference to the synchronic study of linguistic variation:

> It is clear that the data collected in close investigations of live speech communities are much richer than the data preserved from earlier language states, and they are observable in a larger number of dimensions and at a much finer level of detail; thus, the patterns revealed in systematic observations of live speech communities appear to the observer as much more variable and multidimensional than historical patterns (as these are usually reported) (1992: 49).

I would argue that the evidence we have for the pronunciation of English in the later modern period is rich enough to provide evidence for 'variable and multidimensional' patterns. Thus, as I have pointed out elsewhere, this period has been attractive in the past to those scholars who were more interested in socio-historical factors: Strang herself was one of these, along with Wyld (1927; 1936), McKnight (1928) and Schlauch (1959). However, as Jones (1989) has demonstrated, this does not mean that systematic changes did not happen (or are not happening): merely that it is more difficult to perceive them, or, to continue my previous metaphor, to 'see the wood for the trees'. In the main part of this chapter, I shall discuss both types of change: those which appear systematic, and affect the phonological inventory at least of what was to become known as Received Pronunciation, and those which are more obviously socially and/or lexically conditioned, resulting in changes in the distribution of phonemes. Before doing this, it is necessary to consider the nature of the evidence for these changes.

6.2   Evidence for Later Modern English pronunciation

6.2.1   Overview: types of evidence

In the previous section, I referred to James Milroy's statement concerning the comparative 'richness' of data collected from studies of present-day speech communities and historical surveys. One obvious reason for this difference is that studies of linguistic variation and change from the later twentieth century onwards call upon recorded speech data, which can be as 'rich' as the methodology allows. If and when scholars embark on studies of phonological change in twentieth-century English, they will have a wealth of data to draw on, provided measures are taken to preserve and archive these recordings. Even from the earlier twentieth century, there is a certain amount of recorded material available from television and radio broadcasts, films and phonographic recordings, which provides similarly 'rich' data. If we take on board the assumption behind the 'apparent time' methodology used in variation and change studies that a person's phonology does not alter significantly once he or she reaches adulthood, then older, living speakers can also provide evidence for the speech of the earlier twentieth century. For earlier periods, though, we must rely on written evidence of various kinds, which can be either direct or indirect. Direct evidence is provided by those whose overt intention is to inform readers about the language of their own period, whilst indirect evidence comes from a number of sources, all of which involve writers inadvertently providing clues about their own or their contemporaries' pronunciation. Indirect evidence comes from rhymes, puns and spellings. This is the only type of evidence available for Old and Middle English, but, from the sixteenth century onwards, a large amount of direct evidence becomes available in the form of works on spelling and pronunciation by a group of scholars generally termed orthoepists. The relative merits of direct and indirect evidence for the reconstruction of Early Modern English pronunciation have been debated at length in Wyld (1936), Dobson (1955), Kökeritz (1953) and Beal (1999: 38–47). For the later modern period, we rely mainly on direct evidence, partly because there is so much more of this available, but also because indirect evidence from this period is more patchy and less reliable. Rhymes are more likely to be 'eye-rhymes' of the LOVE/PROVE type, the standardization of spelling means that only the most informal letters from less well-educated writers provide evidence of pronunciation, and puns are less ubiquitous after the time of Shakespeare. As MacMahon (1998: 379) points out, there is some useful indirect evidence from this period, such as Keats's rhyme of THOUGHTS/SORTS (Mugglestone, 1991: 58), which provides clear evidence for loss of rhoticity (see Section 6.3.7). However, examples such as this can only be used as a supplement to, and a check on, the direct evidence provided by authors who, for various reasons, set out to give the reader a full account of the pronunciation of at least a prestigious variety of English in their own day.

6.2.2 The reliability of direct evidence for Later Modern English pronunciation

Apart from recorded speech data, there are two types of direct evidence for the pronunciation of English in the later modern period. Like the grammars discussed in Chapter 5, works on pronunciation can roughly be divided into those which are prescriptive or normative and those which are purely descriptive, and the more normative works tend to be produced in the earlier part of the period. However, as with the grammars, I shall argue that the most normative works provide valuable evidence for what was considered 'good' pronunciation, whilst the more 'scientific' works of late nineteenth- and early twentieth-century linguists are not entirely objective.

In the second half of the eighteenth century, when the codification of Standard English grammar was well under way, a number of authors began to turn their attention to 'fixing' a standard of pronunciation. The most popular method of presenting this to the reading public was as a pronouncing dictionary: such works were highly marketable because they provided the definitions and conventional spellings expected in a dictionary, with clear and detailed guidelines concerning the 'correct' pronunciation of every word. I shall discuss the socio-linguistic implications of this in the next chapter: what we need to consider here is the value of the evidence provided by these works as a record of the pronunciation of the time. The orthoepists whose works provide direct evidence for Early Modern English pronunciation have been criticized by some scholars on the grounds that, as Holmberg suggests, 'they were sometimes more anxious to teach what they believed was correct than to record the pronunciation they actually heard or used' (1964: 10). Wyld, in particular, is scathing about both the orthoepists and those linguistic historians who have relied upon them for evidence. His objections are, firstly, that the orthoepists tend to confuse spelling with pronunciation; secondly, that their descriptions are often so vague that several interpretations can be put on them; and, lastly, that they are too conservative. He concludes that 'the descriptions are always some way behind the facts, or made to square with the traditional spelling so that they are quite misleading' (1936: 117). Of course, Wyld himself shows considerable bias here, in describing as 'facts' the conclusions at which he has arrived largely on the basis of indirect evidence, and he has in turn been described as 'a fierce language snob' who laid too much emphasis on RP (Bailey, 1996: 90). He is, however, more charitable towards some of the sources of direct evidence from the eighteenth century: John Walker, whose (1791) *Critical Pronouncing Dictionary* was, as we shall see in Chapter 7, the most influential work of its type for a century, is discussed in a section headed 'A Reliable Witness'. Here, Wyld concludes that 'Walker . . . must be placed with the most reliable and informing writers of his class' (Wyld, 1936: 183). On the other hand, Dobson, whose two-volume work on Early Modern English pronunciation is based largely on direct evidence, dismisses later evidence of this type. He states that 'the eighteenth century produced no writers to compare either with the spelling reformers who are our main source up to 1644 (Hodges), or with the phoneticians who, beginning with Robinson (1617) carry us on from 1653 (Wallis) to 1687 (Cooper's *English Teacher*), (1957: I, 311). His conclusion that this is a pity, since indirect evidence becomes less reliable after 1700, provides another explanation for the relative neglect of Later Modern English phonology by scholars such as Dobson. They simply did not trust the evidence available.

I have argued elsewhere (Beal, 1999; 2003), that we need to re-evaluate the evidence provided by eighteenth-century pronouncing dictionaries, since, providing as they do a record of pronunciation across the whole lexicon, they are potentially very valuable sources of evidence for lexical diffusion. Just as I have argued in Chapter 6 that eighteenth-century grammarians such as Lowth have been unfairly demonized as 'prescriptive' and therefore unreliable, so the authors of eighteenth-century pronouncing dictionaries have had a similarly bad press. I would like to suggest that even the most normative authors of works on pronunciation in this period can be relied upon to provide clear evidence for the phonology of at least one variety of English: what I have termed elsewhere (1999: 60) 'proto-RP'. To demonstrate this, I shall spend some time looking at the evidence provided by the man who is to pronunciation what Lowth is to grammar: John Walker.

John Walker's *Critical Pronouncing Dictionary* (1791) was the most successful and authoritative pronouncing dictionary of the late eighteenth and the nineteenth centuries. Reprinted over 100 times up to 1904, it was also the basis of over 20 other dictionaries published in the nineteenth century, including Smart's *Walker Remodelled* (1836). Walker's *Critical Pronouncing Dictionary* was described as the 'statute book of English orthoepy' (*The Athenaeum*, 1807: 81). Mugglestone tells us that 'by the end of the nineteenth century, John Walker had . . . become a household name . . . he had in effect become one of the icons of the age, commonly referred to as "Elocution Walker", just as Johnson had come to be labelled "Dictionary Johnson" in the public mind' (1995: 41). Walker, like Lowth, suffered a bad press in the twentieth century because of the normative nature of his work. As early as 1869, when reprints of the *Critical Pronouncing Dictionary* were still selling well, Ellis described Walker and other authors of pronouncing dictionaries as 'those word-pedlars, those letter-drivers, those stiff-necked pedantic philosophical, miserably informed, and therefore supremely certain, self-confident and self-conceited orthographers' (1869: I, 155). Webster, too, is scathing about the pronunciations recommended by Walker, but, as we saw in Chapter 3 (p. 50), his criticisms are probably motivated by nationalistic feelings and the desire to establish a separate standard for America. On the other hand, Ellis acknowledges that Walker had done 'good and hard work' (1869), and, when we come to the early twentieth century, both Jespersen and Wyld evaluate Walker more positively as a source of evidence. Wyld, in particular, praises Walker as 'amongst the most reliable and informing writers of his class . . . He appeals . . . to a real type of existing English, and he must be held to mirror the usage of his day among refined and learned, and, though to a lesser extent perhaps, among fashionable speakers, with considerable fidelity' (Wyld: 1936: 183). Sheldon sets up a binary opposition between Walker and his rival elocutionist Sheridan that has echoes of Leonard's contrast of Lowth and Priestley. She asserts that 'while Sheridan reflects the speech of his time better, Walker satisfies the temper of his time better, and its demand for linguistic regulation and reform' (1947: 146). In fact, the explanation for these divergent opinions on Walker can be traced to the different orientations and interests of these scholars. Ellis, as we shall see in Chapter 8, was interested in dialects, and developed his own phonetic script to represent the sounds as precisely as possible, so it is understandable that he would react against Walker's representation of a prestigious standard and, to a certain extent, the fossilization of this eighteenth-century standard in later reprints. Wyld was interested in the development of Standard and Modified Standard pronunciation, and so would be interested in the socio-linguistic information provided by Walker. Sheldon, on the other hand, just had a much greater interest in Sheridan, and went on to write a book about his life and career in the theatre (1967). I wish to argue that, like Lowth and other 'prescriptive' grammarians discussed in Chapter 5, Walker was undoubtedly normative, but this does not mean that the pronunciations prescribed by him were not in use. Rather, he gives a very precise account of the pronunciation in formal registers of an elite group of speakers. Twentieth-century linguists have tended to view eighteenth-century accounts of pronunciation as amateur and unscientific, whilst recognizing the likes of Ellis as fellow professionals. However, whilst it is true that philology as a discipline did not exist before the nineteenth century, Walker and his contemporaries had a tradition of phonetic observation and description behind them, exemplified by the works of seventeenth-century orthoepists such as Cooper. When Walker describes pronunciations, he does so using an articulatory terminology which is by this time well established. There is no sense that his descriptions are vague or confused, as we can see if we look at his rules on the 'Organic Formation of the Letters'. These demonstrate Walker's awareness of articulatory processes and the fact that he has studied the works of earlier phoneticians, notably Holder, whose *Elements of Orthoepy* (1669) he acknowledges as the source of his distinction between voiced and voiceless consonants. Rule 41 states:

> The best method of shewing the organic formation of the consonants will be to class them into such pairs as they naturally fall into, and then by describing one, we shall nearly describe its fellow, by which means the labour will be lessened, and the nature of the consonants better perceived. The consonants that fall into pairs are the following:

p	f	t	s	sh	th	k	ch	chair
b	v	d	z	zh	dh	g	j	jail

> (Walker, 1791: 6).

In rule 43, he goes on to explain the distinction:

> This difference in the formation of these consonants may be more distinctly perceived in the s and z than in any other of the letters; the former is sounded by the simple issue of the breath between the teeth, without any vibration of it in the throat, and may be called a hissing sound; whilst the latter cannot be formed without generating a sound in the throat, which may be called a vocal sound. The upper rank of letters, therefore, may be called breathing consonants; and the lower, vocal ones.
> (Walker, 1791: 6).

Whilst the terminology may seem quaint and the explanations longwinded, this is as good an account of the voiced/voiceless distinction as we might find in many an introductory textbook today. Although Walker was not a 'professional' linguist by today's criteria, he was certainly well informed and well read. He makes reference to a number of orthoepists and elocutionists throughout his *Critical Pronouncing Dictionary*, often to disagree with them. Whilst his tone in these passages is confident to the point of arrogance, his full accounts of the differences between his own recommendations and those of earlier writers provide us with valuable insights into the nature of linguistic variation and change in the eighteenth century. To take one example, let us look at Walker's note to the entry on *merchant*:

> ☞Mr. Sheridan pronounces the *e* in the first syllable of this word, like the *a* in *march*; and it is certain that, about thirty years ago, this was the general pronunciation; but since that time the sound of *a* has been gradually wearing away; and the sound of *e* is so fully established, that the former is now become gross and vulgar, and is only to be heard among the lower orders of the people. It is, indeed, highly probable, that, however coarse this sound of *e* may now seem, it was once, not only the common pronunciation, but the most agreeable to analogy . . . *Sermon. service, vermin* &c. are still pronounced by the vulgar, as if written *sarmon, sarvice, varmint* &c.; and this was probably the ancient manner of pronouncing every *e* in the same situation. This analogy is now totally exploded; and except *clerk, sergeant* and a few proper names, we have scarcely another word in the language where this *e* has not its true sound. But instead of saying with Mr Nares, that *Merchant* has returned to the proper sound of *e*, we may with greater probability assert, that this and every other word of the same form have acquired a sound of *e* which they never had before, and which, though a feebler and a shorter sound, conduces to the simplicity and regularity of our pronunciation. Dr Kenrick concurs, in my opinion, that pronouncing the *e* in this word like *a* is vulgar; and every other orthöepist, who gives the sound of the vowels, marks it as I have done.

Walker's tone is highly prescriptive here; *gross* and *vulgar* are derogatory terms which he often uses. Likewise, he often takes issue with 'Mr Sheridan', whose *General Dictionary of the English Language* (1780) was his main rival in the market for guides to 'correct' pronunciation. Nevertheless, he accuses Sheridan not of being wrong, but of being old-fashioned, and, of course, the distribution of /ɑː/ pronunciations in this set of words is exactly that which prevails in RP and most British varieties today. Evidence from the spellings in letters by the Wentworth family confirm that the /ɑː/ pronunciation was found in *servant*, etc. in the early eighteenth-century, for these contain many instances of spellings such as <sarvant, desarve> etc. (Wyld 1936: 216–22). It seems unjust to accuse Walker either of being conservative or of prescribing 'unreal', idealized pronunciations here. Indeed, as I have observed elsewhere (Beal, 1999;

2003), the pronunciations recommended by Walker are often advanced rather than conservative. MacMahon cites Ellis as particularly critical of Walker's 'usherism': the 'constant references to the habits of a class of society to which he did not belong [and] the most evident marks [in the *Dictionary*] of insufficient knowledge, and of that kind of pedantic self-sufficiency which is the true growth of half-enlightened ignorance' (Ellis, 1869: 624–5, cited in MacMahon, 1998: 378). However, I have argued (2003) that it was precisely Walker's social position on the fringe of 'polite' society and loosely connected to the networks of the powerful and influential (including Garrick and Johnson) which made him, according to social network theory, most likely to be an innovator. I shall discuss Walker's importance as an elocutionist further in Chapter 7: here, I hope to have established that his *Critical Pronouncing Dictionary* is a valuable source of information at least on what was considered prestigious pronunciation in late eighteenth-century England. As we shall see in Chapter 8, his proscriptions also provide insights into the nature of regional and/or non-standard pronunciations. Of course, it would be foolish to rely on Walker alone for an account of eighteenth-century pronunciation, even of educated London English. Fortunately, there are many other pronouncing dictionaries and treatises on pronunciation which can be compared with Walker's to provide a fuller account, not only of London English, but of the 'modified' standards emerging in provincial English cities and in Scotland (see Jones, 1991; 1995; 1997 for accounts of the latter). I shall refer to a number of these in the following sections, including Burn (1786), Kenrick (1773), Sheridan (1780) and Spence (1775).

For the later nineteenth and the early twentieth centuries, we have direct evidence which looks more familiar to us as linguists, and which we are disposed to take at face value. Alexander Ellis, Henry Sweet and Daniel Jones are revered as founding fathers of phonetics, and their works are considered more scientific than those of Walker, Sheridan, etc. However, as we shall see in Chapter 8, these great scholars were not without their own prejudices and, whilst Jones intended his *English Pronouncing Dictionary* as a descriptive work, 'a record of *facts*, not theories or personal preferences' (1917: vii), it was marketed and received as the natural heir to Walker. Moreover, as Crowley points out, and as we shall see in Chapter 7, Jones was instrumental in defining and promoting Received Pronunciation, a variety of which, of course, he spoke himself. Crowley concludes from his discussion of Jones and Wyld:

> It has been shown that the early-twentieth-century linguists Jones and Wyld, just like the earlier nineteenth-century linguists, saw themselves as neutral scientists, observers without discrimination. It has also been shown that, in so

far as this particular concept was concerned their self-images were false, since when they developed their theories concerning the 'Standard Language' they constructed them along the lines of the preferences and prejudices that had been present in the nineteenth century and earlier (2003: 173).

I am not arguing here that we should not make use of these later sources as evidence for nineteenth- and early twentieth-century pronunciation: on the contrary, they provide rich and detailed information. I am simply entering a plea for parity: if we need to read Walker with caution because he is 'prescriptive', then we should extend the same healthy scepticism to our reading of more recent linguists. Above all, we need to bear in mind that most of these sources provide us with accounts of the usage of only one section of society, and of the prestigious pronunciation that was to become known as RP. In the following sections, I shall therefore concentrate on tracing the history of this variety, but will note developments in other varieties as and when evidence of these is available.

6.3   Phonological change

6.3.1 Overview

In the following sections, I shall discuss individual changes in the phonology of English between 1700 and 1945. In the scope of this chapter, I cannot hope to give an exhaustive account of variation and change within this period, so I shall concentrate on developments for which we have a reasonable amount of information. This means that I shall concentrate more on the segmental phonology of the period than on the prosody and intonation, and, rather than giving a complete account of the phonology of any period, I shall concentrate on areas in which change is observable. To give an overview of the pronunciation of what was considered 'correct' English pronunciation in England at two different points in time, I have transcribed (Figure 6.1) a passage often used to exemplify the phonology of different varieties of English: the fable of the North Wind and the Sun. In passage A, I have transcribed each word according to my interpretation of the pronunciation recommended in Walker's *Critical Pronouncing Dictionary*, whilst in passage B I have simply taken the transcriptions provided in the 1937 edition of Daniel Jones's *English Pronouncing Dictionary*.

In these transcriptions, I have indicated variant pronunciations by the use of a forward stroke: the alternative to the left is the one indicated as more usual or favoured by Walker or Jones in each case. Some of the apparent differences between A and B are due to conventions of transcription. Jones does not use the symbols /ɪ/ or /ɒ/, but in his 'table of chief sounds occurring

The North Wind and the Sun

The North Wind and the Sun were disputing which was the stronger when a traveller came along wrapped in a warm cloak.
They agreed that the one who first succeeded in making the traveller take his cloak off should be considered stronger than the other.
Then the North Wind blew as hard as he could, but the more he blew, the more closely did the traveller pull his cloak around him; and at last the North Wind gave up the attempt.
Then the Sun shone out warmly, and immediately the traveller took off his cloak. And so the North Wind was obliged to confess that the Sun was the stronger of the two.

A. Walker (1791)

ðɛ nɔɹθ wɪnd/ waɪnd ænd ðɛ sʌn wɛɹ dɪspjutɪŋ hwitʃ wɒz ðɛ stɹɒŋɡʌɹ hwen eː tɹævɪlʌɹ keːm ælɒŋ ræpt ɪn eː wɔɹm kloːk.

ðeː ægriːd ðæt ði wʌn huː fʌɹst sʌksiːdɛd ɪn meːkɪŋ ðɛ tɹævɪlʌɹ teːk hɪz kloːk ɒf ʃʊd biː kɒnsɪdʌɹd stɹɒŋɡʌɹ ðæn ðiː ʌðʌɹ .

ðen ðɛ nɔɹθ wɪnd/ waɪnd bliu æz hɑːɹd æz hiː kʊd bʌt ðɛ moːɹ hiː bliu ðɛ moːɹ kloːsliː dɪd ðɛ tɹævɪlʌɹ pʊl hɪz kloːk æɹɔʊnd hɪm ænd æt læst ðɛ nɔɹθ wɪnd/ waɪnd geːv ʌp ði ætɛmt.

ðen ðɛ sʌn ʃɒn ɔʊt wɔɹmliː ænd ɪmiːdiːætliː ðɛ tɹævɪlʌɹ tuːk ɒf hɪz kloːk ænd soː ðɛ nɔɹθ wɪnd/ waɪnd wɒz ɒblaɪdʒd / ɒbliːdʒd tuː kɒnfɛs ðæt ðɛ sʌn wɒz ðɛ stɹɒŋɡʌɹ ɒv ðɛ tuː

B. Jones (1937)

ðə nɔːθ wind ænd ðə sʌn wəː dɪspjuːtɪŋ witʃ / hwitʃ wəz ðə stɹɒŋɡə hwen / wen ə tɹævlə keɪm əlɒŋ ræpt in ə wɔːm klouk.

ðei əgriːd ðət ðə wʌn huː fəːst sʌksiːdid in meikiŋ ðə tɹævlə teik hiz klouk ɔːf / ɔf ʃəd bi kənsidəd stɹɒŋɡə ðən ði ʌðə.

ðen ðə nɔːθ wind bluː əz hɑːd əz hiː kʊd bət ðə mɔː hiː bluː ðə mɔː klousli did ðə tɹævlə pʊl hiz klouk əɹaʊnd him ənd ət lɑːst ðə nɔːθ wind geiv ʌp ði ətɛmpt.

ðen ðə sʌn ʃɒn aut wɔːmli ənd imiːdjətli ðə tɹævlə tʊk ɔːf / ɔf hiz klouk ənd sou ðə nɔːθ wind wəz əblaidʒd / oblaidʒd tə kənfes ðət ðə sʌn wəz ðə stɹɒŋɡəɹ əv ðə tuː

Fig. 6.1 Transcriptions of 'The North Wind and the Sun', according to Walker (1791) and Jones (1937)

in the dictionary' (1937: xxi) he indicates that /iː/ differs from /i/ and /ɔː/ from /ɔ/ in terms of quality as well as quantity, the latter symbol being lower than the former in each case. Walker, on the other hand, using superscripted numerals and keywords, distinguishes o^3 in *nor* from o^4 in *not* and e^1 in *meet* from i^2 in *pin*, so I have transcribed them with the symbols more commonly used to distinguish the equivalent sounds in present-day RP as in, for example, Wells (1982). In discussing the sound changes indicated by differences between A and B, and elsewhere in this chapter, I shall use Wells's keywords to denote standard lexical sets. As we shall see in Section 6.3.6, Jones's transcription does create problems with regard to the interpretation of the final unstressed vowel of words such as *warmly* (Wells's *happ*Y set), but otherwise these differences are of little consequence.

There are, however, several differences between A and B which are indicative of changes in the pronunciation of this variety of British English in the later modern period. Perhaps the two most striking differences are that Jones uses schwa, whereas Walker does not, and that Walker's notation suggests a rhotic variety, whilst Jones's is non-rhotic. These two features are related, as a number of the instances of schwa in Jones's transcription are derived from vowels preceding <r>. These changes will be discussed in Sections 6.3.6 and 6.3.7. Walker's notation lacks the diphthongal phonemes /ei/ as in *came, gave* (Wells's FACE set) and /ou/ as in *cloak* (the GOAT set). As we shall see in Section 6.3.2, this is borne out in other accounts of eighteenth-century pronunciation. The contrast between Walker's /læst/ and Jones's /lɑːst/, and between Walker's /ɒf/ and Jones's variation between /ɒf/ and /ɔːf/ suggests changes involving the lengthening of these vowels before fricatives, which will be discussed in Section 6.3.3. Another difference involving alternative pronunciations is that between Walker's /hw/ in *which, when* and Jones's alternative of /w/ as the less usual pronunciation. This would indicate a change still in progress in 1937, at least as far as RP is concerned. As we shall see in Section 6.3.8, the /w/ pronunciation was used in Walker's time, but not, according to Walker, from the best speakers. Changes which seem to affect more restricted sets of words include Walker's long vowel in /tuːk/ contrasting with Jones's /tuk/ and Walker's /bliu/ versus Jones's /bluː/. These will be discussed in Sections 6.3.4 and 6.3.5 respectively. Finally, there is one word whose pronunciation is variable in both transcriptions: *oblige*. We shall consider this, with a number of other individual words (as opposed to lexical sets) which are variable in the later modern period, in Section 6.3.10. Of course, this one passage does not indicate all the differences between the pronunciation of educated southern British speakers in the late eighteenth and mid- twentieth centuries, but it does provide us with some useful starting-points. I shall therefore begin by discussing these features, before going on to examine other areas of change in the phonology of Later Modern English.

6.3.2   The FACE and GOAT sets

Walker, along with all other eighteenth-century sources, clearly indicates that words in the FACE and GOAT sets have monophthongal pronunciations, whereas Jones records diphthongs in both sets. In present-day British English, monophthongal pronunciations of these words are found in a range of regional accents, including many in the north of England, but in both sets the monophthongs described by Walker are the result of the raising of lower vowels in the (Early Modern English) Great Vowel Shift. In FACE, the vowel transcribed in passage A above as /eː/ is the result of the raising of Middle English /aː/. Dobson tells us that this raising went through three stages: [æː], [ɛː], and [eː], and that the last of these 'existed in StE from the beginning of the seventeenth century, but was rare before 1650 and was still not accepted in good speech in the second half of the eighteenth century; it became normal in StE early in the eighteenth century' (1957: 594). Walker describes this sound as follows:

> This is what is called, by most grammarians, its slender sound . . . we find it in the words *lade, spade, trade* &c. and sometimes in the diphthong *ea*, as *bear, swear, pear* &c; nay, twice we find it, contrary to every rule of pronunciation, in the words *where* and *there*, and once in the anomalous diphthong *ao* in *gaol*. It exactly corresponds to the sound of the French *e* in the beginning of the words *être* and *tête* (1791: 10).

MacMahon points out that Walker's use of the French *être* and *tête* as examples suggests a more open vowel, but that his citation elsewhere (1791: xvi) of *fée, épée* as exemplifying the equivalent French sound to 'slender *a*' suggests [eː]. He concludes that Walker's pronunciation of /eː/ was more open than that of present-day RP, but not as open as [ɛː] (1998: 450). What is beyond doubt is that Walker describes this vowel as monophthongal: although he uses the term *diphthong* in the passage cited above where we would use *digraph*, he clearly understands the difference between monophthongs and diphthongs in articulation. This is shown both in the description of diphthongs and in his 'table of the simple and diphthongal vowels') (1791: xvi) in which only *i* in *pine* and *u* in *tube* are described as diphthongal. Diphthongs usually represented in spellings as digraphs, as in *oil, pound*, are described as combinations of two vowels. The first reliable evidence for a diphthongal pronunciation of the FACE set comes from Batchelor (1809). MacMahon points out that Gildon and Brightland state that 'The Diphthongs . . . *ai* . . . *ay* . . . *ey* . . . *oi*

... when they are truly pronounc'd, are compounded of the foregoing, or prepositive Vowel, and the Consonant *y*' (1711: 32). I would be suspicious of this evidence, firstly because it is the only suggestion of a diphthongal pronunciation before Batchelor, and secondly because they only mention diphthongal pronunciations of digraphs. This could, of course, indicate that the variety described by Gildon and Brightland retained a distinction between the reflexes of Middle English [aː] in FACE and [æɪ]/[ɛɪ] in, for example, *play, veil*, as do some accents of British English today. Batchelor is generally cited as the first to provide reliable evidence for the diphthongization (Jones, 1989: 292; Chomsky and Halle, 1968: 283–4), but he is conscious that his predecessors and contemporaries have not noticed this: 'The motions of the tongue can neither be seen nor felt, in some cases, without more attention than grammarians generally think proper to devote to that purpose' (1809: 53, cited in MacMahon, 1998: 450). Later nineteenth-century sources such as Smart (1836) and Sweet (1877) in Britain, and Rush (1827) and Whitney (1875) in America, are increasingly confident about identifying this sound as diphthongal. The early twentieth century sees a reversal of this process in the usage of at least some RP speakers: Barber writes of the 'smoothing of diphthongs' as follows:

> There is . . . a tendency for some of the existing diphthongs to be smoothed out, that is, for the glide to become shorter, so that they are more like pure vowels. This process of monophthongisation is especially seen in ei (the sound of *say, plain* etc.); the glide in this sound is now very slight, and in some people's speech it is not far removed from a long pure vowel of the eː type (1964: 45).

Barber was describing here the speech of the 'past few decades' (1964: v), i.e. the 1940s and 1950s. Corroborating evidence for this early to mid-twentieth-century 'smoothing' comes from Horn and Lehnert (1954: 325). This is part of a general tendency to smoothing, now restricted to a very conservative and upper-class variety of RP, in which the triphthongs /aiə/, /auə/ in *fire, tower* are also smoothed (and merged) to [aː] or [ɑː]. Barber writes that 'this smoothing of aiə and auə is far commoner in R.P. proper than in educated regional speech' (1964: 46). This would appear to have been a development of the 1940s to 1960s, and is now restricted to a few older and/or upper-class speakers in England. The more general pronunciation in educated speech of the south of England, and in general RP, has been diphthongal since the nineteenth century. Likewise, in American English, a diphthongal pronunciation has been characteristic of General American thoroughout this period, with monophthongal pronunciations such as /aː/ found in regional varieties, in this case those of the south.

The development in the GOAT set is parallel to that in FACE: Walker describes the vowel in this set as the 'long open sound' of *o* (1791: xx). We should not conclude from Walker's use of the word 'open' here that he is describing a more open sound than [oː], for he contrasts the 'open' sound with the 'slender' sound of *prove, move, who*, etc., i.e. /uː/. Walker is thus describing his 'first sound' of *o* as 'open' by comparison with /uː/, rather than in more absolute terms. MacMahon points out that the first evidence for diphthongization of GOAT words comes from the Scottish orthoepist William Smith in 1795: 'The English long *o* has in it a shade towards the *oo*' (1795: 20, cited in MacMahon, 1998: 459). As with FACE, the first tentative description of a diphthongal pronunciation comes from the turn of the nineteenth century, with commentators becoming increasingly confident in their remarks on this development as that century progresses. In the case of GOAT, though, there appears to be no 'smoothing' in the early twentieth century. What does happen is that the first element is centralized from [o] to [ə] from the end of the nineteenth century. This was noted by Sweet as giving 'a character of effeminacy or affectation to the pronunciation', suggesting that it was a new and fashionable development at the time, of which he did not approve. We can see in transcription B (Figure 6.1) that Jones transcribes *cloak* as /klouk/. However, in the 'explanations' at the beginning of his dictionary, Jones writes that this diphthong 'varies considerably, generally in the direction of being advanced towards the central position, also to some extent by partial unrounding of the first element' (1937: xxii). It would appear that this centralized pronunciation became more common in RP as the twentieth century progressed, for Gimson introduced the notation /əu/ in 1962. Wells writes of the development that he terms 'GOAT Advancement' that 'it has presumably been current since at least the nineteenth century' but 'has only quite recently (since the Second World War?) ousted [ou], or perhaps rather [öu], as the ideal image of a "correct" or "beautiful" RP GOAT diphthong' (1982: 237, parenthesis in original).

6.3.3   The BATH and CLOTH sets

Like the FACE and GOAT sets discussed above, these two sets develop in parallel during the later modern period, but in this case they diverge at the very end of our period. In both cases, an earlier short vowel is subject to lengthening and backing and/or lowering in a range of phonetic environments. The developments are subject to phonetic, lexical and social conditioning, so accounts of the pronunciation and distribution of variants differ considerably throughout the eighteenth and nineteenth centuries. Today, the BATH set provides one of the most salient markers of the distinction between northern and southern varieties of English English on the one hand, and between English and American English on the other. Whilst RP and most southern varieties in England have /ɑː/ in this set, General American English has /a/, whilst northern English accents have /aː/ in *half, calf, calve*, etc., but /a/ in *bath, laugh, pass* and *dance*. Many southern hemisphere varieties, on the other hand, have /ɑː/ in *half, calf, calve, bath, laugh*, and *pass* but /a/ in *dance*, etc. Even in RP, the distribution of /ɑː/ is lexically conditioned: thus /ɑː/ in *pass*, but /æ/ in *gas*; /ɑː/ in *command* but /æ/ in *expand*, and so on, whilst, for example, *plastic, elastic* vary from one RP speaker to another. As Wells suggests, this distribution 'represents the ossification of a half-completed sound change, which seems to have come to a stop well before completing its lexical diffusion through the vocabulary' (1982: 233). Before orthographic <r> in final or preconsonantal position, all non-rhotic varieties of English have a long vowel. This is now categorical, but was not always so. The first evidence for lengthening both before fricatives and before /r/ comes from the seventeenth century. Daines (1640) shows the new long vowel before <r> followed by another consonant in the words *barn*; *carp*; *sharp*; *smart*; *art*; and *marsh*. Coles (1674) writes that the <a> of *arm*, etc. is like that of *father*, and has a sound midway between *all* and *ale* (the other two 'long' realizations of <a>). Cooper (1685, 1687), tells us that <a> always has the value of a lengthened version of short /a/, i.e [aː] or [æː], when it occurs before preconsonantal /r/, except when the following consonant is /ʃ/. He is also the first to provide evidence of the new long vowel occurring before voiceless fricatives, specifically stating that *past (= pass + ed)* has a long vowel but *pass* (as in *pass by*) a short one. Cooper also shows the long vowel in *path*, but does not suggest that this is generalized to other words in which <a> is followed by /θ/. Evidence for a lengthened vowel before final /r/ is much more scarce: Cocker (1696) has it only in *war*, whilst Dobson (1957: II, 519) cites foreign observers as recording a long vowel in *far* in 1672 and 1678. By the beginning of the eighteenth century, a long vowel from ME /a/ could occur in the following environments:

- before preconsonantal, but not final /r/;
- before preconsonantal, but not final /s/;
- before /θ/;
- before /ð/ followed by either /s/ or syllabic /r/, e.g. *father; rather; lather; paths*;
- (varying with /ɔː/) before preconsonantal /n/ /lf, lm, lv/.

If we were to compare the pronunciations described by Cooper with those of early twentieth-century RP as exemplified by Jones (1937), we might surmise that the lengthening has extended to the environments before final /r/ and before all fricatives in all positions. However, the fact that Walker has /last/ for *last* suggests that the progress of this sound change through the later modern period is not straightforward. In fact, Walker tells us that, although 'Italian *a*' had previously been heard in words such as *glass, fast*, 'this pronunciation seems to have been for some years advancing to the short sound of this letter, as heard in *hand, land, grand* etc. and pronouncing the *a* in *after, answer, basket, plant, mast*, etc. as long as in *half, calf* etc. borders very closely on vulgarity' (1791: 10). Walker here seems to be describing a reaction against the lengthening of /a/ in most subsets of the BATH set. Only seven years earlier, Nares had described a distribution similar to that of present-day RP: he provides what he considers to be an exhaustive list of the words in which this 'open A' occurs, amounting to 140 in all. He then comments:

> A slight review of the above list will shew that this effect is chiefly produced by combinations of particular letters. The consonants *f, l, n,* and *s,* appear to be principally concerned in it: and the words might, for the most part, have been arranged from such considerations; thus, words in *-sk, ask, bask, cask, flask, mask;* words in *-ss, ass, brass, class, glass,* &c. &c. But the whole number of words is so inconsiderable, that classification seemed unnecessary (1784: 6–7).

In fact, as I demonstrate elsewhere (Beal, 1999: 189–92), Nares' list shows a more consistent distribution than that of present-day RP, with 'open *a*' in *ant, asp* and *ass* as well as *grant, clasp* and *class*. Walker has a short vowel in all of these words, and indeed has his 'Italian a' in only 30 of the words in Nares' list. Before fricatives, Walker has the long vowel in *bath, father, lath, master,* and before /n/ only in the context /nd/ as in *chandler, command, countermand, demand, remand, reprimand, salamander,* and in the isolated instances *courant, prance* and (alternating with the spelling *jaunty* pronounced /dʒɔːnti/) *janty*. The other words in this list for which Walker has a long vowel are those in which the vowel is followed by /lf/, /lv/, such as *calf, calm,* or where the vowel is in word-final position as in *ah, aha*. In the second edition of his *Critical Pronouncing Dictionary*, Walker, in a footnote to the comment cited above, notes the 'very elaborate and judicious observations on English pronunciation by Mr Smith' (i.e. William Smith, 1795), and takes issue with these:

> In this work he departs frequently from my judgement, and particularly in the pronunciation of the letter *a*, when succeeded by *ss, st* or *n,* and another consonant, as *past, last, chance,* &c. to which he annexes the long sound of *a*

as in *father*. That this was the sound formerly, is highly probable, from its still being the sound given to it by the vulgar, who are generally the last to alter the common pronunciation: but that the short *a* in these words is now the general pronunciation of the polite and learned world, seems to be candidly acknowledged by Mr Smith himself; and as every correct ear would be disgusted at giving the *a* in these words the full sound of *father*, any middle sound ought to be discountenanced, as tending to render the pronunciation of a language obscure and indefinite [1791] 1856 edn: 25).

Other evidence from the late eighteenth and nineteenth centuries supports Walker's view that a long vowel was considered 'vulgar' in most BATH words. Horn and Lehnert (1954: 343) cite Georg Christoph Lichtenberg, who lived in England in 1770 and 1774–5, telling us that 'zierlichen Mädchen' (dainty young ladies) pronounced the <a> in *nasty* so high that it sounded almost like *nehsti*' and that this was in order to avoid the 'vulgar' [ɑː]. In fact, the change seems to have begun as a lengthened [æː], and not to have invited adverse comment until this lengthened vowel is retracted to [ɑː]. Sheridan (1780) does not even have a fourth 'a' sound, distinguishing only *hat/hate/hall*: presumably, for him, the [æ] / [æː] alternation was sub-phonemic. Walker's description of 'Italian *a*' on the other hand, suggests a more retracted pronunciation, acceptable in *father* but not in *basket*. Mugglestone cites comments echoing Walker's view from most of the nineteenth century. Indeed, Longmuir explicitly acknowledges 'the high character of Walker, and the increasing dislike of anything resembling a drawl in speaking' as influencing the preference for 'Walker's extreme short sound of ... *pass*, like *passive* ... now generally adopted as the proper sound' (1864, cited in Mugglestone, 1995: 93). He goes on to note that 'there is a disposition among literary men and public speakers, to unite on some *intermediate* sound between the intire broadness of the *a* in *father*, and the narrowness of the *a* in *fat*'. Whether this is the 'obscure and indefinite' pronunciation rejected by Walker is difficult to determine, but, as Mugglestone points out, Ellis 'confirms this predilection'. Thus, throughout the nineteenth century, those who aspired to 'correct' pronunciation in England had to steer a very narrow course, avoiding both the 'broad' [ɑː] and the 'mincing' [æ]. By the beginning of the twentieth century, the stigma of 'broad' [ɑː] had been lifted, for Jones (1907) transcribes this vowel as cardinal ɑ, and continues to use this notation in subsequent editions. Since semi-phonetic spellings such as <larst>, <larf> for *last, laugh* have been used since the nineteenth century to represent Cockney speech, the introduction of [ɑː] to RP may well be an instance of 'change from below'.

The parallel lengthening of short *o* to /ɔː/ has had a different fate. In this case, reaction against the lengthening eventually won the day. In tran-

scription B we note that Jones gives [ɔːf] and [ɔf] as alternative pronunciations, with the former more common. In fact, this reversal of the earlier
lengthening can be dated quite precisely, as, in the 1907 edition of his
pronouncing dictionary, Jones has only [ɔːf], whilst, in the 1967 edition
updated by Gimson, [ɔf] is the usual pronunciation, with [ɔːf] described as
'old-fashioned'. Walker explicitly draws a parallel between *a* and *o* before
fricatives:

> What was observed of the *a*, when followed by a liquid and a mute, may be
> observed of the *o* with equal justness. This letter, like *a*, has a tendency to
> lengthen when followed by a liquid and another consonant, or by *s, ss* or *s* and
> a mute. But this length of *o*, in this situation, seems every day growing more
> and more vulgar; and, as it would be gross, to a degree, to sound the *a* in
> *castle, mask* and *plant*, like the *a* in *palm, psalm*, &c. so it would be equally
> exceptionable to pronounce the *o* in *moss, dross* and *frost*, as if written
> *mawse, drawse*, and *frawst* (1791: 22).

As Mugglestone points out, this stigmatization of [ɔːf] pronunciations
parallels that of 'broad' [ɑː] throughout the nineteenth century, with a
similar tendency in literature to depict the speech of Cockney, lower-class
speakers with semi-phonetic spellings like *orf*. In this case, it would appear
that lower- and upper-class speakers used the long vowel at the beginning of
the twentieth century, but that, possibly as a reaction against the stigma of
being perceived as lower-class [ɔːf], in this case the short alternative won
the day. Today, [ɔːf]-type pronunciations in England are the preserve of the
very old and/or very 'posh': citation of these in class never fails to raise
giggles from British students. The histories of these two vowels provide an
object lesson to those who believe that sound change is structurally and
internally motivated. Barber acknowledges this:

> The fact is, this change of ɔː to ɔ is not a phonemic change going on at the
> present time: a change took place almost two centuries ago in certain styles of
> speech, and two kinds of form, one with a long vowel and one with a short,
> have existed side by side in the language ever since; what is happening now is
> that one style is becoming fashionable at the expense of the other . . . This is
> the kind of thing that happens when social groups go up or down in the
> world, and it is possible that the spread of the ɔ-forms in the present century
> is the result of social changes, especially the rise of democracy (1964: 43).

6.3.4   The FOOT and STRUT sets

Wells defines his FOOT set as 'comprising those words whose citation form
in RP and GenAm has the stressed vowel /ʊ/' (1982: 132). In both these

accents, it contrasts with the STRUT set, whose citation forms have /ʌ/. Both these vowels derive from Middle English short /u/ and shortened /oː/, becoming separated by the FOOT–STRUT split which gives us the contrastive phoneme /ʌ/. As we shall see in Chapter 8, within England this latter phoneme is only found in southern accents, and the 'lack' of this distinction was, by Walker's time, already a highly salient feature of northern pronunciation. As we can see from the transcription /sʌn/ in both A and B above, in the reference varieties exemplified in pronouncing dictionaries, the STRUT vowel has remained stable, at least in phonemic terms. Phonetically, there seems to have been some movement, as eighteenth-century sources describe this as a central vowel, and mostly equate it with schwa, whereas early twentieth-century phoneticians suggest that the pronunciation in RP has been fronted towards [a]. Thus Abraham Tucker writes:

> This short 'u' . . . is easiest pronounced of all the vowels . . . and therefore is a great favourite with my countrymen, who tho not lazy are very averse to trouble, wishing to do as much work with as little pain as possible. We can draw it out to a great length on particular occasions, as when the watchman calls 'past ten u-u-u clock', or when a man hesitates till he hits upon some hard name, as 'This account was sent by Mr u-u-u Schlotzikoff, a Russian' (1773: 14).

This is corroborated by Odell's comparison between this sound and the French e in words such as je, me or 'in the final syllables of the words gloirĕ, victoirĕ, &c. when they occur in poetical composition' (1806: 4, cited in MacMahon, 1998: 417). By the early twentieth century (e.g. Jones, 1907), this vowel is given the notation /ʌ/ and marked as distinct from schwa. Barber states that /ʌ/ is 'a phoneme that has changed somewhat in the present century' (1964: 41). Barber points out that Jones describes this phoneme as 'a half open and rather retracted sound . . . decidedly more retracted than the central sounds ə and əː' but that 'to-day, the ʌ-sound seems to be made considerably further forward and lower than this, at any rate by the younger generation' (Barber, 1964). Barber here cites Jones's *Outline of English Phonetics*, but in the 1937 edition of his *English Pronouncing Dictionary* used as the source of transcription B, Jones acknowledges the fronting of /ʌ/, stating that it is 'in some speakers, somewhat advanced in the direction of cardinal (a)' (1937: xxii). However, since these developments are on the sub-phonemic level, they are not reflected in transcriptions A and B. I shall return to the more centralized eighteenth-century pronunciation of the STRUT vowel in Section 6.3.4, but will now turn to the FOOT set.

The word *took* is transcribed as /tuːk/ in A but as /tʊk/ in B, suggesting that the vowel in this set has been shortened between the eighteenth and the twentieth centuries. In fact, the development of this set is rather more complex, and some FOOT words are still subject to variation in present-day RP. For *room*, Jones has the variants /rum/ and /ruːm/ in that order, but notes that 'the use of the variant ruːm appears to be very much on the increase' (1937: 367). Those FOOT words in which the vowel is derived from Middle English /oː/ have been subjected to what Dobson calls 'later shortening', as opposed to the earlier shortening that allowed the resulting /ʊ/ in, for example, *blood, flood* to be caught up in the movement to /ʌ/ which caused the FOOT–STRUT split. This 'later shortening' is a sound change which progressed slowly and was subject to environmental conditioning and lexical diffusion. Dobson describes the evidence from Early Modern English as follows:

> In the seventeenth century only the best observers give evidence of the development of [ʊ] by later shortening of ... [uː] ... But there is sufficient evidence of [ʊ] by later shortening in the following cases. (*a*) Before [d] in *good* ... in *hood* ... and in *stood* ... (*b*) Before [t] in *foot* ... and in *soot* ... but, as in PresE, not in *boot, root* and *shoot*. (*c*) Before [θ] Coles gives [ʊ] in *sooth* and *tooth*, which in PresE have normally [uː], though [ʊ] exists as a variant in *tooth*. (*d*) Before [v] there is no evidence of later shortening to [ʊ]. (*e*) Of other consonants, only [k] regularly causes later shortening; it seems by contrast only rarely to have caused early shortening ... In *book*, [ʊ] is recorded by Hodges, Coles and possibly Cooper ... in *hook, look* and *took* by Hodges and Coles; in *cook* by Hodges; and in *brook, crook* and *shook* by Coles. But Coles has [uː] in *nook* and *rook*, which have [ʊ] in PresE ... Before other consonants the shortening is sporadic; Hodges has [ʊ] in *hoop*, and Cocker seems to have [ʊ] beside [uː] in *fool* (1957: II, 511–12).

Thus there was variation across the lexical set and between different orthoepists' accounts. As Dobson points out, 'in the later seventeenth century, any one word may have [ʌ], [uː] or [ʊ]' (1957: 508). A similar level of variability is found in and between eighteenth-century sources. Bronstein and Sheldon (1951) carried out an exercise involving the comparison of a smaller number of words with ME /oː/ in seven eighteenth-century dictionaries including Sheridan (1789) and Walker (1791) and 15 from the nineteenth century. They conclude:

> Most variation of all appears in the -*ook* words, now, in American dictionaries, stabilized to [ʊ]. The pronunciation [u] predominates slightly for most of these words in the eighteenth century, although *look, shook* and the disyllable *crooked* favor [ʊ]. By the nineteenth century [u] is passing out and [ʊ] has become the favored sound in all the *ook* words except *nook*. This shift

seems to have occurred without occasioning much comment, favorable or adverse, among dictionary editors. In the eighteenth century, Walker gives [u] for all the *ook* words. Jones [= Stephen Jones (1798)], who in almost all other respects follows Walker, protests mildly that 'Mr Walker has marked as similar sounds the double *o* in *look* and *tooth*, *took* and *tool*, though in strictness there is no smaller difference between them than between *long* and *short*' (Preface, p. iii) (1951: 89).

Walker admits the shortened sound in only a few words in which it is represented by the spelling <oo>. He considers the 'regular' pronunciation of this 'diphthong' (i.e. digraph) to be long. However, he notes 'a shorter sound corresponding to the *u* in *bull*, in the words *wool, wood, good, hood, foot, stood, understood, withstood*', and goes on to assert that 'these are the only words where this diphthong has this middle sound' (1791: 35). I have pointed out (1999: 141) that Walker is probably recommending a conservative pronunciation, particularly for *-ook* words, because of his reverence for 'analogy'. To him, the 'regular' pronunciation of <oo> is /uː/ and /ʊ/ both in these words and in, for example, *bull*, is a recent development whose spread should be discouraged. The detailed comparisons of entries in a range of pronouncing dictionaries made by both Bronstein and Sheldon (1951) and me (Beal, 1999), demonstrate that, in reality, there was still a great deal of variability in the pronunciation of these words throughout the eighteenth century. As Bronstein and Sheldon point out in the passage cited above, the /ʊ/ pronunciation becomes more widespread in the nineteenth century, so that, today, /uː/ in *-ook* words is characteristic of some accents of the north of England. However, variation still exists within RP, as *tooth*, *room* and *soot* can all be heard with either a long or a short vowel.

6.3.5 Yod-dropping

The set of words to be discussed in this section is distributed across the sets included under Wells's keywords GOOSE and CURE. In each of these sets, Wells has to distinguish subsets with and without a historical /j/ preceding the vowel. Thus *dupe, mute, truth, blue* and *tooth, loot, loop, boom* are in separate subsets of the GOOSE set, whilst *boor, moor, poor, spoor* and *endure, lure, pure, sure* are in separate subsets of the CURE set. In each case, the second subset is made up of words which have, at an earlier stage, been pronounced with the diphthong /iu/. The first part of this diphthong changes to /j/, which in a number of these words is then either assimilated into the preceding consonant or else dropped. The preceding consonant may be palatalized as part of this process; thus for *sure, sugar* /siu/ develops to /sju/ then /ʃu/. This process is called 'yod-dropping' by Wells, who distinguishes 'early yod-dropping' after palatals, /r/ and consonant clusters with /l/ from 'later yod-dropping' after /t/, /d/, /n/, /θ/, /z/, /s/ and /l/. However, as we shall see, 'yod-dropping' in all these environments is attested in the eighteenth century, although the resulting pronunciations are often proscribed.

Early evidence of yod-dropping by assimilation with a preceding palatalized consonant is found in Cooper (1687), who lists *shugar* as an instance of 'barbarous speaking'. By 1791, this pronunciation has become acceptable: Walker gives the transcription <shu³gu²r>, which we can translate into IPA as /'ʃʊgʌr/. However, he refers the reader to rule 454, in which he discusses 'the tendency of the *s* to aspiration before a diphthongal sound'. Here he sets out the principle that 'the accent or stress naturally preserves the letters in their true sound; and as feebleness naturally succeeds force, so the letters immediately after the stress, have a tendency to slide into different sounds, which require less exertion of the organs' (1791: 54). He then goes on to discuss the words *sure* and *sugar*:

> This analogy leads us immediately to discover the irregularity of *sure*, *sugar* and their compounds, which are pronounced *shure* and *shugar*, though the accent is on the first syllable, and ought to preserve the *s* without aspiration; and a want of attending to this analogy has betrayed Mr Sheridan into a series of mistakes in the sound of *s* in the words *suicide, presume, resume*, &c. as if written *shoo-icide, pre-zhoom, re-zhoom*, &c. but if this is the true pronunciation of these words, it may be asked, why is not *suit, suitable, pursue* &c. to be pronounced *shoot, shootable, pur-shoo*, &c. If it be answered, Custom; I own this decides the question at once . . . But those who see analogy so openly violated, ought to be assured of the certainty of the custom before they break through all the laws of language to conform to it (1791: 54).

Presumably, in the case of *sure* and *sugar*, 'custom' was sufficiently clear to persuade Walker to overcome his distaste for pronunciations which violated his rule of analogy. In the case of *sure*, Walker indicates a palatalized consonant, but the vowel is his <u¹> as in *tune*, either /iu/ or /ju/. Apart from the words *sure* and *sugar*, as Walker's note indicates, there is variation between different eighteenth-century sources as to the pronunciation of <u> after palatal or palatalized consonants. Sheridan seems more prone to accept palatalized pronunciations than many of his contemporaries. The author of *A Vocabulary of such Words in the English Language as are of Dubious or Unsettled Accentuation* (1797), writes under *tune*:

> I have followed Mr Walker in the pronunciation of this word; Mr. Sheridan shounds it tsho³n; and this sound he gives also to the *tu* in *Tuneful, Tuneless*,

Tuner, Tunick, Tunicle, Tutelage, Tutelary, Tutelar, Tutor, Tutorage, and *Tutoress,* while Mr Walker preserves the pure sound of the *tu* as in *Tune,* above marked (cited in Sheldon, 1938: LXXX).

In fact, Sheridan's pronunciation /tʃuːn/ is very advanced for its date: even in 1937, Jones still has /tjuːn/ for this. Sheridan's contemporaries often accused him of introducing Irishisms: in many cases, the accusation is unjust, but the palatalization in *tune,* etc. might be due to influence from Irish English. Jespersen, for instance, points out that 'B. Shaw writes *Choosda* and *schoopid* as Irish for *Tuesday* and *stupid,* (1909–49: I, 347). In unstressed syllables, many eighteenth-century sources regarded the pronunciation with yod-dropping and a reduced vowel (e.g. /ˈneːtər/ for *nature*) as preferable to one in which the /t/ is palatalized. Pronunciations such as /ˈneːtər/ were regarded as acceptable in the seventeenth century: Cooper (1687), for instance, gives *centaury : century; ordure : order; pastor : pasture* and *picture : pick't her* as homophones. Walker condemns this pronunciation:

> There is an incorrect pronunciation of this letter [= <u>] when it ends a syllable, not under the accent which prevails, not only among the vulgar, but is sometimes found in better company; and that is giving the *u* an obscure sound, which confounds it with vowels of a very different kind. Thus we not infrequently hear *singular, regular* and *particular* pronounced as if written *sing-e-lar, reg-e-lar,* and *par-tick-e-lar* (1791: 23).

The author of *A Caution to Gentlemen who use Sheridan's Dictionary* (3rd edn 1790: 6 cited in Sheldon, 1938: 306–7) admits that 'the natural propensity is to abbreviate -u- and to pronounce the word thus nètŭr' (= [ˈnetər]: Sheldon). However, Sheldon adds,

> the author goes on to observe that in polite pronunciation, the u̲ is long and a y̲ is sounded before it, [ˈnetjur]. But -TSHUR and -TSHOUS cannot be tolerated, and if a foreigner or native 'be ambitious for passing for an English gentleman, let him avoid with utmost care, Mr Sheridan's -SH-' (1938: 307).

So eighteenth-century British pronunciation varied between a conservative and informal, but increasingly disfavoured /ˈneːtər/, and advanced /ˈneːtʃər/, a conservative and formal (possibly even hypercorrect) /ˈneːtjuːr/ and, in Walker, a compromise /ˈneːtʃuːr/. For a fuller account of this variation, see Beal (1999: 146–9).

A great degree of variability between eighteenth-century sources is found where /j/ follows /r/. Walker sees /juː/ as the regular sound of long <u>, as well as <ew> and <eu>, but finds the pronunciation /uː/ acceptable after /r/.

He writes of the 'diphthong' <ui>: 'when this diphthong is preceded by *r*, it is pronounced like *oo*, thus *bruise, cruise, fruit, bruit, recruit* are pronounced as if written *broose, crooze, broot, froot, recroot*' (1791: 39). Here, though, Walker is referring only to orthographic <ui>: in other cases where earlier /juː/ or /iu/ follows /r/, Walker's usage varies: he has /uː/ in, for example, *brute, intrude, prune* but /juː/ in *frugal, peruse, quadruple*. Johnston (1764), whilst giving no indication that /uː/ is 'vulgar', shows some inconsistency: he has a rule that /uː/ should be used after /d/, /l/, /n/, /r/, /s/ and /t/, and gives *rude* as an example of this, but in his dictionary entry for *rude*, the pronunciation indicated is /juː/. Elphinston, a Scot living in London, clearly condemns yod-dropping: Jespersen quotes him as writing in 1787 that it is 'vulgar indolence or bluntness' to 'sink the liquefaction' in *peruse, rule*, making them *per-ooz, rool* (1909–49: I, 382). Sylvester Douglas, another Scot, has /juː/ in *Bruce, spruce,* and *truce*. This would suggest that yod-dropping was less advanced in the usage of (Anglicized) educated, middle-class Scots, where more conservative norms applied. In my (1999) study of eighteenth-century English pronunciation, I compared the distribution in four pronouncing dictionaries of /juː/ and /uː/, taking 110 entries for words in which these sounds follow /r/. The dictionaries were those of Spence (1775), Sheridan (1780), Burn (1786) and Walker (1791). Of these four, Walker was the only Londoner: Spence was born in Newcastle upon Tyne, Sheridan was Irish and Burn a Scot. I found that, of these 110 words, Sheridan had only 13 with /juː/, Walker had 29, Spence had 59 and Burn had a near-categorical 102. Thus, if we view yod-dropping after /r/ as a change which was diffusing in the late eighteenth century, Sheridan's usage is the most advanced and Walker's not far behind, but the northerner Spence and the Scot Burn show much more conservative usage. I conclude that this pattern 'shows a reluctance to "sink the liquefaction" which seems to increase with distance from the capital, with Spence having almost twice as many instances of /juː/ as Walker, and Burn almost twice as many as Spence' (1999: 153). However, all these eighteenth-century sources show variation across this set of words. Jespersen identifies Batchelor (1809) as the first to state categorically that 'the long *u* (yuw), properly pronounced, never immediately follows *r* in the same syllable' (1909–49: I, 382). When the following vowel is unstressed though, variation continues well into the twentieth century: Jespersen (1909–49) sees /juː/ as the norm in words like *erudition, garrulous, purulency, purulous,* and *virulent*, whilst Jones (1937) has /juː/ as the less common alternative for all of these words.

The one word transcribed differently in A and B with regard to yod-dropping is *blue*. Strang (1970: 118) refers to 'divided usage' after /l/, but the four eighteenth-century sources compared with regard to variation after

/r/ all have /juː/ regularly in this environment. Jones points out (1991: 63) that Sylvester Douglas regarded the Scots tendency to use /juː/ in the items *blue, pursue, luxury* as well as *build* and *burial* as 'an unacceptable hyper-correction', but in the case of *blue*, at least, this pronunciation seems to have been widespread in late eighteenth-century Britain.

The process referred to by Wells as 'later yod-dropping' was already under way in eighteenth-century London English, but was highly stigmatized as a Cockneyism. Walker writes of the 'diphthong' <ew>: 'this diphthong is pronounced like long *u* and is almost always regular. There is a corrupt pronunciation of it like *oo* chiefly in London, where we sometimes hear *dew* and *new*, pronounced as if written *doo* and *noo*' (1791: 32). These pronunciations are, of course, normal in General American English today, and were spreading into other varieties of British English in the nineteenth and early twentieth centuries. MacMahon points out that 'a yod-less pronunciation of NEWS was regarded by Sweet as "vulgar" (Sweet to Storm 21 Jan. 1889), although Ellis (1899: 601) had noted the pronunciation, alongside /juː/, without adverse comment' (1998: 473). Also included under 'later yod-dropping' are words such as *suit, presume*, in which yod is dropped after /s, z/ without these consonants being palatalized. Jones's entry for *suit* changes from /sjuːt/ only in 1907, to /sjuːt/ with /suːt/ as the less common alternative in 1937. Barber notes this change taking place in the first half of the twentieth century:

> In words where both forms are heard, the forms with uː are gaining ground at the expense of those with juː: . . . After s, the juː is still common, but uː is now respectable: *suit* is frequently pronounced suːt, and from B.B.C. announcers I have heard *assume* and *consume* as əˈsuːm and kənˈsuːm. After z the change is less marked, and until quite recently, the uː forms sounded dialectal; how-ever, they are now beginning to appear in educated speech, and B.B.C. announcers sometimes use such pronunciations as riˈzuːm (resume). As in many things, the process has gone farther in American English than in British English, and many British juː pronunciations sound affected to American ears (1964: 44).

Thus, the contrast between /bljuː/ in transcription A and /bluː/ in B alerts us to a set of changes involving yod-dropping, which have been diffusing socially, lexically and geographically throughout the later modern period.

6.3.6 Unstressed vowels

One of the most striking differences between transcriptions A and B is the lack of schwa in the former. In words such as *traveller, stronger, agreed, considered*, Jones uses /ə/ to transcribe all the vowels in unstressed syllables,

but Walker has his 'short *u*', transcribed here as /ʌ/ for the -*er* in *traveller,*
stronger and the 'full' vowel corresponding to the spelling in the first
syllables of *considered, agreed*. Lass points out that, whilst 'received
wisdom ... is that from the end of the Old English period vowels in weak
position in the foot tended to reduce to schwa' (1999: 133), clear evidence
is hard to find until much later. The only evidence from Middle English is a
tendency for vowels in unstressed syllables to be represented in apparently
random ways or for one vowel grapheme to take the place of others.
However, as Lass points out, there is 'no mention of special qualities in
weak syllables' in the works of sixteenth- and even seventeenth-century
orthoepists. From Wallis (1653) onwards, there is recognition of an
'obscure' vowel, but this is the STRUT vowel, and is identified only in
stressed syllables. By the eighteenth century, this 'obscure *u*' is identified as
a vowel used in unstressed syllables as well as in what we now know as
Wells's STRUT set. However, the pronunciation of unstressed vowels was
one of the most contentious issues discussed in eighteenth-century pronouncing dictionaries and other works on English usage. Walker writes:

> It may, indeed, be observed, that there is scarcely any thing more distinguishes
> a person of mean and good education than the pronunciation of the un-
> accented vowels. When vowels are under the accent, the prince and the lowest
> of the people, with very few exceptions, pronounce them in the same manner;
> but the unaccented vowels in the mouth of the former have a distinct, open
> and specific sound, while the latter often totally sink them, or change them,
> into some other sound. Those, therefore, who wish to pronounce elegantly,
> must be particularly attentive to the unaccented vowels; as a neat pro-
> nunciation of these, forms one of the greatest beauties of speaking (1791: 23).

Remarks such as this have led scholars such as Sheldon (1938; 1947) and
Shields (1973; 1974) to suggest that Walker was reluctant to admit schwa-
like pronunciations. However, the passage cited here is from Walker's
section on the pronunciation of *u* in, for example, *singular, regular,*
particular, which has been discussed in Section 6.3.5 above. Elsewhere, he
provides a great deal of evidence for the 'obscure' vowel in unstressed
syllables. Under *a*, he writes:

> But besides the long and short sounds common to all the vowels, there is a
> certain transient indistinct pronunciation of some of them, when they are not
> accented, that cannot so properly be called obscure, as imperfect: for it seems
> to have no more of the sound of the vowel to which it corresponds than what
> is common to the rest; that is a simple guttural tone, entirely unmodified by
> the organs which distinguish the sound of one vowel from another, and is
> really no more than a commencement of the vowel intended to be pronounced
> (1791: 12).

His description of the sound of *e* before /r/ is more explicit:

> The *e* in *her* is pronounced nearly like short *u*; and as we hear it in the un-
> accented terminations of *writer, reader*, where we may observe that the *r* being
> only a jar, and not a definite and distinct articulation like the other
> consonants, instead of stopping the vocal efflux of voice, lets it imperfectly
> pass, and so corrupts and alters the true sound of the vowel ... It may be
> remarked, that though we ought cautiously to avoid pronouncing the *e* like *u*
> when under the accent, it would be *nimis Aticé*, and border too much on
> affectation of accuracy, to preserve this sound of *e* in unaccented syllables
> before *r* (1791: 13).

Here, Walker rightly recognizes the effect of a weakened /r/ on the preceding vowel. This will be discussed further in Section 6.3.7. Despite the use of
loaded terms like *corrupt, obscure* and *imperfect*, Walker does acknowledge
the existence of a separate pronunciation for unstressed vowels and
identifies the sound as almost, but not exactly, that of /ʌ/. The distribution
of /ʌ/ in transcription A follows Walker's recommendations for careful
pronunciation: the 'obscure' vowel is categorical in the -er of *traveller,
stronger, considered* and *other*, but in other contexts, the 'full' vowel is
given, as in the first syllables of *agreed, considered* and *around*.

Apart from this 'obscure *u*', some unaccented vowels were pronounced as
/ɪ/ in the eighteenth century and earlier. Lass points out that 'as early as the
fourteenth century the incipient standard had at least two reduction vowels
... a higher and fronter one identified with short /i/, and a lower one' (1999:
135). Many eighteenth-century sources show variation between these two
pronunciations in a range of words, with extensive use of /ɪ/ tending to be
identified as northern or Scottish (see Beal, 1999: 156–9 for a fuller
discussion of this). Walker recognizes variation in some of these unstressed
endings, recommending /ɪ/ for some words and /ʌ/ for others. Thus for the
-ace ending, he writes '*menace, palace, pinnace, populace, solace*, might,
without any great departure from their common sound, be written *pallus,
sollus*, &c, while *furnace* almost changes the *a* into *i* and might be written
furnis' (1791: 12–13). Later, he writes '*eo*, when unaccented, has the sound
of *u* short in *surgeon, sturgeon, dudgeon, luncheon, puncheon, truncheon,
burgeon, habergeon*; but in *scutcheon, escutcheon, pidgeon* and *widgeon*,
the *eo* sounds like short *i*' (1791: 31). He also suggests that *marchioness*
should be pronounced as if written *marshunes*, but *cushion* as if written
cushin (1791: 33). In the twentieth century, the /ɪ/ variants have tended to
become increasingly rare, with /ə/ taking over in words such as *menace,
village*, etc. Wyld provides evidence for /ɪ/ in -*est*, -*en*, -*el*, -*less*, -*ness*,
-*le(d)ge*, -*et*, -*age*, -*as* (*purchase, Thomas*), -*on*, -*ot*, but suggests that a
change from /ɪ/ to /ə/ has been taking place in his lifetime. On *purchase*, he

writes 'I remember hearing [pʌtʃɪs] in my boyhood from excellent speakers who preserved the habits of an earlier generation' (1936: 263), and on the spelling <stomick> for *stomach*, 'I have heard the latter word so pronounced by very old speakers whose speech was merely old-fashioned though it contained no vulgarisms' (1936: 263). Barber suggests that this change from /ɪ/ to /ə/ was continuing in the mid-twentieth century:

> Very common are alternations between i and ə; thus *system* can be pronounced 'sistɪm or 'sistəm, *exact* can be igz'ækt or əgz'ækt, *ability* can be ə'biliti or ə'biləti, and similarly with *corporate, become, remain, horrible, waitress, kitchen,* and many others. Forms which I have heard from B.B.C. announcers, and which have struck me as unusual, are *women* ('wimən), *useless* ('juːsləs), and *engine* ('endʒən) (1964: 49).

Jones (1917) gives /'sistəm/ as the less usual alternative for *system*, but has only /i/ for the other words in Barber's list. Fabricius demonstrates that 'the tendency to drift from KIT values to schwa values within weak syllables' (2002: 213) has accelerated in the second half of the twentieth century. As Barber points out, 'American and Australian speech have gone further than British' (1964: 49), but the use of schwa in words where Barber thought it 'hardly possible' in RP, e.g. *damage, boxes, ended*, is certainly heard from younger RP speakers today. Fabricius notes that these words are first recorded with schwa in the *Longman Pronouncing Dictionary* of 1990.

Another area of variation and change in late twentieth-century RP discussed by Fabricius is what Wells calls 'happY-tensing' – 'an increasing tendency throughout the English-speaking world to use a closer quality, [i (ː)], and for speakers to feel intuitively that *happy* belongs with FLEECE rather than with KIT' (1982: 256–7). Fabricius notes this change as first recorded in the *Longman Pronouncing Dictionary* of 1990, but the evidence from transcriptions A and B suggests that happY-tensing has been around much longer. Walker clearly equates the final vowel of *happy* with FLEECE, for he gives both the annotation <e¹> as in *me*. Jones, on the other hand, gives us no clear evidence for either a tense or a lax vowel, since his notation does not distinguish /i/ from /ɪ/. Elsewhere (Beal, 2000), I point out that happY-tensing cannot be a recent change spreading from southern to northern accents, since Spence (1775), who, as noted above, was born in Newcastle, also has the same vowel in FLEECE and happY. Although Fabricius is correct in noting the increasing use of tense vowels in the happY set by younger RP speakers, it would appear that there has been variability since at least the late eighteenth century.

Although this section is concerned with unstressed vowels, it is worth mentioning here that, whilst Jones has a stressed schwa in *were*, /wəː/,

Walker has /weɹ/. This is because centralization of the vowel in this environment, as exemplified in Jones's transcription, depends on loss of rhoticity, which is the subject of the next section.

6.3.7   Weakening and loss of /r/

Along with the differences in the representation of unstressed vowels, the distribution of /r/ is one of the most striking distinctions between transcriptions A and B. That these two areas are linked is hinted at in Walker's statement (quoted above, p. 51) that the 'obscure' vowel appears in the termination -er because the /r/ is 'only a jar, and not a definite and distinct articulation like the other consonants' (1791: 13). Walker has often been cited as providing the first clear evidence of the development which, above all others, led to what Wells (1982: 211) has termed the 'great divide' between reference varieties of English and American English: the loss of rhoticity in the former. Transcription A shows /r/ realized in all positions because this is how Walker marks the words concerned. He is quite clear in his statement that /r/ should always be pronounced whenever it appears in the orthography. However, his description of the variant realizations of /r/, both in different dialects and in different environments, is very revealing, and worth quoting in full.

> As this letter is but a jar of the tongue, sometimes against the roof of the mouth and sometimes at the orifice of the throat, it is the most imperfect of all the consonants ... There is a difference in the sound of this letter, never noticed by any of our writers on the subject, which is, in my opinion, of no small importance; and that is the rough and the smooth r. The rough r is formed by jarring the tip of the tongue against the roof of the mouth near the fore teeth: the smooth r is a vibration of the lower part of the tongue, near the root, against the inward region of the palate, near the entrance of the throat. This latter r is that which marks the pronunciation of England, and the former that of Ireland. In England, and particularly in London, the r in *lard, bard, card, regard*, is pronounced so much in the throat, as to be little more than the middle or Italian a lengthened into *baa, baad, caad, regaad* while in Ireland, the r in these words is pronounced with so strong a jar of the tongue against the fore part of the palate, and accompanied with such an aspiration or strong breathing at the beginning of the letter, as to produce that harshness we call the Irish accent. But if this letter is too forcibly pronounced in Ireland, it is often too feebly pronounced in England, and particularly in London, where it is sometimes entirely sunk; it may, perhaps, be worthy of observation that, provided we avoid too forcible a pronunciation of the r, when it ends a word or is followed by a consonant in the same syllable, we may give as much force as we please to this letter at the beginning of a word, without producing any harshness to the ear. Thus *Rome, river, rage*, may have the r as forcible as in

Ireland, but *bar, bard, card, hard* &c. must have it nearly as soft as in London (Walker, 1791: 50).

Here, Walker distinguishes two allophones of /r/ and hints at the total loss of /r/ in postvocalic position, at least in the non-standard pronunciation of London. In the ideal system recommended by Walker, prevocalic /r/ is described as an alveolar trill or flap [r] or [ɾ] , whilst preconsonantal /r/ is an approximant [ɹ]. However, Walker acknowledges that Irish English has the 'forcible' /r/ in all environments, whilst Londoners have lost the /r/ in, for example, *bar, bard*, with consequent lengthening of the vowel. Walker here is describing a change 'from below' which was in progress in the late eighteenth century: weakening of /r/ in preconsonantal position (including word-final position when the following syllable begins with a consonant) is attested from the seventeenth century (Jonson, 1640), but Walker's (albeit reluctant) admission that it becomes 'little more than the middle or Italian a' gives us clear evidence for loss of rhoticity in late eighteenth-century London. This does not mean that Walker's transcription is idealized, though, for educated Londoners are described as having a rhotic pronunciation well into the nineteenth century. Smart (1842) describes much the same distribution as Walker, with a trilled /r/ in, for example, *ray* and *pray*, but a different notation for the <r> in *regulator, ears, asunder, thunder, bear, armed* and *starts*. MacMahon notes that the latter 'appears to indicate non-rhoticity', but that Smart 'clearly confirms the existence of rhoticity in "well-bred London society" with the observation of "the tongue being curled back during the progress of the vowel preceding it, the sound becomes guttural, while a slight vibration of the back part of the tongue is perceptible in this sound"' (1836: vii, cited in MacMahon, 1998: 474).

On the other hand, the non-rhotic pronunciation continues to be stigmatized in England throughout most of the nineteenth century. Mugglestone (1995: 98–103) shows that, throughout the nineteenth century, vocalization of /r/ was as highly stigmatized as 'h-dropping': as late as 1880, Gerard Manley Hopkins criticized Keats for his 'rhyming open vowels to silent *r*s, as *higher* to *Thalia*: as long as the *r* is pronounced by anybody, and it is by a good many yet, the feeling that it is there makes this rhyme most offensive, not indeed to the ear, but to the mind' (Abbot, 1935: 37, cited in Mugglestone, 1995: 101). Here, Hopkins perhaps protests too much: his statement that /r/ is 'pronounced . . . by a good many yet' suggests that it is disappearing, and 'the feeling that it is there' hints at an underlying rather than an actual /r/. In the same year, though, the highly prescriptive handbook already referred to in Section 5.3, *Don't: a Manual of Mistakes* warns its readers: 'Don't drop the sound of *r* where it belongs, as *ahm* for *arm*,

wahm for *warm, hoss* for *horse, govahment* for *government*. The omission
of *r* in these and similar words – usually when it falls after a vowel – is very
common' (1880, cited in Bailey, 1996: 107).

Whether 'common' here means 'ubiquitous' or 'common as muck' is not
entirely clear, but either way it shows that non-rhotic pronunciations were
frequent, but still stigmatized at the end of the nineteenth century. By this
time, though, more descriptive phoneticians such as Sweet were describing
the variety then emerging as RP as non-rhotic. McMahon cites Sweet's
correspondence with the Norwegian linguist Johan Storm, in which the
former states: 'I make no r-glide in liberty, & judging from the incapacity of
Englishmen in general to do so, I doubt whether any of them do so, except
provincials' (Sweet to Storm, 23 Feb. 1880, cited in MacMahon, 1998:
475). Here, then, we have three pieces of evidence from the same year,
1880: Hopkins suggesting that, whilst some speakers still pronounce
postvocalic /r/, others feel that it should be there, *Don't* warning readers
against the 'common' non-rhotic pronunciation, and Sweet telling Storm
that the rhotic pronunciation is 'provincial'.

MacMahon provides further evidence for 'considerable variation
between rhoticity and non-rhoticity, with intermediate semi-rhoticity,
especially during the later nineteenth century in the educated South of
England' (1998). Such extreme variability is typical of what we can expect
to find in a cosmopolitan city when there is a sound change in progress
(Milroy, 1982: 96–7). Rhoticity by this stage was associated with both the
upper classes and with 'provincials', but, crucially, the non-rhotic variety
was used by those who were at this time defining Received Pronunciation.
Since Jones was himself one of this group, it is not surprising that the
pronunciation transcribed in B is unambiguously non-rhotic. Bailey sums
up this evidence as follows:

> the history of noninitial *r* in the nineteenth century encapsulates some of the
> dynamism of sound change characteristic of the period. Despite attempts to
> manipulate pronunciation through schooling and books of linguistic etiquette,
> change took place, so that *r*-less speech became the norm for London-based
> varieties (1996: 109).

Whilst I would broadly agree with this conclusion, as we shall see in
Chapter 7, RP itself became a prescribed variety in the twentieth century,
when 'schooling' and 'books of etiquette' began to proscribe the rhotic
pronunciations formerly recommended.

A feature which is related to the loss of rhoticity, and which is likewise
first attested in the second half of the eighteenth century, is intrusive /r/.
Once the rule has been established that /r/ is pronounced intervocalically,

but not preconsonantally, then words ending in orthographic <r> will have variant realizations according to whether the following syllable begins with a vowel or a consonant. Thus *far* will be pronounced /fɑː/ in present-day non-rhotic varieties, but *far away* /fɑːrəwei/. Once this pattern is established, an analogous alternation develops in words ending in vowels, so that *law* is pronounced /lɔː/ but *law and order* is /lɔːrənɔːdə/. This was first noticed by Sheridan, who states that in Cockney proper names ending in *a*, for example, *Belinda*, are pronounced with a final /r/ (1762: 34). Spence notes this as a vulgarism which could be avoided if only the lower classes could learn how to spell: 'Why should People be laughed at all their lives for betraying their vulgar education, when the Evil is so easily remedied. How ridiculous it is to hear People that can read saying *Any Think – A Horange – Idear – Noar*' (Spence, 1814). Although Spence was born in Newcastle, he had by 1814 been living in London for over 30 years: all the features mentioned as betraying a 'vulgar education' here were characteristic of London speech at the turn of the nineteenth century. Intrusive /r/ continues to be condemned throughout the nineteenth and twentieth centuries, but less prescriptive commentators are increasingly willing to admit that it occurs in the colloquial usage of educated southern English speakers. Alford, like Spence in the above quotation, equates intrusive /r/ with h-dropping as the twin shibboleths of speech 'enough to make the hair of any one but a well-seasoned Cockney stand on end' (1864: 50). Even those from whom we might expect a more objective approach turn prescriptive when it comes to intrusive /r/. As Mugglestone points out, 'Alexander Ellis ... shares in these patterns of proscription, and the language of subjective inequality rather than objective observation features highly in his comments' (1995: 157). Ellis writes: 'illiterate speakers – those who either do not know how to spell, or ignore the rules of spelling in their speech – usually interpose an (r) between any back vowel, as (a, A, ɑ) and a subsequent vowel' (1869–89: I, 201, cited in Mugglestone, 1995). Sweet takes a more descriptive approach: 'I know as a fact that most educated speakers of Southern English insert an *r* in *idea(r) of, India(r) Office*, etc. in rapid speech, and I know that this habit, so far from dying out, is spreading to the Midlands; and yet they all obstinately deny it' (1890: viii, cited in Mugglestone, 1995). On the other hand, Jones, in the first edition of the *English Pronouncing Dictionary* states that most educated speakers did not use intrusive /r/. Sources from the mid-twentieth century such as Ward (1945) and Jones (1960) note the increasing frequency of its use among educated speakers, and Barber remarks that, especially after schwa, 'it is regularly used by B.B.C. announcers, for example, after words like *India* and *Ghana*' (1964: 60). He goes on to state that 'it is less common after other vowels, and was formerly considered sub-standard in such positions; however, this distinction now seems to be breaking down, and many speakers of R.P. are beginning to use intrusive **r** in phrases like *the law of the sea* (ðə 'lɔːr əv ðə 'siː)' (Barber, 1964). However, intrusive /r/ remains a shibboleth to this day: Burchfield writes under 'Law and order':

> It is important not to insert an intrusive /r/ between *law* and *and*. Avoid the same fault in other cases: Say *drawing* not *draw-ring*, *idea of*, not *idea-r-of*, *law abiding* , not *law-r-abiding*. But be careful to make correct liaisons, as in *a pair_of, for_all I know*' (1996: 444).

6.3.8 H-dropping

In transcription A, Walker's recommended pronunciations of *which, when* are transcribed /hwitʃ, hwɛn/ but in B, Jones's transcriptions lack the initial /h/. The sound at the beginning of these words, in varieties such as Scots and American English, which do not have initial /w/ here, is today sometimes transcribed as a single phoneme /ʍ/. However, Walker clearly transcribes it as a sequence of /hw/ and viewed the simplification to /w/ as an instance of what Wells has described as 'the single most powerful pronunciation shibboleth in England', commonly known as 'h-dropping' (1982: 254). I shall therefore deal with these two developments together, even though they have had a different history in the twentieth century. There is evidence of both 'h-dropping' and loss of /h/ in initial /hw/ from at least the sixteenth century, and probably much earlier. In both cases, the process was almost certainly accelerated as a result of contact with (h-less) French speakers after the Norman Conquest. However, there is no sign of any adverse comment about 'h-dropping' before the eighteenth century. The first writer to explicitly condemn this practice is Sheridan, who writes: 'There is one defect which more generally prevails in the counties than any other, and indeed is gaining ground among the politer part of the world, I mean the omission of the aspirate in many words by some, and in most by others' (1762: 34). Walker (1791: xii–xiii) includes in the list of 'faults of the Cockneys' that of 'not sounding *h* where it ought to be sounded, and inversely'. Both Walker and Sheridan equate 'h-dropping' with the simplification of /hw/ to /w/. Thus Walker writes of <h>:

> This letter is often sunk after *w*, particularly in the capital, where we do not find the least distinction of sound between *while* and *wile*, *whet* and *wet*, *where* and *wear*. Trifling as this difference may appear at first sight, it tends greatly to weaken and impoverish the pronunciation, as well as sometimes to confound words of a very different meaning. The Saxons, as Dr Lowth

observes, placed the *h* before the *w*, as *hwat*, and this is certainly its true place; for in the pronunciation of all words, beginning with *wh*, we ought to breath forcibly before we pronounce the *w*, as if the words were written *hoo-at*, *hoo-ile* &c. and then we shall avoid that feeble, cockney pronunciation, which is so disagreeable to a correct ear (1791: 46).

Like 'h-dropping', this pronunciation was not stigmatized until the late eighteenth century: John Jones (1701: 118) makes the neutral observation '*what, when,* etc., sounded *wat, wen,* etc., by some', whilst William Johnston (1764: 9) suggests that the aspiration is weakened rather than lost: '*Wh* sounds *whee* before *a, e,* and *i* . . . where the *h* is very little heard.' The history of these two variants diverges towards the end of the nineteenth century. Whilst 'h-dropping' continues to be so stigmatized that whole handbooks are written just to advise readers how to avoid this stigma (see Mugglestone, 1995: 107–50 for a full discussion of these), initial /w/ in *which, what,* etc. eventually becomes accepted as educated southern English usage. MacMahon points out that, although Sweet transcribes these words with (wh), he admits that this is 'an artificial sound for the natural (w) of South English' (1877: 112, cited in MacMahon, 1998: 468). Ellis points out that 'by far the greater number of educated people in London say (w)' in *wheat* (1874: 1144–5, cited in MacMahon, 1998). In the early twentieth century, /hw/ could still be heard from conservative RP speakers, but /w/ increasingly became the norm. Barber writes that 'the general tendency . . . is for **hw** to die out and be replaced by **w**; indeed, **hw** probably persists only because of the spelling, and of the belief in some schools that **hw** is a more refined pronunciation than **w**. Most people say wɛə and wɔt' (1964: 56). The simplification to /w/ is characteristic of RP and most other English accents, but Scots, American and some (Scots-influenced) New Zealand accents retain /hw/. We have already noted that the London-based Scot Elphinston viewed /w/ in *which,* etc. as a 'fault of the English'. At the end of the eighteenth century, the pronunciation of <wh> in Scots was [χw] rather than the 'weaker' [hw]. Sylvester Douglas writes under *W*: 'The Scotch pronounce the *wh* like their guttural *ch*, followed in like manner by a *u*, losing itself in the succeeding vowel . . . When they endeavour to correct this fault they are apt to omit the *h*, so as to pronounce *whit* and *wit, whig* and *wig* in the very same manner' (Jones, 1991: 141). This suggests that, in the eighteenth century, some Scots speakers might pronounce /ʍ/ as /w/ thinking it to be more correct than the very un-English sounding [χw]. Jones (1997) suggests that there may be evidence of this tendency in James Robertson's *The Ladies' Help to Spelling,* a book published in Glasgow in 1722. Robertson pairs together as words that 'sound alike' *while/wile; whore/woer* (= *wooer*: J.B.); *white/Wight; who/woe.* Jones writes of this:

It is difficult to imagine [hw] onsets in items like <woe>, <woer> and <wile>. We might therefore tentatively suggest that [h]-less forms are being recommended by Robertson to the young Ladies of Glasgow, a female usage directly opposed to that of London. Since [hw] forms were regarded as particularly Scottish (especially their 'Commonly Pronounced' <chot> *'what'* and <chuen> *'when'* types with their syllable initiating [χ]/[ç]) then their replacement by [w] might be expected in a work recommending at least local prestige usage (Jones, 1997: 448–9).

At a time when the speech of educated Scots was being Anglicized, /w/ might seem the lesser of two evils, but, since there is still a lingering feeling even in England that /hw/ is more correct, this pronunciation persists amongst educated Scots.

As far as initial /h/ is concerned, as we saw above, there is no evidence for the stigmatization of 'h-dropping' until the second half of the eighteenth century. Walker considers h-dropping and h-insertion as equally incorrect and Spence (1814) likewise gave 'a *Horange*' as an example of a vulgarism that could be corrected by teaching the poor to spell. Thus it was important to know in which words with orthographic initial <h> it was correct to 'sink' this consonant. Many late eighteenth-century pronouncing dictionaries provide such lists: Walker's is *heir, heiress, herb, herbage, honest, honestly, honesty, honour, honourable, honourably, hospital, hostler, hour, hourly, humble, humbly, humbles, humour, humourist, humourous, humourously, humoursome* (1791: xiii). Elphinston seems to sanction the restoration of /h/ in some of these words when he writes: 'Dhey dhat think *uman, umor* and dhe like, look too *umbel*, may innocently indulge the seeming aspiration' (1786: 15). Four years later, in 1790, *human* is absent from Elphinston's list of words with silent <h>. Thus, the sensitization to h-dropping as a social shibboleth seems already by the end of the eighteenth century to have led to the recommendation that <h> be pronounced in certain words where it had formerly been silent. In 1846, Smart's *Walker Remodelled*, explicitly states that it is better to err on the side of pronouncing <h> where it could be silent than vice versa:

> In some pronouncing dictionaries, *herb* and *hospital* are included among the words whose initial *h* is silent; but the *h* may be aspirated in these and their derivatives without the least offense to polite ears; and even in *humble* and *humour*, the sounding of *h* is a fault, far less grating than it would be in *heir*, *honest* and the other words stated above' (quoted in Mugglestone, 1995: 148).

Wyld writes of the words *humour, humoured* that 'the restoration of the aspirate . . . is a trick of yesterday, and I never observed it until a few years ago, and then only among speakers who thought of every word before they uttered it' (1936: 295). These comments suggest that the 'restoration' of /h/ is a hypercorrection introduced in order to avoid the greater stigma of h-dropping. American English retains more of these words with silent *h*, including *herb* and its derivatives, probably because 'h-dropping' in stressed syllables is not a feature of General American, and so the 'restoration' of /h/ in words of French origin is not an issue. In twentieth-century RP, 'function words' such as the pronouns *he, her him, his* and the auxiliaries *has, have, had* are pronounced without /h/ when unstressed. Barber notes that 'in rapid familiar speech the **h** disappears from many words even in the most highly educated and socially impeccable speakers, though they may not be conscious of it. But in educated speech **h** is only lost at the beginning of an unstressed syllable or word' (1964: 56). He goes on to predict that h-dropping may eventually become acceptable even in stressed syllables, but this does not seem to be happening in RP, or in the usage of middle-class speakers of regional varieties.

6.3.9   The velar nasal

The representation and distribution of the velar nasal is identical in transcriptions A and B, and these are indeed the pronunciations recommended by Walker and Jones for the words concerned. However, this masks the fact that there was an important shift in the social distribution of /ŋ/ in the course of the later modern period. Walker clearly differentiates /n/ from /ŋ/: 'N has two sounds; the one simple and pure, as in *man, not*, &c. the other compounded and mixed, as in *hang, thank*, &c.' (1791: 48). He goes on to warn that 'when they are unaccented in the participial termination *ing*, they are frequently a cause of embarrassment to speakers who desire to pronounce correctly' and gives the following detailed advice:

> We are told, even by teachers of English, that *ing*, in the words that *ing*, in the word *singing, bringing* and *swinging*, must be pronounced with the ringing sound, which is heard when the accent is on these letters, in *king, sing*, and *wing*, and not as if written without the g as *singin, bringin, swingin*. No one can be a greater advocate than I am for the strictest adherence to orthography, as long as the public pronunciation plays the least attention to it; but when I find letters given up by the Public, with respect to sound, I then consider them as cyphers; and, if my observation does not greatly fail me, I can assert, that our best speakers do not invariably pronounce the participle *ing*, so as to rhyme with *sing, king* and *wing* (1791: 48–9).

Walker suggests here that there is already a tendency for 'teachers of English' to insist on /ŋ/, but that 'our best speakers' sometimes pronounce *-ing* as /ɪn/. This latter pronunciation, incorrectly referred to as 'dropping the *g'* was to become as great a shibboleth of working-class speech as h-dropping in the course of the nineteenth century. By 1836, Smart's *Walker Remodelled* recommended /ɪŋ/ in all contexts and, as Mugglestone (1995: 152–3) points out, both spellings with <in'> for /ɪn/ and 'hypercorrect' forms such as *ribbing* for *ribbon* parallel the treatment of /h/ in nineteenth-century novelists' depiction of working-class speech. However, in the case of /ɪŋ/ the usage of the 'best speakers' suggested by Walker persists in upper-class usage into the early twentieth century. As in many other cases, it is the middle classes, ever conscious of spelling and eager to avoid vulgarity, who are at the vanguard of change. The aristocratic pronunciation began to be condemned towards the end of the nineteenth century. Gwynne, for instance, writes of 'a greater blemish, where we have a right to look for perfection, than the peculiarities of the provinces in those who reside there' (1869: 60, cited in Mugglestone, 1995: 154). The stereotype of the aristocratic *huntin', shootin' and fishin'* pronunciation seems to have become a source of humour in the early twentieth century. Ross writes that it 'certainly survived into the 'twenties but, even then, sounded silly and affected unless used by the very old U [upper class]. Now it exists only as a joke, usually made by the non-U against the U' (1970: 16). Wyld is rather more tetchy on this subject: 'such pronunciations as *huntin', shillin'* , &c., which for some reason are considered as a subject of jest in certain circles, while in others they are censured, are of considerable antiquity' (1936: 289). By the middle of the twentieth century, then, a change 'from above', initiated by the middle classes, had led to such stigmatization of the /ɪn/ variant that even the supposed rulers of the country could not escape censure for using this.

6.3.10 Changes in the pronunciation of individual words

One difference between transcriptions A and B which cannot be discussed in terms of general phonological change is that concerning the recommended pronunciations of *obliged* and *wind*. In the case of *wind*, Walker gives both alternatives, but suggests that /wɪnd/ is normal 'except in the territory of rhyme'. He does not condemn /waɪnd/, but notes that 'in prose, this regular and analogical pronunciation borders on the antiquated and pedantic'. In the case of *obliged* Walker is much more assertive. He gives two alternative pronunciations here, one following the French pronunciation /ˈɒbliːdʒd/ and the Anglicized /ˈɒblaɪdʒd/. I have placed them in the order ɒblaɪdʒd/ɒbliːdʒd in transcription A because Walker, in a very extensive section under 'Different Sounds of the Letter *I*', makes his preference clear:

There is an irregular pronunciation of this letter, which has greatly multiplied within these few years, and that is, the slender sound heard in *ee*. This sound is chiefly found in words derived from the French and Italian languages; and we think we show our breeding by a knowledge of those tongues, and an ignorance of our own . . . When Lord Chesterfield wrote his letters to his son, the word *oblige* was, by many polite speakers, pronounced as if written *obleege*, to give a hint of their knowledge of the French language; nay, Pope has rhymed it to this sound:

> 'Dreading ev'n fools, by flatterers *beseig'd*
> 'And so *obliging*, that he ne'er *oblig'd*.'

But it was so far from having generally obtained that Lord Chesterfield strictly enjoins his son to avoid this pronunciation as affected (1791: 15).

Walker goes on to give a very detailed account of the recommendations of a host of fellow orthoepists: Sheridan, Johnston, Barclay, Scott, Kenrick, Buchanan, Perry, Fenning and Nares, whose opinions differ, some favouring /'ɒblaɪdʒ/, some preferring /'ɒbliːdʒ/, others giving only one or other of these alternatives. However, his references to affectation, and his use of Lord Chesterfield as an authority, hint at Walker's personal preference, and he suggests that the publication of Chesterfield's letter has been so influential with 'the polite world' that 'we not unfrequently hear [*oblige*] now pronounced with the broad English *I*, in those circles, where, a few years ago, it would have been an infallible mark of vulgarity' (Walker, 1791). Walker here provides ample evidence for variability in the pronunciation of this word by 'the polite world', and gives the alternative pronunciations in the dictionary entry, but the reader directed to principle 111 as cited above will be left in no doubt as to where Walker's preference lies. Wyld (1936: 226) notes this variation in spellings from the seventeenth and early eighteenth centuries, but suggests that Chesterfield in fact intended to state that /'ɒbliːdʒd/ was the 'correct' pronunciation. If this is so, then Walker's misinterpretation of Chesterfield has had far more influence than Chesterfield's own pronouncement, for, whilst variable pronunciation persisted throughout the nineteenth century, /'ɒbliːdʒd/ was increasingly disfavoured. Mugglestone cites Graham's anecdote about the actor, John Kemble: 'When George II said to him: "Mr Kemble, will you 'obleedge' me with a pinch of your snuff?" [Kemble] replied: "With much pleasure, your Majesty; but it would become your royal lips much better to say 'oblige'"' (1869: 158, cited in Mugglestone, 1995: 218). Mugglestone goes on to note that nineteenth-century novels regularly use the spelling <obleeged> in the language of servants, where, of course, the use of this word is in itself sycophantic. Yet Wyld cites *The Bookman* of May 1907, stating that Wilkie Collins himself used the /iː/ variant. It would appear that the preference for /aɪ/ was introduced and disseminated by precisely those people who would be most likely to consult Walker in cases of uncertainty: the middle classes. This tendency to be guided by authorities such as Walker also led to the reduction of variation in a number of other words. In many cases, pronunciations influenced by the orthography (spelling pronunciation) prevailed over long-established variants. Strang notes: 'from the mid-19c dates a tendency to restore /w/ forms in such words as *woman*, *swore*, *swollen*, *quote* ... *Edward*, *upward*, *Ipswich*' (1970: 81). Yet Walker clearly marks the /w/ in these and other words, and, in the case of *swoon* explicitly condemns the alternative pronunciation: 'In *swoon* ... this letter is always heard; and pronouncing it *soon* is vulgar' (1791: 57). However, Walker is not always in favour of spelling pronunciation: in the case of *waistcoat*, he gives the pronunciation /'wɛskɔt/ but strongly hints that the pronunciation with the 'full' pronunciation of each part of the compound might be preferable: 'it would scarcely sound pedantick if both parts of the word were pronounced with equal distinctness'. Under *cucumber*, he again barely hints at what was to become the accepted pronunciation:

> In some counties of England, especially in the west, this word is pronounced as if written *Coocumber*: this, though rather nearer to the orthography than *Cowcumber*, is yet faulty, in adopting the obtuse *u* heard in *bull* rather than the open *u* heard in *Cucumis*, the Latin word whence *Cucumber* is derived ... But however this may be, it seems too firmly fixed in the sound of *Cowcumber* to be altered.

Mugglestone notes that, in the course of the nineteenth century, *cowcumber* increasingly became marked as 'unfashionable', put into the mouths of such characters as Dickens' Mrs Gamp. She cites Levante as stating 'none but the most illiterate now pronounce this word other than as it is written' (1869: 148, cited in Mugglestone, 1995: 219). The increasing preference for spelling-pronunciations in the nineteenth century is a result of increasing literacy, and a corresponding veneration for the written word.

Other changes apparently affecting individual words reflect the 'residue' (Wang, 1969) caused by earlier competing or uncompleted sound changes. In two cases, this involves the apparent reversal of earlier mergers, which has been the subject of much scholarly debate concerning the principle of irreversibility of mergers (see, for instance, Labov, 1975; Milroy and Harris, 1980). The word *great* notoriously varied between /griːt/ and /greːt/ in the eighteenth century, whilst words such as *boil, join* might be pronounced with /ɔɪ/ or /aɪ/. In the case of *great*, the prevailing /eɪ/ pronunciation is a result of this word, along with *break* and *steak*, being 'left behind' when the majority of words with ME /ɛː/ (often spelt <ea>), became homophonous with reflexes of ME /eː/ (as in *meet*). These words had previously been homophonous with reflexes of ME /aː/ (as in *mate*). Thus earlier *mate/meat* homophony gave way to *meet/meat*. In the eighteenth century, there is evidence that, at least for the word *great*, both pronunciations were current, but the one homophonous with *grate* was gaining ground. Johnson is quoted as having been told by Lord Chesterfield that *great* should rhyme with *state*, but that Sir William Yonge told him that it should rhyme with *seat* and 'none but an Irishman would pronounce it *grait*' (Boswell, cited in Wyld, 1936: 212). Walker expresses a preference for the former variant:

> The word *great* is sometimes pronounced as if written *greet*, generally by people of education, and almost universally in Ireland; but this is contrary to the fixed and settled practice in England. That this is an affected pronunciation, will be perceived in a moment by pronouncing this word in the phrase *Alexander the Great*; for those who pronounce the word *greet* in other cases will generally in this rhyme it with *fate*. It is true the *ee* is the regular sound of this diphthong; but this slender sound of *e* has, in all probability, given way to that of *a*, as deeper and more expressive of the epithet *great* (1791: 30).

Walker's reasoning here is quite specious, of course, and it is more than likely that he attributes the *greet* variant to Irish English simply because he personally prefers the alternative. However, it could well be the case that both variants were heard in Ireland as well as in England. Milroy points out that, in present-day Belfast 'Hib-E [= Hiberno-English] speakers appear to have access to two systems . . . one in which *meat* merges with *mate* and one in which *meat* merges with *meet*' (1992: 157). The eventual preference in RP and many other English varieties for /greɪt/ could well be at least in part due to the influence of Walker and his like on the choices between competing variants made by 'the polite world' in the late eighteenth and the nineteenth centuries. In the case of *oil, join*, etc., the matter is less complicated, in that the pronunciations which prevailed in RP all reflect the spelling. In the later eighteenth century, the reversal of an earlier merger of ME /ɔɪ/ as in *foil* and /iː/ as in *file* was in process, and apparently proceeding word by word. Kenrick writes that it 'would now appear affectation' to pronounce *boil, join*, otherwise than *bile, jine*, but that the same pronunciation in *oil, toil* is 'a vicious custom' which 'prevails in common conversation' (1773, cited in Jespersen, 1909–49: I, 330). Walker, though, allows no such variation. Under the heading *OI* he writes:

> The general, and almost universal sound of this diphthong, is that of *a* in *water*, and the first *e* in *metre*. This double sound is very distinguishable in *boil, toil*,

spoil, joint, point, anoint, &c. which sound ought to be carefully preserved, as there is a very prevalent practice among the vulgar of dropping the *o*, and pronouncing these words, as if written *bile, tile, spile,* &c. (1791: 35).

Wyld suggests that 'the [*oi*] pronunciation ... represents probably an artificially "restored" pronunciation due to the spelling, and this is the Received Pronunciation at the present time' ([1936] 1956: 250). He points out that this 'restored' pronunciation is unetymological in the case of *boil* ('a swelling') and *joist*, both of which had /iː/ in ME. What Wyld fails to point out is that, for *boil*, there are doublets in eighteenth-century pronouncing dictionaries. Walker lists *bile* (pronounced /baɪl/) as 'a sore angry swelling' and adds 'Improperly *Boil*' whilst Spence (1775) simply lists *boil* and *bile* as separate entries with the same meaning but different pronunciations. In either case, the recommended pronunciation accords with the spelling, even where the latter is 'improper'. The so-called 'reversal' of the *oi/i* merger seems to have involved variation between merged and unmerged alternatives from about the sixteenth century, with the variant most closely linked to the spelling eventually winning out due to the influence of literacy, and of pronouncing dictionaries such as Walker's.

6.3.11   Changes in twentieth-century English

Apart from the changes discussed above, there is evidence for some developments which have affected present-day RP, but which do not begin until the turn of the twentieth century. One of these is the glottalization of /t/, a feature associated today with a range of regional accents and, above all, with 'Estuary English' (Rosewarne, 1994). Evidence for glottalization of intervocalic /t/ in 'uneducated southern English speech' is provided by Rippmann (1906: 32), and by 1945 Ward notes this in more general usage, although, as MacMahon points out (1998: 487), she seems not to approve of this pronunciation. Both Jones (1960) and Gimson (1962) admit that glottalization occurs in some contexts for some speakers of RP. Barber notes of the glottal stop:

This is perhaps a sound that is spreading more widely in educated speech ... The glottal stop is heard in some sub-standard English dialects, and notably in Cockney, where it is used in place of t ... and sometimes in place of other voiceles plosives (as when *knock* is pronounced [nɔʔ]). It is also heard in educated speech, but only before certain consonants, and only in place of t, never of any other voiceless plosive' (1964: 69–70).

Evidence for glottalization in other urban dialects of English also first appears in the late nineteenth/early twentieth century. In Scotland, clear evidence comes from Wilson, who writes that 'the glottal catch in place of *t* between two vowels . . . is more common in Fife' (1926: 17), and O'Connor clearly marks it in his IPA transcription of the speech of an adolescent boy from the West End of Newcastle (1947). Jesperson noted the use of the glottal stop in several dialects of Scots and Northern English in 1887 (see below, p. 208). Thus, whilst it would be tempting to view the spread of glottalization in late twentieth-century English as a change originating in lower-class London English, it appears to have surfaced in several urban dialects in the late nineteenth/early twentieth century. The extension to RP noted by Jones, Gimson and Barber is a consequence of social, rather than geographical, diffusion.

Another example of the social diffusion of a variant previously restricted to lower-class usage is l-vocalization. This, according to Wells, was first noticed by Jones, who attributed it to 'London dialectal speech' ([1909] 1956: §298, cited in Wells, 1982: 259). There seems to be no evidence of this development before the twentieth century, but it was spreading to RP by the early 1960s. Barber notes: 'there are slight signs that this tendency is beginning to affect educated speech, even speakers of R.P. sometimes say 'ʃæu wiː for *shall we?*; I have heard B.B.C. announcers pronounce *Wales* as 'wæuz and on the Third Programme I have heard a distinguished elder scientist (apparently a speaker of R.P.) use forms like ðəm'seuvz for *themselves*' (1964: 48). Wells goes further, in predicting that 'it seems likely that it will become entirely standard in English over the course of the next century' (1982: 259).

6.4   Conclusion

In this review of changes in the pronunciation of English during the later modern period, I have concentrated largely on the reference variety which was to become known as Received Pronunciation. We have seen that developments in eighteenth-century London English, such as loss of rhoticity, mark the beginning of what Wells (1982: 211) calls the 'great divide' between British (or, rather, English) and American English. Other innovations of this period, such as lengthening of /a/ in BATH words, contribute to that other 'great divide' between English regional accents, the 'north–south divide', and are variably realized in, for example, Australian English, which typically has /baːθ/ but /dæns/. A complete history of changes in all varieties of English would be beyond the scope of this volume, but I shall consider the historiography of some of these varieties in Chapter 8. What has also been evident in the course of this chapter is that many of the authors who provide direct evidence for the pronunciation of earlier periods are not simply passive observers of the language. Walker and Jones were both highly influential in defining and describing the reference varieties of their time. Walker, especially, had an uncanny knack of picking winners from among competing variants (*cowcumber* being a rare aberration), so he must have been either a very astute observer of current trends, or a trendsetter, or, more likely, both. Jones, whilst professing objectivity, by his very selection of his own (public-school) pronunciation, set the norms of RP, and in successive editions tracked changes in that variety. In the next chapter, we will look at the role played by pronouncing dictionaries and other guides to 'correct' pronunciation in defining and disseminating Received Pronunciation.

7

Defining the standard of pronunciation: pronouncing dictionaries and the rise of RP

7.1 Introduction

In Chapter 5, I argued that the later modern Period saw what, following Haugen's (1971) model, we may call the codification and implementation stages in the standardization of English grammar. With regard to the standardization of pronunciation, the process of selection had begun in the sixteenth century, but serious attempts at codification and implementation were not made until the second half of the eighteenth century, when the pronouncing dictionaries referred to in Chapter 6 began to appear. The notion of a 'standard' pronunciation is necessarily more fluid than that of a standard grammar or orthography, since it concerns the spoken rather than the written language. Whilst it is feasible to conform to externally imposed norms in writing, where revision and correction is possible, this is much more difficult in speech. The details of phonological change discussed in the previous chapter demonstrate that the standard of pronunciation was far from fixed at any point in the later modern period: changes from 'above' and from 'below' bear witness to the influence of different social groups at different times. However, the growing market for 'accent-reduction' classes in the USA, and more recently in Britain, testifies to the fact that, where there is a class of people with social aspirations and a recognized prestige pronunciation, there will be a market for schemes promising to make that pronunciation available. Holmberg recognized this when he wrote: 'it is in the eighteenth century that the snob value of a good pronunciation began to be recognised' (1964: 20). The key word here is 'value': it was at this point that a prestigious accent became a marketable commodity, due to the appearance of a socially aspiring middle class, who could afford the elocution lessons and pronouncing dictionaries which were being produced in order to make this 'proper' pronunciation available. In this chapter, I shall first examine the role of pronouncing dictionaries and other guides to 'correct' usage in defining and disseminating this standard of pronunciation, and then go on to discuss the rise (and fall) of that peculiarly English phenomenon, Received Pronunciation.

7.2 Defining 'a proper pronunciation'

7.2.1 Early definitions

Although serious attempts at implementing the standard pronunciation did not begin until the second half of the eighteenth century, the idea that one variety of spoken English was more prestigious than any other is clearly stated in two works produced in 1589. Puttenham, in his *Arte of English Poesie*, defines the locus of this standard very clearly: 'ye shall take the usuall speech of the Court and that of London and the shires lying about London within lx myles' (1589: 121). He also defines it in social terms as the usage of 'men civill and graciously behavoured and bred' rather than that of artisans or tradesmen, and states that this usage will not be found in the 'marches and frontiers', in ports, or in the far north and west. Hart, in his *Orthographie*, likewise locates the 'flower' of speech in London, and identifies the far north and west as areas so far beyond the influence of this standard that, were his reformed spelling implemented, they could not be blamed for spelling according to their own norms of pronunciation: 'if any one were minded at Newcastell upon Tine, or Bodman in Cornewale, to write or print his minde there, who could justly blame him for his Orthographie, to serve hys neighbours according to their mother speach' (1589: ff. i^r–ii^v). Neither Hart nor Puttenham makes any attempt to define this standard in terms of the actual pronunciations recommended: it is taken for granted that, in order to acquire this prestigious pronunciation, a person would have to associate with those who speak it; therefore provincials cannot be blamed for their outlandish speech.

The orthoepists of the seventeenth century are much more explicit in their descriptions of what they term the 'proper' pronunciation, but this is because they have a scientific interest in phonetics and choose to describe the reference variety of their day, much as late twentieth-century introductory texts on English phonology might do. Like their predecessors, they locate this pronunciation in London, but they tend to name the universities as well. For instance, Price states that he 'has not been guided by our vulgar pronunciation, but that of *London* and our *Universities*, where the language is purely spoken' (1655: A3ᵛ), and Coles bases his description on 'the present proper pronunciation in OXFORD and LONDON' (1674: title page). However, the introduction of the word 'vulgar' is significant here, as it was to become a keyword for the shibboleths which eighteenth-century pronouncing dictionaries helped their readers to avoid. The notion that some pronunciations are, like the unacceptable words in Johnson's dictionary, to be 'branded with some note of infamy', comes in towards the end of the seventeenth century. Cooper, as Dobson notes (1957: 309), is tolerant of dialectal differences, but he describes some pronunciations as 'barbarous' and advises his readers to avoid them. These 'barbarous pronunciations' are described more neutrally in his Latin version as 'facilitas causa' (for the sake of ease), but they foreshadow the proscriptions of eighteenth-century authors such as Walker. One example of what Cooper refers to as 'Barbarous Speaking' which, though also proscribed by Walker, has eventually become acceptable even in RP, is *shugar,* but others, such as *wuts* for *oats,* have remained dialectal or non-standard. Although Cooper lists these 'barbarous' pronunciations, he does not attribute them to speakers from any class or region. Sheldon is probably right in stating that 'no 17th century grammarian advises his reader to avoid this or that pronunciation because it is heard only among the lower classes. It is clear that the feeling had not yet grown up that pronunciation was a class shibboleth' (1938: 198).

7.2.2 Proper and polite speech: eighteenth-century standards

Sheldon, after the statement cited above, goes on to suggest that the idea of pronunciation as a 'class shibboleth ... was to come later, when the suddenly well-to-do bourgeois were trying to rise above their stations' (Sheldon, 1938). This is true to a certain extent: as I have already indicated (p. 168), the proliferation of pronouncing dictionaries and other guides to 'correct' pronunciation in the late eighteenth century depended on there being a market for such a commodity. However, not all pronouncing dictionaries were aimed at the 'well-to-do', and factors other than class came into play in creating this market for a 'good' pronunciation. Just as we saw with regard to the market for grammars (Section 5.1.1), factors such as the rise of provincial towns and cities, the consequences of the Act of Union, and the expansion of education also need to be considered.

The locus of what was considered 'proper' or 'polite' speech in the eighteenth century ('proper' and 'polite' being key words at this time), was, in essence, no different from that identified by Puttenham and Hart.

William Perry writes in the preface to his *Royal Standard English Dictionary*:

> Those who ... with the correctness and precision of true learning, combine the ease and elegance of genteel life, may justly be styled the only true standard for propriety of speech.
>
> It is from the practice of men of letters, eminent orators, and polite speakers in the metropolis, that I have deduced the criterion of the following work, on the merit of which the learned part of mankind are capable of determining for themselves (1775, cited in Sheldon, 1938: 285).

Most eighteenth-century writers agree with this definition of 'proper' speech. Johnston describes it as 'that pronunciation ... in most general use, amongst people of elegance and taste of the English nation, and especially of London' (1764: 1), and Kenrick claims to describe 'the actual practice of the best speakers; men of letters in the metropolis' (1773: vii). Walker, whose *Critical Pronouncing Dictionary* was reprinted over 100 times between 1791 and as late as 1904, set down similar criteria, albeit with a nod to general 'custom':

> But what is this custom to which we must so implicitly submit? Is it the usage of the greater part of speakers, whether good or bad? This has never been asserted by the most sanguine abettors of its authority. Is it the majority of the studious in schools and colleges with those of the learned professions, or of those who, from their elevated birth or station, give laws to the refinements or elegancies of a court? To confine propriety to the latter, which is too often the case, seems an injury to the former, who, from their very profession, appear to have a natural right to a share, at least, in the legislation of language, if not to an absolute sovereignty ...
>
> Perhaps an attentive observation will lead us to conclude, that the usage, which ought to direct us, is neither of these we have been enumerating, taken singly, but a sort of compound ratio of all three. Neither a finical pronunciation of the court, nor a pedantic Græcism of the schools, will be denominated a respectable usage, till a certain number of the general mass of speakers have acknowledged them; nor will a multitude of common speakers authorise any pronunciation which is reprobated by the learned and polite.
>
> As those sounds, therefore, which are the most generally received among the learned and polite, as well as the bulk of speakers, are the most legitimate, we may conclude that a majority of two of these states ought always to concur, in order to constitute what is called good usage (1791: vii–viii).

However, whilst the sixteenth-century orthoepists were content to locate the 'best' speech, the authors of these pronouncing dictionaries deliberately set out to define and 'fix' an explicit standard. Thomas Sheridan is very clear on this point in the preface to his *General Dictionary of the English Language*, where he asks 'whether many important advantages would not accrue both to the present age, and to posterity, if the English language were ascertained, and reduced to a fixed and permanent standard?' (1780: B1). Here Sheridan is deliberately echoing the words of Swift (who had been his teacher in Dublin), Lowth and other eighteenth-century grammarians, but advocating that the same process of codification should be applied to pronunciation. He evokes the 'Golden Age' of Queen Anne, and suggests that, since the accession of a foreign family to the throne, the language had gone into decline:

> From that time the regard formerly paid to pronunciation has been gradually declining; so that now the greatest improprieties in that point are to be found among people of fashion; many pronunciations, which thirty or forty years ago were confined to the vulgar, are gradually gaining ground; and if something be not done to stop this growing evil and fix a general standard at present, the English is likely to become a mere jargon, which every one may pronounce as he pleases (1780: B3).

Whilst Puttenham and Hart recognized the inevitability of regional dialects, especially for those living in Newcastle and Bodmin, Walker and Sheridan set out to eradicate them. Sheridan writes:

> Almost every county in England has its peculiar dialect ... One must have preference, this is the court dialect, as the court is the source of fashions of all kinds. All the other dialects, are sure marks, either of a provincial, rustic, pedantic or mechanical education, and therefore have some degree of disgrace annexed to them (1761: 29–30).

Walker likewise notes that 'there is scarcely any part of England remote from the Capital where a different system of pronunciation does not prevail' (1791: xiii). Both Sheridan and Walker go on to enumerate the 'faults' of various categories of speaker, and provide advice as to how these might be corrected. Sheridan, himself an Irishman, albeit one who had been taught by Swift, included a set of 'Rules to be observed by the Natives of Ireland, in order to obtain a just Pronunciation of English'. Walker took these over wholesale, advertising on the title page of his *Critical Pronouncing Dictionary* that it included 'Rules to be observed by the Natives of Scotland, Ireland and London, for avoiding their respective Peculiarities'. The 'natives of London' referred to here were Walker's 'countrymen, the Cockneys', who, being 'the models of pronunciation to the distant provinces, ought to be the more scrupulously correct' (1791: xii). We shall see in Chapter 8 that the proscriptions of Walker and his ilk provide us with a good deal of useful information about the regional and/or non-standard pronunciations current in the eighteenth century: what is of interest here is a hardening of attitudes towards any pronunciation deemed 'improper'. Two keywords are used to describe the kind of pronunciation to be avoided: *vulgar* and *provincial*. *Vulgar* refers to a sociolect, the lower-class speech of London, particularly reprehensible because, as Walker points out, the 'Cockneys' have access to 'polite' speakers, and therefore have no excuse. 'Vulgar' speech was regarded as uneducated and a definite bar to social advancement. Those who were upwardly mobile would be especially keen to avoid this stigma, but activists such as the Radical Thomas Spence saw 'vulgar' pronunciations as a barrier to the progress of the labouring classes. His *Grand Repository of the English Language* (1775) was principally intended to introduce his scheme for reformed spelling (Beal, 1999; 2002). However, he states on the title page that it provides 'the most proper and agreeable pronunciation', and, in his last publication, Spence suggests that the stigma of 'vulgar' pronunciation should not be borne. He asks: 'Why should People be laughed at all their lives for betraying their vulgar education, when the Evil is so easily remedied. How ridiculous it is to hear People that can read saying *Any Think – A Horange – Idear – Noar*' (Spence, 1814). As we saw in Chapter 6, the pronunciations which 'betray' the speaker here are all features which Spence would have encountered in London rather than his native Newcastle: h-dropping, the 'hypercorrect' use of /ŋk/ for /ŋ/ and intrusive /r/.

The word *provincial* is used to describe both regional accents of England, especially those of the north and west, and the national varieties of Ireland, Scotland and Wales. Sheridan explicitly called for 'the establishment of an uniformity of pronunciation throughout all his Majesty's British dominions' (1762: 205), and George Campbell argued that what he called 'National language' could be heard from 'the upper and the middle ranks, over the whole British empire' (1776: 133). Sheridan, of course, was Irish, and Campbell a Scot, as was Buchanan, whose desire to unite England and 'North Britain' by means of a uniform standard we have already noted in Section 5.1.4. Buchanan states in the preface to the *Linguae Britannicae Vera Pronuntiatio* that 'the people of North Britain seem, in general, to be almost at as great a loss for proper accent and just pronunciation as foreigners'. He promises that, after studying his work, 'they may in a short time pronounce as properly and intelligibly as if they had been born and bred in London and be no more distinguished by that rough and uncouth brogue which is so harsh and unpleasant to an English ear' (1757: xv). The stigmatization of Scots was exacerbated by the increased contact between educated Scots and English speakers after the Act of Union (1707). Scottish members of parliament were lampooned, and ambitious, upwardly mobile Scots soon learned that their accent could prove to be a disadvantage. Sylvester Douglas, a Scot practising law in London, states this very clearly:

> There are, I believe, few natives of North-Britain, who have had occasion either to visit or reside in this country, that have not learned by experience the disadvantages which accompany their idiom and pronounciation [sic]. I appeal especially to those whose professions or situations oblige them to speak in public. In the pulpit, at the bar, or in parliament, a provincial phrase sullies the lustre of the brightest eloquence, and the most forceful reasoning loses half its effect when disguised in the awkwardness of a provincial dress (Jones, 1991: 99).

Both Sheridan and Walker were invited to give lectures on elocution in Edinburgh, and in both cases the lectures were a great success. After Sheridan's visit in 1761, the Select Society of Edinburgh, a literary and philosophical society whose members included the flower of the Scottish Enlightenment, published a set of regulations 'for promoting the reading and speaking of the English Language in Scotland':

> As the intercourse between this part of GREAT-BRITAIN and the Capital daily increases, both on account of business and amusement, and must still go on increasing, gentlemen educated in SCOTLAND have long been sensible of the disadvantages under which they labour, from their imperfect knowledge of the ENGLISH TONGUE, and the impropriety with which they speak it (cited in Jones, 1997: 271).

As Jones points out, the Select Society set out to bring teachers from England 'to instruct gentlemen in the knowledge of the ENGLISH TONGUE, the manner of pronouncing it with purity, and the art of public speaking' (1997: 272). They succeeded in doing this, and schools were set up in Edinburgh, Glasgow, Dundee and Aberdeen. The consequence of this was not a total eradication of Scots pronunciation, but rather the partial Anglicization of the speech of educated, middle-class Scots to create what Adams called 'the tempered medium, generally used by the polished class of society' (1799: 157). This would be a predecessor of the prestigious Scottish English varieties spoken by educated, middle-class Scots in cities like Glasgow ('Kelvinside') and Edinburgh ('Morningside') today. Whatever the consequence, the motivation of Scots learning 'English' in schools, attending lectures on elocution, or buying pronouncing dictionaries such as those of Buchanan (1757), Johnston (1764) or Burn (1786), all of whom were Scots, was to sound as English as possible. A combination of political and social factors thus conspired to create a market for pronouncing dictionaries and lectures on elocution, all promoting a uniform 'polite' pronunciation based on educated London usage. Before going on to consider how notions of 'correct' pronunciation developed through the nineteenth century, it is worth looking at some of these resources in more detail.

The advantage of a pronouncing dictionary was that it could provide a clear guide to the 'correct' pronunciation of every word. Readers could study the 'principles' of correct pronunciation by regular study, and could use the dictionary as a reference-book in cases of uncertainty. Walker recommended that readers refer to pronouncing dictionaries as guides to pronunciation in the same way that they would consult Johnson's dictionary. In Chapter 6, we saw how some of the 'principles' provided by Walker provide evidence for sound changes in progress at the time, such as loss of rhoticity and lengthening of /a/ in BATH words. His individual entries provided clear information on the recommended pronunciation of each word: taking a system invented by Sheridan but first used in a dictionary by Kenrick (1773), Walker used superscripted numbers and keywords to represent different vowel sounds, and a combination of semi-phonetic spelling and italics to distinguish consonants. Figure 7.1 is an extract from Walker's *Critical Pronouncing Dictionary* from CAPTIVE to CARNAL. The keywords are placed at the top, running across two pages, so that the reader can always refer to them, but the numbers referring to sections of the 'principles' in which these are described in detail are placed next to them. Like any dictionary, this provides definitions and an indication of part of speech (*s* = substantive, *a* = adverb, etc.). The head-word is first given in capitals in conventional spelling, then spelt according to Walker's system. Although this is not a truly phonetic system in the sense of 'one sound = one spelling' (see Beal, 1999: 78–80 for further discussion of this), it is a usable and practicable system. In *carbuncle*, Walker signals the velar nasal by <ng> and the gemination of the /k/ by <k_k>, whilst the vowels are indicated as <a^2> (as in *far*) and <u^2> (as in *tub*), thus /kɑːrˈbʌŋkkl/. After some words, Walker places a number referring to one of the 'principles' which precede the dictionary proper. Thus, after *card*, he places number 92, which refers to a section in which he discusses the tendency, in polite pronunciation, for initial /k/ or /g/ to be 'softened by the intervention of a sound like *e*' (1791: 13). This subtle distinction was presumably not important enough to be signalled in the main entry, but it is characteristic of Walker's keen ear for phonetic variation that he includes this comment. The pronunciation to which he refers is no longer present in RP, but does occur in some Caribbean varieties. After some entries, Walker gives a more substantial note, signalled by the pointing hand symbol. These refer to areas of disagreement or controversy: after *carabine*, Walker discusses the opinions of a

CAP   CAR

☞ 559. Fàte 73, fâr 77, fåll 83, fåt 81—mé 93, mèt 95—pine 105, pìn 107—nô 162, môve 164

CAPTIVE, kåp'tĭv, s. 140. One taken in war ; one charmed by beauty.

CAPTIVE, kåp'tĭv, a. Made prisoner in war.

CAPTIVITY, kåp-tĭv'ĕ-tĕ, s. Subjection by the fate of war, bondage ; slavery, servitude.

CAPTOR, kåp'tûr, s. 165. He that takes a prisoner, or a prize.

CAPTURE, kåp'tshûre, s. 461. The act or practice of taking any thing ; a prize.

CAPUCHIN, kåp-û-shèèn', s. 112. A female garment, consisting of a cloak and hood, made in imitation of the dress of capuchin monks.

CAR, kår, s. 78. A small carriage of burden ; a chariot of war.

CARABINE, or CARBINE, kår-bìne', s. A small sort of fire-arms.

☞ Dr Ash, Bailey, W. Johnston, Entick, and Buchanan, accent *Carabine* on the last syllable, and Dr Johnson and Mr Perry on the first ; while Mr Sheridan, Dr Ash, Buchanan, Dr Johnson, and Bailey, accent *Carbine* on the first ; but Mr Scott, Entick, Perry, and Kenrick, more properly on the last. The reason is, that if we accent *Carbine* on the first syllable, the last ought, according to analogy, to have the *i* short ; but as the *i* is always long, the accent ought to be on the last syllable, 140.

CARBINIER, kår-bè-nèèr', s. A sort of light horseman.

CARACK, kår'åk, s. A large ship of burden, galleon.

CARAT, } CARACK, } kår'åt, s. A weight of four grains ; a manner of expressing the fineness of gold.

CARAVAN, kår-å-vàn', s. 524. A troop or body of merchants or pilgrims.

CARAVANSARY, kår-å-vàn'så-rè, s. A house built for the reception of travellers.

CARAWAY, kår'å-wå, s. A plant.

CARBONADO, kår-bò-nå'dò, s. 92. 77. Meat cut across to be broiled.

To CARBONADO, kår-bò-nå'dò, v. a. To cut or hack.—See *Lumbago.*

CARBUNCLE, kår'bùngk-kl, s. 405. A jewel shining in the dark ; red spot or pimple.

CARBUNCLED, kår'bùngk-kld, a. 362. Set with carbuncles ; spotted, deformed with pimples.

CARBUNCULAR, kår-bùng'kù-lùr, a. Red like a carbuncle.

CARBUNCULATION, kår-bùng-kù-là'shùn, s. The blasting of young buds by heat or cold.

CARCANET, kår'kå-nèt, s. A chain or collar of jewels.

CARCASS, kår'kås, s. 92. A dead body of an animal ; the decayed parts of any thing ; the main parts, without completion or ornament ; in gunnery ; a kind of bomb.

CARCELAGE, kår'sè-lĭdje, s. 90. Prison fees.

CARD, kård, s. 92. A paper painted with figures, used in games ; the paper on which the several points of the compass are marked under the mariner's needle ; the instrument with which wool is combed.

To CARD, kård, v. a. To comb wool.

CARDAMOMOM. This word is commonly pronounced kår'då-mûm, s. A medicinal seed.

CARDER, kår'dûr, s. 98. One that cards wool, one that plays much at cards.

CARDIACAL, kår-dì'å-kål, } a. CARDIACK, kår'dè-åk, } a. ... having the quality of invigorating.

CARDINAL, kår'dè-nål, a. 88. Principal, chief.

CARDINAL, kår'dè-nål, s. One of the chief governors of the church.

CARDINALATE, kår'dè-nå-låte, } s. CARDINALSHIP, kår'dè-nål-shĭp, } s. The office and rank of a cardinal.

CARDMATCH kård'måtsh, s. A match made by dipping a piece of card in melted sulphur ; a party at cards.

CARE, kåre, s. Solicitude, anxiety, concern ;

caution ; regard, charge, heed in order to preservation ; the object of care, or of love.

To CARE, kåre, v. n. To be anxious or solicitous ; to be inclined, to be disposed ; to be affected with.

CARECRAZED, kåre'kråzd, a. 359. Broken with care and solicitude.

To CAREEN, kå-rèèn', v. a. To calk, to stop up leaks.

CAREER, kå-rèèr', s. The ground on which a race is run ; a course, a race ; full speed, swift motion ; course of action.

To CAREER, kå-rèèr', v. n. To run with a swift motion.

CAREFUL, kåre'fûl, a. Anxious, solicitous, full of concern ; provident, diligent, cautious ; watchful.

CAREFULLY, kåre'fûl-lè, ad. In a manner that shows care ; heedfully, watchfully.

CAREFULNESS, kåre'fûl-nès, s. Vigilance, caution.

CARELESLY, kåre'lès-lè, ad. Negligently, heedlessly.

CARELESSNESS, kåre'lès-nès, s. Heedlessness, inattention.

CARELESS, kåre'lès, a. Without care, without solicitude, unconcerned, negligent, heedless, unmindful, cheerful, undisturbed, unmoved by, unconcerned at.

To CARESS, kå-rès', v. a. To endear, to fondle.

CARESS, kå-rès', s. An act of endearment.

CARET, kå'rèt, s. A note which shows where something interlined should be read, as ʌ.

CARGO, kår'gò, s. The lading of a ship.

CARIATIDES, kå-rè-åt'è-dèz, s. The Cariatides in architecture are an order of pillars resembling women.

CARICATURE, kår-ĭk-å-tsbûre', s. 461.

☞ This word, though not in Johnson, I have not scrupled to insert, from its frequent and legitimate usage. Baretti tells us, that the literal sense of this word is *certa quantità di munizione che si mette nell' archibuso o altro*, which, in English, signifies the charge of a gun : but its metaphorical signification, and the only one in which the English use it, is, as he tells us, *dichesi anche di ritratto ridicolo in cui sensi grandemente accresciute i diffetti* when applied to paintings, chiefly portraits, that heightening of some features, and lowering of others, which we call in English overcharging, and which will make a very ugly picture, not unlike a handsome person : whence any exaggerated character, which is redundant in some of its parts, and defective in others, is called a Caricature.

CARIES, kå'rè-ĭz, 99. } CARIOSITY, kå-rè-ôs'è-tè, } s. Rottenness.

CARIOUS, kå'rè-ûs, a. 314. Rotten.

CARK, kårk, s. Care, anxiety.

To CARK, kårk, v. n. To be careful, to be anxious.

CARLE, kårl, s. A rude, brutal man, a churl.

CARLINE THISTLE, kår'lĭne-*th*ĭs'sl, s. A plant.

CARLINGS, kår'lĭr gz, s. In a ship, timbers lying fore and aft.

CARMAN, kår'mån, s. 88. A man whose employment it is to drive cars.

CARMELITE, kår'mè-lĭte, s. 156. A sort of pear ; one of the order of White Friars.

CARMINATIVE, kår-mĭn'å-tĭv, s. Carminatives are such things as dispel wind and promote insensible perspiration.

CARMINATIVE, kår-mĭn'å-tĭv, a. 157. Belonging to carminatives.

CARMINE, kår-mĭne', s. A powder of a bright red or crimson colour.

☞ Dr Johnson, Sheridan, Ash, and Smith, accent this word on the first syllable ; but Mr Nares, Dr Kenrick, Mr Scott, Perry, Buchanan, and Entick, more properly on the last : for the reason, see *Carbine.*

CARNAGE, kår'nĭdje, s. 90. Slaughter, havock ; heaps of flesh.

CARNAL, kår'nål, a. 88. Fleshly, not spiritual ; lustful, lecherous.

72

Fig. 7.1   A page from Walker's *Critical Pronouncing Dictionary*

number of authorities on the accentuation of the word, then provides a rationale for his decision to place the accent on the second syllable. In the case of *caricature*, Walker uncharacteristically focuses on lexical rather than phonological matters, but it is interesting to note that he feels the need to justify adding any word not found in Johnson. Not all eighteenth-century pronouncing dictionaries were as detailed or as large as Walker's: Spence's *Grand Repository of the English Language* (1775) was designed for the 'labouring part of the people' and so was smaller and therefore, presumably, cheaper. Spence did not use the system of superscripted numerals, instead introducing a truly phonetic script of his own devising, illustrated in Figure 7.2. Here, Spence writes: 'to read what is printed in this alphabet, nothing is required but to apply the same sound immutably to each character (in whatever position) that the alphabet directs'. Spence provides keywords, so that we can determine the number of phonemic contrasts in the system of pronunciation recommended here. Thus we can see that he has no STRUT/FOOT contrast, since his <u> sounds are exemplified by *tune* and *tun* (presumably /iu/, /juː/ and /ʊ/). As we shall see in Chapter 8, this provides evidence for what was considered 'proper' speech in the north of England, but, to Spence's readers, it would simply have provided a fairly clear guide to pronunciation without the complication of Walker's 'principles'. Spence intended his work for those with limited time and money: the artisan and labouring classes who would only have time to study in the evenings. These two very different pronouncing dictionaries had contrasting fortunes: Spence's *Grand Repository* was never reprinted, and only two copies are extant today. Yet it must have had some influence, for one of those copies made its way to America, and the 'new alphabet' created by 'Mr Spence of Newcastle' is mentioned by William Perry in the preface to his *Royal Standard Dictionary* (1775: vi). Walker's dictionary was, however, to be the most influential of its time, continuing as the major authority on English pronunciation until the appearance of Daniel Jones's pronouncing dictionary in 1917. The *Critical Pronouncing Dictionary* was reprinted over a hundred times up to 1904 and was the basis of over 20 other dictionaries published in the nineteenth century, including B. H. Smart's *Walker Remodelled* (1836). It was successful and influential in America as well as Britain, the first American edition appearing in 1803. Walker was acknowledged to have 'settled all doubts on the subject' of English pronunciation, and his *Critical Pronouncing Dictionary* came to be regarded as the 'statute book of English orthoepy' (*The Athenaeum*, 1807: 81). By the end of the nineteenth century, Walker had become a byword for linguistic correctness, so that those who used an affected pronunciation

The N E W   A L P H A B E T.

Capi-tals. Letters	Small Letters	Names		
A	A	ă	as in mane, (MAN)	
Λ		ă	as in man, (MΛN)	
A		ah	as in father, (FAHIR)	
ЛU		au	as in wall, (WAUL)	
B	в	ib or bĭ		
D	d	id or dĭ		
E	e	ē	as in mete, (MET)	
Є		ĕ	as in met, (MET)	
F	ғ	if		
G	G	ig or gĭ		
H	н	hă		
I	ı	ī	as in fite, (SIT)	
		Ĭ	as in fit, (SIT)	
J	J	idge or jĭ		
K	k	ik or kĭ		
L	L	il		
M	м	im		
N	и	in		
O	o	ō	as in note, (NOT)	
C		ŏ	as in not, (NCT)	
P	p	ip or pĭ		
R	я	ir		
S	s	iſs		
T	т	it or tĭ		
U	v	ū	as in tune, (TUN)	
Ʊ		ŭ	as in tun, (TUN)	
V	v	iv		
W	w	wĭ	as in way, (WA)	

Capi-tals. Letters	Small Letters	Names	
Y	ʏ	yĭ	as in young, (YUIG)
Z	z	iz	
⅏		oo	as in moon, (MꝹN)
Oſ		oi	as in oil, (OIL)
OJ		ou	as in houſe, (HOUS)
SI		iſh	as in ſhell, (SHEL)
ʒI		izh	as in viſion, (VIʒIN)
ΘI		itch	as in child, (CHILD)
TI		ith	as in think, (THINK)
IЄ		ith	as in they, (THA)
WI		whĭ	as in which, (WHICH)
NG		ing	as in loving, (LUVING)

⁎⁎⁎ The vowels in this alphabet are A Λ A ЛU E Є I I O C U Ʊ ⅏ Oſ OJ; and the conſonants B D F G H J K L M N P R S T V W Y Z SI ʒI ΘI TI IЄ WI NG.

☞ To read what is printed in this alphabet, nothing is required but to apply the ſame ſound immutably to each character (in whatever poſition) that the alphabet directs.

N. B. In the following work, n. ſtand for name, or ſubſtantive;—q. for quality, or adjective;—v. for verb;—part. for participle;—ad. for adverb;—conj. for conjunction;—prep. for prepoſition;—interj. for interjection.

A

Fig. 7.2 The 'New Alphabet' from Spence's *Grand Repository of the English Language*

were accused of trying to 'out-Walker Walker' (Mugglestone, 1995: 41). The pronouncing dictionaries of the eighteenth century, especially Walker's, were thus very successful in defining the standard of pronunciation, and in disseminating this standard amongst the aspiring classes throughout the British Isles and even in America. That they were not able to 'fix' the pronunciation is demonstrated by the details of variation and change discussed in Chapter 6, for which these pronouncing dictionaries provide the richest source of direct evidence.

7.2.3 Standards and shibboleths

We saw in Section 5.3 that, in the nineteenth century, whilst the major grammars of the preceding century continued to be published in new

AN ACCURATE

NEW SPELLING and PRONOUNCING

ENGLISH DICTIONARY.

A

A, An article, placed before names of the fingular number that begin with a founded confonant.

A'bacus, (\BIK\S) n. a counting table; the uppermoft member of a pillar.

Abáft, (IB\FT) ad. behind; to the ftern.

Abáifance, (\BAZINS) n. a bow or curtefy; refpect.

Abándon, (\B\NDIN) v. to forfake; to defert.

Abáfe, (\BAS) v. to bring down; to humble.

Abáfement, (\BASMINT) n. depreffion; humiliation.

Abáfh, (\B\SH) v. to put to the blufh.

Abáte, (\BAT) v. to diminifh; to leffen.

Abátement, \BATMINT) n. an allowance made.

Abb, (\B) n. the warp threads of cloth.

A'bbacy, (\BISE) n. the rights, privileges, or jurifdiction of an abbot.

A'bbefs, (\BIS) n. the governefs of an abbey inhabited by women.

A'bbey, (\BE) n. a monaftery, governed by an abbot or abbefs.

A'bbot, (\BIT) n. the chief of an abbey inhabited by men.

A B B

Abbréviate, (\BREVEAT) v. to abridge; to fhorten.

Abbreviátion, (\BREVEASIIN) n. fhortening; a contraction.

Abbréviature, (\BREVEITUR) n. a mark ufed for the fake of fhortening.

A'bdicate, (\BDIKAT) v. to renounce; to refign.

Abdicátion, (\BDIKASIIN) n. refignation.

Abdómen, (\BDOMIN) n. the lower part of the belly.

Abdóminous, (\BDOMINIS) q. belonging to the abdomen; big-bellied.

Abdúce, (\BDUS) v. to draw away.

Abecedárian, (ABESEDAREIN) n. one who teaches the alphabet.

Abecédary, (ABESEDIRE) q. belonging to the alphabet.

Abèrrance, (\BERINS) n. an error.

Abèrrant, (\BERINT) q. going wrong.

Abérring, (\BERING) part. going aftray.

Aberrátion, (\BIRASIIN) n. wandering.

Abét, (\BET) v. to aid, or affift.

Abétment, (\BETMINT) n. encouragement.

A 2

Fig. 7.3   The first page of Spence's *Grand Repository of the English Language*

editions, a new market emerged for simpler guides to 'correct' usage, often combined with advice concerning other areas of life. The same trend can be observed with respect to guides to pronunciation: alongside new and/or revised editions of Walker, we see the emergence of cheap handbooks offering advice on how to avoid the worst shibboleths such as h-dropping, aimed at the newly emerging lower middle class whose white-collar and service-based jobs demanded a veneer of gentility. Works such as *Don't* (Censor, *c.* 1880) and *Enquire Within Upon Everything* (Anon, 1878) also included advice on 'correct' pronunciation, which increasingly became seen as another aspect of etiquette. Towards the end of the century, the emergence of philology as a scientific discipline led to a number of descriptive works by scholars such as Ellis (1869) and Sweet (1877) which, whilst aiming at objectivity, played their part in defining Received Pronunciation. Thus, with guides to pronunciation as with grammars, the nineteenth century sees the beginning of the prescriptive/descriptive division that is still with us today. As we saw with respect to grammars, though, there is a continuum rather than a binary distinction: pronouncing dictionaries are descriptive in so far as they describe the pronunciation of real, albeit elite, speakers, and the philological works promote that elite variety.

We noted in Chapter 6 that, in the nineteenth century, certain features of 'vulgar' pronunciation proscribed by Walker and other eighteenth-century authorities take on the character of shibboleths. Bailey refers to this tendency more generally when he writes: 'if there is one heritage of the nineteenth-century language culture that survives most vigorously, it is the institutionalization of hierarchy among linguistic variants. The nineteenth century is, in short, a century of steadily increasing linguistic intolerance' (1996: 82). For a large part of the population, the lower middle class, there was no prospect of acquiring the prestige accent that would become known as Received Pronunciation. However, they, more than any other social group, would want to avoid the stigma of what Spence termed a 'vulgar education'. His group formed the market for the cheap manuals, often devoted to one or two shibboleths of pro-nunciation, which appeared in multiple editions through the nineteenth century. Mugglestone (1995) gives a full account of these, noting that works such as *Poor Letter H: Its Use and Abuse* (1854), *Harry Hawkins' H Book* (1879) and *Mind Your H's and Take Care of Your R's* (1866) were so popular that 'books of accompanying exercises were swiftly devised to supplement the main text, a means by which the "vulgar", whether rich or otherwise, might monitor their conformity to a linguistic norm presented as integral to good standing in the eyes of the world' (1995: 130). These handbooks are full of humorous cautionary tales, exemplifying the social embarrassment of being exposed as 'vulgar' by the omission or misplacement of /h/. *Poor Letter H* contains the follow-ing anecdote:

> I have heard a person who was very well dressed, and looked like a lady, ask a gentleman who was sitting behind her, if he knew whether Lord Murray had left any *Heir* behind him:– the gentleman almost blushed, and I thought stopped a little, to see whether the lady meant a *Son* or a *Hare* (1866: 16–17, quoted in Mugglestone, 1995: 131).

What is notable here is that the person exposed to embarrassment is a lady, and that she is 'very well dressed': women were particularly vulnerable to criticism, since a lack of overt gentility would be equated with impropriety. As we noted in Chapter 5, manuals for young ladies included lessons in grammar and speech along with dress and household management. *Enquire Within upon Everything* (Anon, 1878) includes an extensive section on the use of /h/, employing the same kind of humorous anecdote as that cited above. Indeed, the story of 'Mrs Alexander Hitching, – or, as she frequently styled herself, with an air of conscious dignity, Mrs HALEXANDER 'ITCHING' takes up the best part of five pages under the heading 'H OR NO H?' (Anon, 1878: 70–4). Like the lady in the anecdote from *Poor Letter H* cited above, Mrs Hitching is portrayed as a figure of fun because, despite her airs and graces, she betrays her vulgar origins by her use of /h/. The introduction to the story tells us a great deal about a woman's place at this time:

> Her husband was a post-captain of some distinction, seldom at home, and therefore Mrs. A.H. (or, as she rendered it, Mrs. *H.I.*) felt it incumbent upon herself to represent her own dignity, and the dignity of her husband also. Well, this Mrs Hitching was a next-door neighbour of ours – a most agreeable lady in many respects, middle aged, good looking, uncommonly fond of talking, active, almost of fussy habits, very good tempered and good natured, but with a most unpleasant habit of misusing the letter H to such a degree that our sensitive nerves have often been shocked when in her society (1878: 70–1).

In Mrs Hitching, we can see a comic type whose pedigree can be traced back to Mrs Slipslop and Mrs Malaprop: the respectable, middle-aged matron who betrays her lack of education through her speech. However, cautionary tales such as this would be aimed at younger women, whose value on the marriage market depended on their ability to exhibit 'proper' behaviour in speech as in all aspects of life. *Private Education; or a Practical Plan for the Studies of Young Ladies* provides the following advice: 'the manner of expressing yourself should be particularly attended to as well as your pronunciation. How would it sound at your own table if you should say "will you take a little *air*" for hare. "Do you ride on *orseback* for horseback?"' (1816: 280–1, cited in Mugglestone, 1995: 179). Hill, writing in *The Aspirate* (1902), makes this point explicitly: 'so important indeed is the question of the use of h's in England ... that no marriage should take place between persons whose ideas on this subject do not agree' (1902: 13, cited in Mugglestone, 1995: 186). The same sentiment is voiced in *How to Choose a Wife*, in which men are warned: 'perpetual nausea and disgust will be your doom if you marry a vulgar and uncultivated woman' (1854: 51, cited in Mugglestone, 1995). (For a fuller discussion of these 'guides for ladies', see Mugglestone, 1995: 160–207.) The assumption behind all these statements is that pronunciation reflects status and since, in nineteenth-century (and later) society, a wife reflected her husband's status, 'vulgar' speech would be an acute social embarrassment. There was also the view, affecting both sexes, that the shibboleths of 'vulgar' speech would betray social climbers. This is expressed very clearly in the following advice from *The Letter H, Past, Present and Future*:

> H, in speech, is an unmistakable mark of class distinction in England, as every person soon discovers . . . I remarked upon this to an English gentleman, an officer, who replied – 'It's the greatest blessing in the world, a sure protection against cads. You meet a fellow who is well-dressed, behaves himself decently enough, and yet you don't know exactly what to make of him; but get him talking and, if he trips upon his H's that settles the question. He's a chap you'd better be shy of' (Leach 1881: 10–11, cited in Mugglestone, 1995: 78).

Twentieth-century socio-linguists such as Labov (1966) and Trudgill (1974) were able to demonstrate that the proportional use of prestige variants such as /h/ in Norwich and rhoticity in New York is higher in the speech of women and members of the second-highest social class. We see in the extracts cited above the influences which led to this social stratification. As Mugglestone points out, philologists such as Sweet were able to provide a more objective witness to this phenomenon. Sweet notes that 'the Cockney dialect seems very ugly to an educated Englishman or Woman' because 'he – and still more she – lives in a perpetual terror of being taken for a Cockney, and a perpetual struggle to preserve that *h* which has now been lost in most of the local dialects of England' (1890: vi–vii, cited in Mugglestone, 1995: 194).

This tendency to focus on a small number of shibboleths continues into the twentieth century. In a mid-twentieth-century edition of *Don't* (*c*. 1950), the following advice is given:

> DON'T clip final consonants. DON'T say *comin'*, *goin'*, *singin'*, for *coming*, *going*, *singing*. DON'T say *an'* for *and*, nor *nothink* for *nothing*.
> DON'T omit the correct use of the letter '*h*'; but pronounce it with a slight aspirate, and with a full breath from the chest. To sound it at the back of the mouth gives force enough for correctness. There is no greater mark of vulgarity than an obtrusive effort to make other people understand that the speaker is not one of the common people who do not know where to use the '*h*'s'. In this, as in other matters, correctness should appear to be natural and instinctive.

DON'T, on the other hand, put in an '*h*,' where that valuable letter should be omitted. It is very unpleasant to the cultivated ears of others to hear of '*a horange*' or '*a hanimal*'. Consult a pronouncing dictionary if you are at all uncertain whether that tricky eighth letter of the alphabet should be silent or sounded (Censor, *c.* 1950: 35–6).

7.3 Received pronunciation

The advice to 'consult a pronouncing dictionary' here reminds us that handbooks such as *Don't* and *Enquire Within* were not intended to provide the reader with a full account of 'proper' pronunciation. They merely set out to warn him, or more likely her, against the worst social gaffes, in speech as in other aspects of behaviour. *Enquire Within* advises the reader 'to listen to the examples given by good speakers, and by educated persons' (1878: 61), whilst *Don't* exhorts them to 'listen carefully to the conversation of cultivated people, and, if in doubt, consult the dictionaries' (*c.* 1950: 34). The type of person likely to provide a model of 'good' speech was the same as that out-lined in Section 7.2.2 above: in *Enquire Within*, the 'Rules and Hints for Correct Speaking' are 'founded upon the authority of scholars, the usages of the bar, the pulpit, and the senate' (1878: 54). This is not very different from Perry's 'men of letters, eminent orators, and polite speakers in the metropolis', but it echoes even more closely the words of an authority contemporary with *Enquire Within*: Alexander Ellis. The following quotation is often cited as the first instance of the term 'received pronunciation':

> In the present day we may ... recognise a received pronunciation all over the country, not widely differing in any particular locality, and admitting a certain degree of variety. It may be especially considered as the educated pro-nunciation of the metropolis, of the court, the pulpit and the bar (Ellis 1869: 23).

In fact, Ellis was not the first person to use the phrase 'received pro-nunciation', as this collocation of words is used more than once by Walker. For example, he refers to 'a corrupt, but received pronunciation' of the letter [*a*] 'in the words *any, many, catch, Thames*, where the *a* sounds like short *e*, as if written *enny, menny, ketch, Thames*' (1791: 12). Walker's use of the phrase is different from Ellis's though: the former refers to a pronunciation of an individual vowel which happens to be 'received', whilst the latter is describing a whole variety. Walker's usage does, however, give some insight into the origin of this rather curious term: if *received* was already in use with the meaning 'acceptable in polite society', and was being used in relation to speech, then it is easy to see how the phrase 'received pronunciation' came to have its current meaning.

Whatever the origin of the phrase, though, there has been a shift from the view put forward by Smart earlier in the century that 'imitation of a Londoner, or of a person who pronounces like one, is the only method by which a just utterance can be acquired' (1812, cited in Holmberg, 1964: 53). From being located in the capital, the model of pronunciation described by Ellis has become a sociolect used all over the country by a particular class of person. Ellis does not suggest that this sociolect is homogeneous: on the contrary, he states that 'in as much as all these localities and professions are recruited from the provinces, there will be a varied thread of provincial utterance running through the whole' (Ellis, 1869: 23).

As the nineteenth century progresses, the notion that the standard accent of British English is that which gives the least hint as to the regional origin of the speaker is consolidated. Sweet defines Standard English as 'that dialect of English which is approximated to, all over Great Britain, by those who do not keep to their own local dialects, namely, the educated speech of London and Southern England' (1882: 7). Sweet, like Ellis, locates the standard in London, but concedes that there are people of a certain social class 'approximate' to this, wherever they live within Britain. By the end of the century, the emphasis has shifted to stress the non-localized nature of this standard, when Lloyd writes that 'the perfect English is that which is admittedly correct, while giving the least possible indication of local origin' (1894: 52). In the early twentieth century, the sociolectal nature of this standard becomes even more important. Daniel Jones set out to describe the pronunciation of English rather than to prescribe 'correct' or 'proper' speech. In the preface to the first edition of his *English Pronouncing Dictionary*, he states:

> The object of the present book is to record, with as much accuracy as is necessary for practical linguistic purposes, the pronunciation used by a considerable number of cultivated Southern English people in ordinary conversation ... the book is a record of *facts*, not theories or personal preferences. No attempt is made to decide how people *ought* to pronounce (1917: vii).

Sweet likewise sets out an agenda that is clearly descriptive: 'language only exists in the individual, and ... such a phrase as "standard English pronunciation" expresses only an abstraction. Reflect that it is absurd to set up a standard of how English people *ought* to speak, before we know how they actually *do* speak' (1890: 3). However, in confining their descriptions of 'English' pronunciation to that of their own social group, Jones and Sweet unwittingly promoted RP as the norm both for British readers and for foreign learners of English. In the preface to his *English Pronouncing Dictionary*, Jones sets out his definition of the model of speech provided:

> The pronunciation used in this book is that most usually heard in everyday speech in the families of Southern English persons whose men-folk have been educated at the great public boarding-schools. This pronunciation is also used by a considerable proportion of those who do not come from the South of England but who have been educated at these schools. The pronunciation may also be heard, to an extent which is considerable though difficult to specify, from Natives of the South of England who have not been educated at these schools. It is probably accurate to say that a majority of Londoners who have had a university education, use either this pronunciation or a pronunciation not differing greatly from it (1917: viii).

Wyld's definition of 'Received Standard' is very similar:

> This form of speech differs from the various Regional Dialects in many ways, but most remarkably in this, that it is not confined to any locality, nor associated in any one's mind with the area; it is in its origin, as we shall see, the product of social conditions, and is essentially a *Class Dialect*. *Received Standard* is spoken, within certain social boundaries, with an extraordinary degree of uniformity, all over the country . . . If we were to say that Received English at the present day is *Public School English*, we should not be far wrong (1920: 3–4).

Jones's definition seems wider than Wyld's, but it has to be borne in mind that, in the early twentieth century, a far greater proportion of university students would have had a public-school education than is the case today. To speak RP at the beginning of the twentieth century, you had to move in a very restricted social circle: that of the public-school educated. It is this association with a social group rather than a location that accounts for the non-localized nature of RP. As we saw in the preceding sections, 'proper' English from the sixteenth to the late eighteenth century was associated with the south of England and, more specifically, London. A trend develops in the eighteenth century for ambitious parents in the provinces to send their children south for their schooling, specifically in order to rid them of the 'marks of disgrace' associated with their native accents. Hughes notes that, in 1748, a Mr Carr of Whitworth sent his son 'to a very private school at Craike to wear off the Newcastle tone which he learned at Houghton' (1952: 363). Evidence that schoolmasters paid particular attention to this matter is provided in another letter included here. Two boys from Gateshead had been sent to a school at High Wycombe when they were both under the age of nine. The headmaster wrote to the boys' father:

> It was impossible their manner of Reading should have escaped you; it has long been a subject of conversation here, sometimes of mirth, at other times we have treated it very seriously particularly to Master Ellison. He can inform you that he has hardly ever said a lesson or read an English book to me without my talking a great deal to him about it. I have only observed that he generally spake the last syllable in a sentence nearly a third above the last but one. I have made him repeat the concluding syllables after me and have sunk my voice which he exactly imitated and therefore [I] doubt not but we shall acquire a proper cadence in time (Hughes, 1952: 365).

What started as an individual practice became an expected norm of behaviour for the upper and upper-middle classes with the establishment of the public-school system from 1870. Honey notes that 'between 1870 and 1900 this expectation became so well established that few could resist it, and various kinds of disability were experienced by those who did. A new caste was created in British society, the caste of "public school man"' (1988: 210). The linguistic consequence of sending all the boys from the highest strata of society away from their home environment into a close-knit network of peers would be uniformity of speech. Jones recognizes the inevitability of this process:

> For centuries past boys from all parts of Great Britain have been educated together in boarding-schools. If a boy in such a school has a marked local peculiarity in his pronunciation, it generally disappears under the influence of the different mode of speaking which he hears continually around him; he consequently emerges from school with a pronunciation similar to that of the other boys ([1917] 1937: ix).

Boys would be sent away to public schools at precisely the age (pre-adolescent) at which they would be most susceptible to peer pressure, and still able to change their accent. Quite apart from the efforts of school-teachers, the not-so-gentle pressure of fellow pupils, of whom a majority would already speak the 'received' accent of the south, would ensure that it would be a brave lad indeed who dared to retain his 'provincial' accent. Any reader who has moved house as a child of this age, or has children of this age, will recognize the intense pressure to conform amongst pre-adolescents and adolescents of both sexes. Given the expectation that any son of an upper- or upper-middle-class family would attend a public school, and the pressure from teachers and peers to conform that would be exerted, it was inevitable that the elite pronunciation known as RP would evolve. Of course, once it became known that a 'public-school man' could be recognized by his accent – the linguistic equivalent of the 'old school tie' – then those with social aspirations would want to emulate this. RP became a model, not only within Britain, but throughout the Empire, because positions of power and influence would mostly be held by 'public-school men'. This association of RP with public-school education perhaps accounts for the tendency, even today, for British (or at least English) people to regard speakers with marked regional accents as less educated or intelligent than RP speakers. RP would perhaps have remained 'public-school English' had it not been for the advent of broadcasting in the early twentieth century. The BBC from the outset made a deliberate decision to employ announcers who spoke with similar accents. Guidelines on pronunciation were set out 'to secure some measure of uniformity in the pronunciation of broadcast English, and to provide announcers with some degree of protection against the criticism to which they are, from the nature of their work, peculiarly liable' (James 1926, cited in Bolton and Crystal, 1969: 112). Although James here argues that 'there is no standard of pronunciation' (Bolton and Crystal, 1969: 103), he goes on to write of a 'narrow band' of variants, 'more alike as we ascend' the social scale. In practice, the BBC employed RP speakers with such regularity that RP was to become known popularly as 'BBC English'. Strang, as late as 1970, was able to write: 'if we can agree to use RP for the variety of speech heard from British-born national newscasters on the BBC we shall have a general idea of the kind of accent we are talking about' (1970: 45). In the first half of the twentieth century, the majority of Britons would be exposed to RP, as more and more households possessed a radio: the remotest farmer would listen to the Home Service to obtain news and, more importantly, the weather forecast. During World War II, the BBC would be the main source of information for families anxious for news from the front, so that RP became associated in their minds with authority and integrity. Dialectologists in the immediate post-war period saw this as a cause for concern: exposure to RP and Standard English via the BBC would, they feared, lead to the disappearance of 'traditional' dialects. This concern gave impetus to the *Survey of English Dialects*, begun in 1948. However, this anxiety about the fate of traditional dialects was not new: the introduction of universal primary education in 1870 led to fears that schoolteachers would set out to eradicate dialect. These fears were understandable, as there is evidence that English schools in the late nineteenth century employed a policy of discouraging dialect use. Honey tells us that HMIs (= Her Majesty's Inspectors of Schools) after 1870 increasingly advocated eradication of local accent and dialect. In 1886, one HMI recommended the 'kindly and judicious use of ridicule' on the 'inarticulate utterances' of schoolboys in South Yorkshire. Another instance arises in 1894, when an HMI addressing a committee on teacher training at Armstrong College, Durham, stated that students at this northern college needed help to 'overcome the peculiarities of local pronunciation' (1988: 221–2). Further evidence of this educational policy comes from Daniel Jones, who states that *The Pronunciation of English* was intended for:

> English students and teachers, and more especially for students in training-colleges and teachers whose aim is to correct cockneyisms or other undesirable pronunciations in their scholars. At the same time it is hoped that the book may be found of use to lecturers, barristers, clergy, etc., in short all who desire to read or speak in public. The dialectal peculiarities, indistinctiveness and artificialities which are unfortunately so common in the pronunciation of public speakers may be avoided by the application of the elementary principles of phonetics (1909, cited in Crowley, 1991: 165–6).

In this way, not only would the hegemony of RP be consolidated, but there would be a trickle-down effect, whereby teachers all over the country would attempt to eradicate those same 'marks of disgrace' identified by eighteenth-century authorities such as Walker and Sheridan. At the very least, these teachers would instil into their pupils a sense of the inferiority of their native accent and dialect. This consensus as to the superiority of RP seems to hold until the end of World War II. The prestige of this variety seems to be at its height in the 1950s when broadcasters spoke in an accent which never fails to invoke amusement when heard today. Abercrombie describes a situation of which we sense he does not entirely approve:

> The existence of RP gives accent judgements a peculiar importance in England, and perhaps makes the English more sensitive than most people to accent differences. In England, Standard English speakers are divided by an 'accent bar', on one side of which is RP, and on the other side all the other accents . . . there is no doubt that RP is a privileged accent, your social life, or your career, or both, may be affected by whether you possess it or not ([1951] 1965: 13).

His use of the term 'accent bar' is deliberately chosen as analogous to the then-current 'colour bar', a term used in the 1950s and 1960s to voice concerns about the discrimination against persons of colour in a Britain which had as yet no equal opportunities legislation. Abercrombie's 'accent bar' was not destined to survive much longer: just 11 years later, Gimson wrote: 'RP itself can be a handicap if used in inappropriate social situations, since it might be taken as a mark of affectation, or a desire to emphasize social superiority' (1962: 84). Barber, too, notes this shift, in a very interesting section in which he considers the expansion of secondary education after the 1944 Education Act, the experiences of World War II, and the increasing democratization of British society, as possible causes. He cites the 'Angry Young Men' of post-war fiction and drama, such as Jimmy Porter in

John Osborne's *Look Back in Anger,* the heroes of Kingsley Amis's *Lucky Jim* and John Braine's *Room at the Top* as exemplifying this new class of grammar-school-educated graduate. He concludes:

> The great success of these three works with the English public shows the extent to which they are canalising current feelings; the new working-class intellectual and his resentment of the Establishment are certainly realities of our time. And this resentment can also be directed at Received Standard as the language of the Establishment (1964: 27).

We have already gone beyond the chronological scope of this book in tracing the demise of RP in the post-war period, but, writing as I do at a time when 'dialect levelling' is a topic of great interest amongst linguists (see, e.g. Kerswill and Williams, 1994) and 'Estuary English' is of even greater interest to laypersons (Rosewarne, 1994), I cannot resist ending this chapter with Barber's vision of the future:

> What is perhaps most likely . . . is that one of the regional standards will come to be recognised as the new national standard, perhaps coalescing with the present R.S. [= Received Standard] in the process. The regional standard which is taking on this role is that of the most populous and influential part of England, London and the south-east, which of all the regional standards is the one closest to R.S. (so much so, indeed, that many people cannot distinguish between them). Many people, if asked to define Received Standard English, would in fact define it as the speech of the educated classes of the south of England, and not, as I have done, as the speech of the English gentry (1964: 28).

Thus, by the mid-twentieth century, we seem to have come full circle, back to 'the usuall speech . . . of London and the shires lying about London within lx myles'. Attitudes to regional dialects have been cited at various points in this chapter as evidence for the greater prestige of RP and its predecessors. In the next chapter, I shall focus on the study and representation of regional dialects of British English, and of the other national varieties which became established in the course of the later modern period.

8

Beyond Standard English: varieties of English in the later modern period

8.1 Introduction

So far, I have concentrated on discussing changes in the Standard (English) variety of English during the later modern period, noting for each level of language how developments in this reference variety affect and are affected by the prescriptions and proscriptions of normative writers. In each chapter, there have been references to other regional or national varieties, both within and outside the British Isles, usually as lexicographers, grammarians and orthoepists condemn words, structures and pronunciations that they considered 'vicious', 'barbarous' or as displaying some 'marks of disgrace'. Whilst the intention of these works was to discourage or even eradicate the use of dialect, they do provide us with some insights into features of non-standard English which were particularly salient at the time. In some cases, these normative works provide early evidence of variables which were to become major markers of dialect differences at a later stage, such as the lack of the FOOT-STRUT contrast in northern English varieties noted by Walker (see p. 43). Alongside these normative works we see, from the eighteenth century onwards (and earlier in some cases), various kinds of literary representation of dialect. Some of these are humorous 'dialogues' by authors such as John Collier (aka Tim Bobbin), whose *Tummus and Meary* was first published in 1746 and went into 19 editions. Others, such as the poems of William Barnes, are more serious attempts to capture the language of rural folk at a time when the countryside was under threat from enclosures and industrialization. Apart from this 'dialect literature' (i.e. literature written wholly in dialect), we see representations of non-standard varieties in the literary dialect of authors such as Emily Brontë, Elizabeth Gaskell and

Thomas Hardy. These novelists tended to use Standard English for the authorial voice, but used dialect as a marked variety to represent the speech of certain rural and/or lower-class characters. Other insights into regional dialects can be found in travellers' tales such as Defoe's *Tour Through the Whole Island of Great Britain* (1724–76), tourist guides such as West's *A Guide to the Lakes*, and other works such as Marshall's *The Rural Economy of Norfolk* (1787). Whilst some of these representations of dialect are at the level of stereotype, they can still provide insights into both the nature of regional variation at this time, and attitudes towards these varieties.

As we move into the later nineteenth century, the emergence of philology as a scientific discipline creates an interest in regional dialects as linguistic systems which are worthy of study in their own right. Works such as Wright's *Grammar of the Dialect of Windhill in the West Riding of Yorkshire* (1892) started from the assumption that regional dialects were not 'ungrammatical', but had their own grammars which were of interest to philologists. Alexander Ellis's *On Early English Pronunciation* (1869–89) contains a wealth of information on the phonetics and phonology of regional accents, but has been largely neglected because the phonetic script devised by Ellis, 'paleotype', has been viewed as too difficult to decipher, but see Shorrocks (1991) for a defence of Ellis's system. At the same time as the Philological Society was beginning the *New English Dictionary* project, Wright, under the auspices of the equally august English Dialect Society was preparing his *English Dialect Dictionary* (1898–1905) and *English Dialect Grammar* (1905). Alongside these monumental works, glossaries and dictionaries of individual dialects were produced throughout the nineteenth and early twentieth centuries: examples of these are Hunter's *Hallamshire Glossary* (1829), Easther's *Glossary of the Dialect of Almondbury and Huddersfield* (1883), Heslop's *Northumbrian Words* (1892) and Nicholson's *The Folk Speech of East Yorkshire* (1901). These in turn owed a debt to earlier compilations of non-standard vocabulary, such as Ray's *Collection of English Words, Not Generally Used* (1674), which included many northern words, and Grose's *Provincial Glossary* (1787). From all these sources, we can compile a picture of regional variation in British English through the later modern period, and attitudes towards those varieties.

Where other national varieties are concerned, we have seen some voices raised against the hegemony of Standard English, notably by Noah Webster and his fellow Americans (pp. 50–3). This reaction was, of course, motivated by the political imperative towards linguistic autonomy following the American Revolution, marking what Wells (1982: 211) terms the 'great divide' between British and American English. The late eighteenth and the nineteenth centuries saw the colonization by English speakers of most parts of the world, with national varieties evolving in Australia, Canada, New Zealand, South Africa and many other 'minor anglophone locations' (Trudgill, 2002: 44). To provide a full account of the history of all, or indeed any, of these varieties would be beyond the scope of this book. What I hope to do in this chapter is to trace the development of attitudes to and awareness of these, from 'barbarous' colonial dialects to independent national varieties.

8.2   Regional dialects of British English

8.2.1   'Marks of disgrace': evidence from normative works

In Chapters 6 and 7, evidence from pronouncing dictionaries and from other normative works such as *Enquire Within upon Everything* was used mainly as evidence for the development of the accent of English which was prescribed by these works as 'proper'. However, they also proscribed certain pronunciations which they termed 'provincial' or 'vulgar', and we saw that some of these proscriptions provide evidence for the regional and/or non-standard dialects of the time. I have discussed the usefulness of these sources for historical dialectology more fully elsewhere (Beal, 2004): here, I shall provide examples from a range of eighteenth and nineteenth-century sources to illustrate the ways in which they can provide early evidence for variation and change in non-standard varieties of British English. In some cases, the proscriptions of eighteenth- and nineteenth-century authors amount to little more than the rehearsing of well-established stereotypes. Sheridan's remarks on Welsh English, for instance, probably owe more to Shakespeare than to the author's own observation:

> The peculiarity of the Welsh pronunciation arises chiefly from their constantly substituting the three pure mutes, in the room of the three impure; and the three aspirate semivowels in the place of the three flat. Thus instead of *b* they use *p*; for *g* they use *k*, or hard *c*; and for *d* they employ *t*. Thus instead of *blood* they say *plut*, for *God, Cot*, and for *dear, tear*. In like manner, in the use of the semivowels, they substitute *f* in the place of *v*; *s* in the place of *z*; *etħ* in the room of *eth* and *esh* in that of *ezh*. Thus instead of *virtue* and *vice*, they say *firtue* and *fice*; instead of *zeal* and *praise*, *seal* and *praisse*, instead of *these* and *those, tħesse* and *tħosse*, instead of *azhur, osier, ashur, oshir* . . . Thus there are no less than seven of our consonants which the Welsh never pronounce (1780: 62).

Here, the spelling < tħ> stands for /θ/ and <zh> for /ʒ/: Sheridan comments here on the devoicing of initial plosives and fricatives that has been a stereotype of Welsh English at least since Shakespeare's Fluellen spoke of 'Alexander the Pig'. Another long-standing stereotype evoked by Sheridan is that of south-western voicing of initial and medial fricatives: 'for *father* they say *vather*, for *Somersetshire*, *Zomerzetshire*, for *thin*, *thin*' (Sheridan, 1780). In other cases, eighteenth- and nineteenth-century authors provide us with evidence for features which, in the course of the later modern period, move from being markers of a particular variety to stereotypes, and eventually disappear. Here, I use the terms *marker* and *stereotype* in the senses used by Labov. In his classic account of the mechanism of a sound change, Labov identifies several stages. A variable becomes a *marker* when it has developed into 'one of the norms which define[s] the speech community'. At a later stage 'under extreme stigmatization, a form may become the overt topic of social comment, and may eventually disappear. It is thus a *stereotype*, which may become increasingly divorced from the forms which are actually used in speech' (1972: 179, 180). The Welsh devoicing and south-western voicing remarked upon by Sheridan were stereotypes in that they had long been the topic of 'extreme stigmatization' but have not disappeared. One feature noted by Walker does seem to make the transition from marker to stereotype and finally disappear. The 'second fault' of the Cockneys is, according to Walker, that of 'pronouncing w for v and inversely':

> The pronunciation of *v* for *w*, and more frequently of *w* for *v*, among the inhabitants of London, and those not always of the lower order, is a blemish of the first magnitude. The difficulty of remedying this defect is the greater, as the cure of one of these mistakes has a tendency to promote the other (1791: vii–viii).

This feature of London speech is also noted by Elphinston (1787), who, unlike Walker, states that it is confined to 'vulgar' speakers. By the end of the eighteenth century, this feature of 'Cockney' speech must have been well established, for Wyld notes instances of both <v> for /w/ and vice versa in texts from the fifteenth century onwards. Henry Machyn, whom Wyld describes as 'the Cockney Diarist', provides the following examples: *vomen* for 'women', *Volsake* for 'Woolsack', *welvet* for 'velvet' and *woyce* for 'voice' (Wyld, 1936: 292–3). Machyn uses these forms with no awareness of stigma, and comments on the 'Cockney' character of this feature do seem to stem from the eighteenth century, so by this stage it must have been a marker. However, the 'extreme stigmatization' induced by the proscriptions of Walker and his ilk swiftly led to this feature becoming a stereotype. In *Enquire Within upon Everything*, under the heading 'Hints to "Cockney" Speakers', we are told that 'the most objectionable error of the Cockney, that of substituting the *v* for the *w* and *vice versa*, is, we believe, pretty generally abandoned' (1878: 63). This tallies with the account given by Wyld:

> This was formerly a London vulgarism, but is now apparently extinct in the Cockney dialect. Personally, I never actually heard these pronunciations, so well known to the readers of Dickens, Thackeray, and of the earlier numbers of *Punch*. My time for observing such points begins in the late seventies or early eighties of the last century, and I never remember noticing this particular feature in actual genuine speech, though I remember quite well, as a boy, hearing middle-aged people say *weal* for *veal* and *vich* for *which*, jocularly, as though in imitation of some actual type of speech with which they were familiar. I used to wonder why these people introduced this peculiarity in jest, and whose pronunciation it was supposed to imitate. I have since come to the conclusion that my boyhood friends must have heard these pronunciations in their youth – say from twenty to thirty years before my time, which would bring us back to the forties and fifties of the last century (1936: 292).

The reference to 'jest' and to the use of this feature by novelists such as Dickens does suggest that /w/–/v/ interchange had become a stereotype by the mid-nineteenth century and had disappeared by the twentieth.

Another feature which seems to have become a stereotype during this period is the so-called 'Northumbrian burr' (Påhlsson, 1972). This variant had been noticed first by Defoe in his *Tour Through the Whole Island of Great Britain*. This is a key text for evidence of the awareness of dialectal variation at the beginning of the eighteenth century. Like the sixteenth-century authors who singled out Newcastle and Bodmin as the two places in which the dialect was so outlandish as to be beyond the pale, Defoe only comments on the dialects of Northumberland and the south-west. On the former, he writes:

> I must not quit *Northumberland* without taking notice, that the Natives of this Country, of the antient original Race or Families, are distinguished by a *Shibboleth* upon their Tongues in pronouncing the Letter *R*, which they cannot utter without a hollow Jarring in the Throat, by which they are as plainly known, as a foreigner is in pronouncing the *Th*: this they call the *Northumberland R*, or *Wharle*; and the Natives value themselves upon that Imperfection, because, forsooth, it shews the Antiquity of their Blood (1724–7: III, 232–3).

Defoe's tone here is not exactly normative: the 'wharle' is presented as an object of curiosity rather like a traditional story or a folk-custom. The elocutionists of the later eighteenth century were not so tolerant. Sheridan in his *Lectures on Elocution* refers to the 'difficulties of those who wish to cure themselves of a provincial or vitious pronunciation', and uses the northern /r/ as an example of such an affliction:

The letter R is very indistinctly pronounced by many; nay in several of the Northern counties of England, there are scarce any of the inhabitants, who can pronounce it at all. Yet it would be strange to suppose, that all those people, should be so unfortunately distinguished, from the rest of the natives of this island, as to be born with any peculiar defect in their organs; when this matter is so plainly to be accounted for, upon this principle of imitation and habit (1761: 24).

Sheridan sees the burr as an unfortunate habit that can be cured, presumably by attending his lessons on elocution. Kenrick likewise describes the Northumbrian /r/ as a speech defect:

In the northern parts of England, particularly in and about Newcastle, we find the r deprived of its tremulating sound, and very awkwardly pronounced somewhat like a w or oau. *Round the rude rocks the ragged Rachel runs* is a line frequently put into the mouths of Northumbrians, to expose their incapacity of pronouncing the r, as it is sounded by the inhabitants of the southern counties: and indeed their recital of it has a singular and whimsical effect (1773: 31).

Stephen Jones is equally derogatory, but seems to give a different description of the phonetic characteristics of the burr: 'the rough sound of r, as it is pronounced by the natives of Durham, who sound it in their throats with a disagreeable rattling' (1798: 49). Jones thus describes the 'burr' as 'in the throat', possibly uvular, whereas Kenrick's description suggests a labial articulation. In fact, twentieth-century recordings of this variant in Northumbrian speech reveal that it has both characteristics: it is a uvular [R] with secondary lip-rounding. Other sources indicate that the burr was used by Northumbrians in the eighteenth and nineteenth centuries, and that they were either unaware of the stigma, or defiant of it. Thomas Spence's biographer Frances Place writes that Spence 'had a strong "burr in his throat" and a slight impediment in his speech" (BL Add. MS 27,808, fo. 154), and Heslop (1903) tells us that Lord Eldon, who was a native of Newcastle and chancellor of the exchequer in the early nineteenth century, also used the burr. Here, then, we have a feature which becomes noticed as a marker of Northumbrian speech in the eighteenth century, and which is highly stigmatized by authors from outside the region towards the end of the century, but which Northumbrians themselves see as a marker of local identity. By the end of the nineteenth century, however, middle-class Northumbrians were attempting to rid themselves, or at least their children, of this feature. Heslop quotes Murray, writing in 1880, as stating that 'most people of Northumberland, who can afford it, send their children south for education to cure them of the burr. I know many a man, who himself burrs, all whose children pronounce *r* like other Englishmen' (1903: 16–17). Typically, the middle classes ('those who can afford it') were, by the end of the nineteenth century, reacting to the stigmatization of the burr, whilst the upper classes (Lord Eldon) and the lower classes were not. In the twentieth century, the burr was to become increasingly recessive, becoming confined to the speech of rural areas and/or older, working-class speakers. Although the burr is found throughout Northumberland in the *SED*, there is no trace of it in O'Connor's (1947) transcription of the speech of working-class Newcastle youths, and both Warkentyne (1965) and Viereck (1965) report that it was not found in the speech of young people. Påhlsson's (1972) study of Thropton, a village in northern Northumberland so renowned for its 'burrers' that the burr is referred to as the 'Thropton *r*', also shows that the burr is recessive. Further evidence that the burr had become a stereotype by the twentieth century is provided by the jocular references to it in popular literature, such as Scott Dobson's *Larn Yersel' Geordie*:

> **The first sound to learn is the Geordie 'R'**
> This is both rolling and guttural, combining the best effects of Doctor Finlay [a Scottish doctor in a popular TV drama] at his homeliest with the sound of a very old nanny-goat being sick . . . The sound is very rarely heard outside the Geordie enclave although certain vintage records of Mr Maurice Chevalier do contain an approximation (1969: 8).

Like the Cockney /w/–/v/ inversion, the Northumbrian burr becomes a joke, a party-piece which allows the speaker to participate in local identity without bearing the stigma in everyday life. The burr has not yet gone the way of the Cockney inversion: it can still be heard in the remote hills of the Cheviots and the fishing villages on the Northumbrian coast, but its eventual extinction is a near certainty.

In both these cases, eighteenth-century sources provided the first evidence of features which followed the path of Labov's *stereotype* from being the object of overt comment and criticism to recede and eventually disappear. In other cases, normative works provide evidence that some features which, to this day, remain as markers of certain varieties, had attained that status in the later modern period. We saw in Chapter 6 that Walker, like Jones, had the STRUT vowel /ʌ/ in the word *sun*. The absence of the FOOT–STRUT distinction has become the most salient and stable marker of the northern English varieties. Whilst evidence of a new vowel described as 'obscure *u*' is found in southern sources from the mid-seventeenth century, overt comment on the northerners' lack of this vowel comes later in the eighteenth century. As we might expect, Walker has something to say on this point:

> If the short sound of the letter **u** in *trunk, sunk* etc., differ from the sound of that letter in the northern parts of England, where they sound it like the **u** in *bull*, and nearly as if the words were written *troonk, soonk,* etc., it necessarily follows that every word where that letter occurs must by these provincials be mispronounced (1791: xiii).

However, Walker was not the first to notice this: John Kirkby, a Cumbrian, notes that his 'seventh vowel', found in *skull, gun, supper, figure, nature*, 'is scarce known to the Inhabitants of the North, who always use the short sound of the eighth vowel [= /ʊ/] instead of it' (1746: 7). Kirkby's remarks are much more neutral than Walker's, and we can see in Figure 7.2 that Spence, who was also a northerner, simply gives us the unsplit /ʊ/ without comment. Kenrick notes the lack of FOOT–STRUT split in William Ward's (1767) *An Essay on Grammar:*

> It is further observable of this sound, that the people of Ireland, Yorkshire, and many other provincials mistake its use; applying it to words which in London are pronounced with the **u** full as in no. 3 of the Dictionary: as *bull, wool, put, push*, all of which they pronounce as the inhabitants of the Metropolis do *trull, blood, rut, rush*. Thus the ingenious Mr Ward of Beverley, has given us in his grammar the words *put, thus* and *rub* as having one quality of sound; but unless by the word *put* he meant the substantive, a Dutch game of cards so called, or the ludicrous appellation given to provincials of *country put*, it is never so pronounced (1773: 36).

Of course 'Mr Ward', like Kirkby and Spence, was himself a northerner. What is apparent here is that derogatory remarks about the northerners' lack of the FOOT–STRUT split only come from southerners. This is in marked contrast to, for example, Sheridan's 'Rules to be observed by the natives of Ireland' or Walker's 'faults of the Cockneys' in which the authors proscribe the usage of their compatriots. In the eighteenth century, as now, northerners do not seem to view their lack of a separate STRUT vowel as a handicap.

In the cases discussed above, eighteenth-century normative texts have provided early evidence for the existence of variables which have since either become stereotypes, eventually to disappear, or have developed into stable markers of dialect distinctions in British English. These sources are particularly valuable to scholars investigating variation and change in present-day English when they indicate the origin of variants which have been observed to be spreading rapidly in the late twentieth century. In the 1990s, there was a great deal of scholarly and popular interest in the phenomenon of 'Estuary English' (Rosewarne, 1994). This is an accent originally based, as the name suggests, around the Thames Estuary, but said to be spreading throughout the south-east of England. Furthermore, certain features associated with 'Estuary English' have been observed in the speech of younger people in urban centres all over England, and even in Scotland (Stuart-Smith, 1999). There is an assumption that the features which characterize 'Estuary English' are innovations of the twentieth century, because they do not appear in earlier dialect surveys such as the *SED*. However, some of these can be traced back to the London speech of the eighteenth and nineteenth centuries with the help of evidence from normative texts. One of the features which has been observed to be 'spreading rapidly in all directions' (Przedlacka, 2001: 45) is what Wells (1982: 96–7) calls 'TH fronting'. This is the tendency for /θ/, /ð/ to be pronounced as /f/, /v/. Wells explains 'the prevalence of these pronunciations among adult working-class Londoners' as 'a persistent infantilism' (1982: 96), but this cannot explain the apparent spread of this feature to other cities and towns in the late twentieth century. Kerswill and Williams (2002: 93) describe TH fronting as 'at least a century old in London', but earlier evidence is provided by Elphinston (1787), who notes that the 'low English ... say *Redriph* for *Rotherhithe* and *loph* for *loth*'. We can take Elphinston's remark as evidence that TH fronting was present in lower-class London speech towards the end of the eighteenth century, and, whilst its rapid spread might be recent, the phenomenon itself is not. Careful examination of eighteenth- and nineteenth-century sources might shed more light on this phenomenon. Another feature of 'Estuary English', likewise observed to be spreading to other urban dialects of Britain (Foulkes and Docherty, 2000), is the labiodental [ʋ] for /r/. Foulkes and Docherty note the recent emergence of this variant in the speech of young working-class males in a number of English towns and cities, including Derby and Newcastle upon Tyne. They suggest that this is an example of 'accent-levelling', and that the labialized variant originated in Cockney speech, as a result of contact with Yiddish speakers from the 1880s onwards. The earliest evidence they find of any comment on what appears to be labiodental [ʋ] comes from H. Christmas's edition of Samuel Pegge's *Anecdotes of the English Language* (1844: 66). Jespersen cites Christmas as stating that 'people unable to pronounce *r* invariably substitute a *w*' (1909–49: I, 355). Jespersen precedes this with his own statement that 'a great many Southerners habitually round all their [r]s' (1909–49: I, 354). The quote from Christmas does not indicate any geographical origin for this feature, but rather implies that labiodental [ʋ] is a speech defect. Foulkes and Docherty go on to note that there are a number of comments from the late nineteenth and early twentieth centuries noting the existence of this variant as a speech defect and/or in the speech of children in London, but state that there is no evidence from this period of labiodental [ʋ] being associated with

Cockney speech in general. They claim 'to have evidence pointing to the gradual emergence of [ʋ] as a perceived accent feature over the last thirty years or so' (2000: 37). However, in *Enquire Within upon Everything* (Anon, 1878), there is evidence that this labiodental variant was already a recognized feature of 'Genteel Cockney'. In a series of extracts from *Punch*, representations of Cockney speech in semi-phonetic spelling are produced. We are told that these come from 'a very able schoolmaster at work during the past thirteen years ... no other than the loquacious Mr *Punch*, from whose works we quote a few admirable exercises' (1878: 63). Two of these involve the spelling <w> for standard <r>, a clear indication of labialized /r/:

> GENTEEL COCKNEY (*by the sea-side*) – *Blanche.* 'How grand, how solemn, dear Frederick, this is! I really think the ocean is more beautiful under this aspect than under any other!' –
>
> *Frederick.* 'H'm – ah! Per-waps. By the way, Blanche, there's a fella schwimping. S'pose we ask him if he can get us some pwawns for breakfast to-mowaw mawning?'
>
> MILITARY COCKNEY. – *Lieutenant Blazer* (*of the Plungers*). – 'Gwood gwacious! Here's a howible go! The Infantwy's going to gwow a moustache!' *Cornet Huffy* (*whose face is whiskerless*). 'Yaw don't mean that! Wall! There's only one alternative for us. We must shave!' (1878: 63–4).

These extracts are presumably adapted from cartoons in *Punch*, an excellent source of linguistic stereotypes in the nineteenth century (see, for instance, the cartoon reproduced in Bailey, 1996: 89). What is particularly interesting is that the labialization is only represented in the speech of middle-class males: the 'genteel' Cockney and the lieutenant. The wife in the first sketch is represented as having no peculiarities of accent, but using rather pretentious discourse. I would not wish to argue that this evidence in any way undermines the main thesis of Foulkes and Docherty's paper, but it would appear that labiodental [ʋ], like TH fronting, seems to have been present, at least in London speech, for some time. Whilst it would be impossible to build up a full picture of dialectal variation in eighteenth- and nineteenth-century British English from normative texts alone, the examples provided in this section demonstrate that such texts can be a very useful source of information on individual variants, providing necessary time-depth to supplement 'apparent-time' studies.

8.2.2   Dialect literature and literary dialect

In discussing /w/–/v/ interchange above, I noted that this feature was probably already a stereotype, and recessive in actual speech when Dickens used it to mark the speech of some of his characters. Literature of various kinds, from the novels of Dickens, Elizabeth Gaskell, Hardy, etc., to the more 'popular' genres of magazines, songs and 'recitations' for the music halls, provide a good source of evidence for the most salient regional and social variants in the later modern period. In many cases, these sources reflect the same norms that pronouncing dictionaries and self-help books such as *Enquire Within upon Everything* attempt to enforce. As Mugglestone points out, 'authors are, in this as in other ways, a product of the age in which they live; that consciousness of the spoken word and its needful proprieties operates upon them just as on other members of the population' (1995: 210). Literary sources often provide clear evidence of the social stratification of salient variants. For example, we saw in Section 6.3.9 that Walker recommended the use of /n/ in the -*ing* suffix when the stem of the words also ended in -*ing*, and that, whilst this was retained both as an aristocratic and a lower-class usage until the beginning of the twentieth century, the stigmatization of 'dropping the *g*' led to the adoption of /ɪŋ/ by middle-class speakers. Evidence that this variant was highly salient, and that its social distribution was well known in the late nineteenth century, is provided by a number of literary sources. Bailey reproduces a particularly telling cartoon from *Punch*, dated 6 September 1873:

> *Lord Reginald.* 'AIN'T YER GOIN' TO HAVE SOME PUDDIN', MISS RICHARDS? IT'S *SO* JOLLY!'
>
> *The Governess.* 'THERE AGAIN, REGINALD! "*PUDDIN*" – "*GOIN*" – "*AIN'T YER*"!!! THAT'S THE WAY JIM BATES AND DOLLY MAPLE SPEAK – AND JIM'S A *STABLE-BOY,* AND DOLLY'S A *LAUNDRY-MAID!*'
>
> *Lord Reginald.* 'AH! BUT THAT'S THE WAY FATHER AND MOTHER SPEAK, *TOO* – AND FATHER'S A *DUKE,* AND MOTHER'S A *DUCHESS!!* SO *THERE!*' (in Bailey, 1996: 89).

Here, the upper-class young boy answers the pretensions of his middle-class governess with his own superior norms, which just happen to be identical to those of the working-class servants to whom the governess thinks herself superior. Dickens likewise represents the contrasting norms of middle class and working class in the speech of David and Barkis in *David Copperfield*: Barkis is represented as saying to David 'If you was writin' to her, p'raps you'd recollect to say that Barkis was willin'', which David repeats as 'That Barkis is willing?' (1850, cited in Mugglestone, 1995: 211). Mugglestone provides many more examples of literary representations of these and other nineteenth-century norms in literature, demonstrating the value of this source of evidence (1995: 208–57).

Not all literary representations of dialect in the later modern period set out to reflect or reinforce the norms of 'proper' speech. At exactly the same time that pronouncing dictionaries such as Walker's were being produced to satisfy the demand for guides to 'correct' usage from the aspiring middle classes, other forces in society were working towards a more positive appraisal of dialect. In 1781 Robert Burns published *Tam o' Shanter*, a Scots poem written in defiance of the proscriptions against 'Scotticisms', and in 1798 Wordsworth and Coleridge published their *Lyrical Ballads*, marking the beginning of the Romantic movement in English literature. Whilst neither of these two poets wrote in dialect, their work reflects what Burke describes as 'the discovery of the people' across Europe from the late eighteenth century:

> This new and more positive attitude to the culture 'of the people' dwelt upon language as perhaps the central means by which the historical unfolding of cultures was to be revealed. The scholars of the German Enlightenment were crucial . . . in Herder, language is the revelation of the spirit of the 'folk'. There was a new interest in spoken as well as written language, in the illiterate, and in dialect (1978: 9).

This interest was, as we shall see in the next section, most clearly manifested in the works of nineteenth-century philologists and dialectologists such as Ellis and Wright, but many literary authors took a scholarly interest in accurately portraying the language of 'the people'. Elizabeth Gaskell's husband, William Gaskell, was a dialectologist who placed emphasis on the 'antiquity' and 'purity' of the Lancashire dialect. In *Two Lectures on the Lancashire Dialect*, he writes:

> There are many forms of speech and peculiarities of pronunciation in Lancashire that would yet sound strange, and, to use a Lancashire expression, strangely 'potter' a southern; but these are often not, as some ignorantly suppose, mere vulgar corruptions of modern English, but genuine relics of the old mother tongue. They are bits of the old granite, which have perhaps been polished into smoother forms, but lost in the process a great deal of their strength (1854: 13–14).

His wife clearly made use of this expertise in her representations of the speech of working-class Lancastrians, as we see in the following extract from *North and South*:

> 'Why, yo' see, there's five or six masters who have set themselves again paying the wages they've been paying these two years past, and flourishing upon, and getting richer upon. And now they come to us, and say we're to take less. And we won't. We'll just clem them to death first; and see who'll work for 'em then. They'll have killed the goose that laid 'em the golden eggs, I reckon.'

'And so you plan dying, in order to be revenged upon them!'
'No', said he, 'I dunnot. I just look forward to the chance of dying at my
post sooner than yield. That's what folk call fine and honourable in a soldier,
and why not in a poor weaver-chap?' ([1854] 1973: 134).

Here, Elizabeth Gaskell does not attempt to represent the regional
pronunciation, but uses lexical (*clem*) and morphological (*dunnot*) features
to represent the articulate, but non-standard, speech of the striking weaver.
Both these features are included in later glossaries of Lancashire dialect such
as Taylor (1901). The Dorset poet William Barnes was also a serious scholar
of dialect and Old English. He believed that 'Saxon speech is the speech best
understood by Saxons' (Jones, 1962: 10), i.e. that words derived from
classical languages should be avoided. He believed that dialect could be
understood by common people and 'found that many a dialect word and
idiom which seemed out of place in polite society could claim a pure Saxon
pedigree' (Jones, 1962: 11). Barnes's poetry ostensibly portrays a rural idyll,
but is a means of protest against enclosures and the mechanization of
agriculture. His poem *The Common A-Took In* was first published in 1834,
entitled *Rusticus Dolens, or Inclosures of Common, a Dorsetshire Eclogue
in the Dorset Dialect, by a Native of the County.*

> Oh! no, Poll, no! Since they've a-took
> The common in, our lew wold nook
> Don't seem a bit as used to look
> When we had runnen room;
> Girt banks do shut up ev'ry drong,
> An' stratch wi' thorny backs along
> Where we did use to run among
> The vuzzen an' the broom.

Many of the features here are familiar from both earlier and later accounts
of south-western dialects: the initial/v/ in *vuzzen* (= 'furze') suggests that
the feature of initial voicing pointed out by Sheridan was still being used.
This and other features such as the metathesis in *girt* and the *a-* prefix for
the past participle *a-took* are still attested in twentieth-century accounts of
south-western speech such as the *SED*. There is, however, a symbiotic relationship between literary works such as this and the dialect dictionaries of
the same period and later: in at least one instance, the only citation to support an entry in Wright's *English Dialect Dictionary* (1905) comes from
Barnes. This resurgence of dialect writing from the late eighteenth century
onwards applies to national as well as regional varieties: Maria Edgeworth,
for instance, had been much influenced by the philosophy of Rousseau, as is
evident in her *Practical Education* (1798). In her novel *Castle Rackrent*

(1800), Edgeworth attempted to portray the Irish-English dialect of its lower-class characters, not in terms of humorous stereotype, but as realistically as possible. Walter Scott cited Edgeworth as an influence on his use of Scots in his novels from *Waverley* onwards:

> It has been my object to describe these persons, not by a caricatured and exaggerated use of the national dialect, but by their habits, manners and feelings, so as in some distant degree to emulate the admirable Irish portraits drawn by Miss Edgeworth (cited in Tulloch, 1980: 167).

In the case of Scots writers, the same forces which led to the publication of lists of 'Scotticisms' to be avoided led to what Robinson terms a 'back-lash of patriotic nostalgia which found an outlet in antiquarianism' (1973: 42). I have noted elsewhere (Beal, 1997) that literature in Scots from the eighteenth and nineteenth centuries can provide valuable evidence to supplement or pre-date the findings of scholars such as Murray (1873) and Grant and Main Dixon (1921). Tulloch (1980) provides a full account of the language of Walter Scott's novels, noting a number of features which continue to be used in present-day Scots. One example of this is the use of the -*s* inflection for all persons in the present tense. Tulloch explains the rule as follows:

> When the subject is something other than a personal pronoun (e.g. a noun, adjective or relative), or when the pronoun is separated from the verb, the third person singular form may be used for all persons . . . the -s inflection of the third person is, however, used in all cases, even with the pronoun adjacent to the verb, when the tense is the historic present used for the past (1980: 287).

Tulloch provides a number of examples from Scott's novels to exemplify this rule: 'It's gude ale, though I shouldna say that brews it' (*Old Mortality*, 487–8); 'So there's hope Planestanes may be hanged, as many has for a lesser matter' (*Redgauntlet*: 209); 'In troth, I says to him, an' that be the case, Davie, I am misdoubting' (*The Antiquary*: 81). This rule is confirmed by both Murray (1873: 212) and Grant and Main Dixon (1921: 112), and, indeed, is still operating, at least in vernacular Scots, according to Miller (1993: 109) and Macaulay (1991: 161–2). Thus, the literary usage of Walter Scott gives us evidence for the continuity of this rule in Scots throughout the later modern period.

Apart from this 'antiquarian' interest in dialect, the eighteenth, and to a greater extent the nineteenth century, saw the emergence of literature in the urban dialects evolving in the major towns and cities of the Industrial Revolution. The enclosures and mechanization of agriculture against which

Barnes protested had led to migration from the countryside to urban areas, where industrial work was available. The poignancy of this forced migration is evoked in popular songs such as *The Dalesman's Litany*:

> It's hard when fowks can't finnd their wark
> Wheer they've bin bred an' born;
> When I were young I awlus thowt
> I'd bide 'mong t' roots an' corn.
> But I've bin forced to work i' towns,
> So here's my litany:
> Frae Hull, an' Halifax, an' Hell,
> Gooid Lord, deliver me!
> (Moorman, 1918)

This song comes from a collection entitled *Songs of the Ridings* and is typical of a genre of popular writing in urban dialect which emerged from the late eighteenth century. The growth of the urban population in towns and cities such as Newcastle, Manchester, and indeed Halifax, led to the creation of a market for popular forms of literature in dialect. This took forms such as almanacs, columns in local newspapers, and songs and 'recitations' in the mechanics' institutes and music halls that were opened for the entertainment of the urban population. Twentieth-century scholars differ in their views on these forms of dialect literature: Harker (1972) and Vicinius (1974) see these comic dialect works as colluding in the southern and/or middle-class view of dialect as an object of humour or curiosity. Joyce, on the other hand, argues that dialect literature forged an identity for the northern working classes. He writes that 'the intellectual climate in which dialect literature developed was one in which language and literature carried versions of nation and people that offered the labouring classes the possibility of inclusion in the body of society rather than the exclusion so evident in other respects' (1991: 160). I have pointed out elsewhere (Beal, 2001) that these popular writings can give us some insight into the salience of certain features of urban dialect, which are represented by semi-phonetic spelling. One of the most popular songs in the dialect of Tyneside is 'The Blaydon Races', first performed by its composer George 'Geordie' Ridley, at Balmbra's Music Hall in Newcastle on the 5 June 1862. This was included in Thomas Allen's book of *Tyneside Songs* (1891), from which the extract below is taken:

> The rain it poor'd aw the day, an' myed the groon'd quite muddy
> Coffy Johnny had a white hat on – they war shootin' 'whe stole the cuddy'
> There wes spice stalls an munkey shows, an' wives sellin' eiders
> And a chep wiv a happeny roond aboot shootin' now, me boys, for riders

The most frequent feature here is the use of <oo> to represent the pronunciation /uː/ for words such as *shouting* (<shootin'>,and *roundabout* (roond aboot). This pronunciation is a feature of most traditional dialects of the north of England and of Scotland, but in the course of the twentieth century has receded to the very far north as far as English dialects are concerned. It remains a stereotype in Tyneside English, but retains such local resonance, that the spelling <Toon> (and the pronunciation /tuːn/) is used when referring either to the city of Newcastle, or to Newcastle United Football Club (where, incidentally, 'The Blaydon Races' is still sung by supporters). The presence of this feature in nineteenth-century dialect literature suggests that it was already a marker, if not a stereotype, in the Tyneside English of the period. Other features in this extract indicate the presence in the Tyneside dialect of the nineteenth century of features which are today increasingly confined to the usage of working-class males. These include the use of <ye> in *made*, to represent the centring glide /iə/, and <wiv> for *with*, indicating, not TH fronting, but a morphological alternation between vowel and vowel plus /v/ in certain prepositions and auxiliary verbs such as *dae/div; hae/hav, by/biv*, etc. (Beal, forthcoming). Whatever the motivation behind the dialect literature of the late eighteenth and nineteenth centuries, these texts provide us with valuable insights into the features of regional and national dialect that were salient at the time. The evidence is particularly valuable when it comes from representations of urban dialects, because the more scholarly works of this and later periods tended to concentrate on more traditional, rural varieties.

8.2.3   Dialect studies

Whilst, as we have seen in Section 8.2.1 above, normative texts continued to condemn regional dialect throughout the nineteenth and early twentieth centuries, a new, scholarly approach to the study of dialect led to these varieties being viewed as linguistic systems of a validity equal to, if not greater than, Standard English. The impetus towards this view of dialect came from the European scholars of comparative philology, who advocated a historical view of language, according to which dialects are viewed as 'branches' of a parent language and worthy of study in their own right. The 'Neogrammarian Manifesto' (Osthoff and Brugmann, 1878) advocated the study of dialects as 'living' language as opposed to the earlier obsession with reconstructing hypothetical Indo-European ancestor languages. In response to this call Georg Wenker initiated the first dialect survey of German in 1876. Although British scholarship has often been described as lagging behind that of the continent, the English Dialect Society was founded in 1873, and one of the most important works on English dialects was, by this time, already under way. Ellis's *On Early English Pronunciation* (1869–89) contains a vast amount of information on regional pronunciation, but has often been overlooked as a source of evidence because his idiosyncratic notation has deterred scholars. The other great English dialectologist of the nineteenth century, Joseph Wright, was certainly influenced by Neogrammarian thinking. He produced his *Grammar of the Dialect of Windhill* (1892), undertook work for the *English Dialect Dictionary* on behalf of the English Dialect Society (1896–1905) and also produced the *English Dialect Grammar* (1905). These latter two works are still important points of reference for anybody undertaking research into the history of English dialects in England. Although they were certainly 'scientific' in their espousal of the principles of comparative philology, like the *OED* and other great linguistic works of the late nineteenth and early twentieth centuries, they were by no means ideologically or theoretically neutral. Görlach reproduces a letter signed by W. W. Skeat, 'Professor of Anglo-Saxon in the University of Cambridge', requesting funds from the Treasury to support Wright's work on the *English Dialect Dictionary*. The project is presented as a matter of national prestige, as 'a work of the highest interest to many of our fellow-countrymen in all parts of the Empire ... such as no other nation is ever likely to produce, and one which cannot fail to reflect very great credit upon the nation which it most concerns' (Görlach, 1999: 213). Far from being a 'disgrace', as Sheridan thought them, regional dialects, or at least the study of them, are here presented as a matter of national and imperial pride. The philological interest in the historical 'roots' of dialects led to an emphasis on the 'purity' of isolated, rural dialects. This is often expressed as a sense of urgency: a fear that the dialects will be lost unless they are recorded soon. The letter from Skeat stresses this: 'The dialects are dying, and the competent helpers who understand them are waxing old. In a few years it will be too late' (in Görlach, 1999: 213). Apart from Wright's monumental effort, many dictionaries and glossaries of individual dialects were produced by interested and well-educated amateurs: clergymen, schoolmasters and gentlemen. All tell the same story: the dialect must be recorded because it is under threat from the influences of education and urbanization. A few examples here should suffice to convey the prevalent attitude:

> The march of education must sooner or later trample down and stamp out anything like distinctive provincial dialect in England; but when this result shall have been effected, much that is really valuable will be lost to our language, unless an effort is promptly made to collect and record words which, together with the ideas which first rendered them necessary, are rapidly falling into disuse (Parish, 1875: i).

> There can scarcely be a doubt that the genuine South Lancashire dialect, the Folk-Speech of our grandfathers and grandmothers, is fast dying out so far as oral communication is concerned. Railways and compulsory state education are making havoc of the old words (Taylor, 1901: V).

> Before the construction of roads and railways, and more perfect drainage, the towns and villages of east Yorkshire, especially in the low-lying parts, between the Wolds and the sea, were isolated and cut off from communication one with another, by the boggy marshy state of the country; and thus an archaic form of speech has been preserved (Nicholson, 1889: vi).

The last of these is superficially more cheerful, but only because Nicholson has managed to find an area that is still so isolated that 'you may yet find an aged person who has never been out of the village ("toon" he very properly calls it) in which he was born' (1889: vi). This isolation and antiquity is the book's main selling-point. Nicholson later takes up the familiar refrain: 'Railways, telegraph, and School Boards – steam, electricity, and education – are surely killing dialects, even though of late years, much attention has been directed to their preservation in Glossaries and dictionaries – perservation [sic] in books, as antiquarian discoveries' (1889: 1). Many of these dictionaries and glossaries are dependent on earlier sources, such as Ray (1674), Grose (1787) and the kinds of dialect literature referred to in Section 8.2.2 above. Their interest in proving the antiquity of the dialect might lead them to include items no longer used, or to exclude the usage of younger people. Nicholson is so keen to stress the Scandinavian influence on his chosen dialect that he provides a parallel text in Holderness dialect and North Jutland dialect as a frontispiece. He explicitly excludes the dialect of Hull from his account: 'In East Yorkshire there is only one large town, and that, being a sea-port, is cosmopolitan, and contains but a small percentage of dialect-speaking people' (1889: 1–2). Despite these short-comings, these dictionaries and glossaries do provide important evidence for dialectal diversity in nineteenth-century Britain. Wright's *English Dialect Dictionary* goes beyond England and even the British Isles to provide information on a feature which has been observed to be spreading amongst urban dialects in England and Scotland in the late twentieth century: plural *yous*. Macafee considers this to have entered Glasgow speech as a result of Irish-English influence and to be 'now general in Glasgow dialect and apparently spreading from there into other Central dialects' (1982: 45). It has also been observed in the dialects of Liverpool (Hughes and Trudgill, 1996: 96), Newcastle (Beal, 1993: 205) and inner-city Manchester (Cheshire, Edwards and Whittle, 1993: 81). Wright confirms the Irish-English origin of this feature, but also the fact that, by 1905, it had already spread to American and Australian English (the USA and Australia, along with Glasgow, Newcastle, Liverpool and inner-city Manchester, are all homes of the Irish diaspora) (1905: 590):

> YOUS. Pron. Irel Amer. Aus. Also in forms *youse*. Amer. Aus. *Yowz* Don. You, used when speaking to more than one person, cf YEES.
>
> Ir. Boys, boys – look yous at that. BARLOW, *Lisconnel* (1895) 225.
>
> Don. Done! An yows, boys, are all witnesses in this. *Pearson's Mag.* (July 1900).
>
> Amer. Youse fellys is getting' that mule all excited. LLOYD. *Chronic Loafer* (1901) 57.
>
> Aus. We can wait till Hamlet comes, if youse fellows are game. *Longman's Mag.* (Aug. 1901) 301.

The major works on the phonology and phonetics of English produced in the nineteenth and early twentieth centuries also provide early evidence for the occurrence of features which, because they are not found in surveys of rural dialects such as the *SED*, have been assumed to be of more recent origin. We saw in Sections 8.2.1 and 8.2.2 above that TH fronting and labiodental [ʋ] can be found earlier than had been suggested in recent sociolinguistic studies. The same can be said for the glottalization which is perceived as one of the most prominent features of 'Estuary English'. What is more, these early sources suggest that the diffusion of this feature has taken place in a geographical direction opposite to that claimed by, for example, Kerswill and Williams (2002). Bailey (1996: 76) points out that the first person to notice the glottal stop in English was Alexander Melville Bell, who observed in 1860 that it accompanied the sound of *t* in dialects of the west of Scotland. Ellis likewise noted examples of this from central Scotland, in the words *Saturday, better, water, butter* and *wanting*. Jespersen, who according to Bailey visited Britain in 1887, made the following observations:

> The glottal stop ['] produced by a closure of the vocal chords ... is not a regular element of the English sound system. It may sometimes be heard in the beginning of a word before a vowel, though extremely rarely in the South of England; Scotchmen and Americans seem more inclined to use it in this position, though it is never of so regular occurrence as in North German. After a vowel it is found pretty often in the North of England and in Scotland, especially among the uneducated, but by no means exclusively among dialectal speakers ... I have heard it in the following words: in Sheffield *tha't* (very often), *can't, thin'k, po'pe, boo'k*; in Lincoln *I'ts, migh't, cer'tainly, u'p, wha't, bough't, thin'k, si't*; in Glasgow *don't, wan't, o'pen, go't, tha't, brigh'tening, no't*; in Edinburgh in a great many similar words. Sometimes we have the further development that the mouth stop is omitted, as in [wɔ'er] for *water* (Edinburgh) (1909–49: I, 414).

Jespersen's evidence points to preglottalization of all voiceless plosives having spread from Scotland to the borders of the north and the east midlands (Sheffield, Lincoln) by the beginning of the twentieth century, with full glottal replacement of /t/ beginning to occur in Scotland. This is directly contradictory to the principle set out in Kerswill and Williams (2002) that consonants involved in dialect levelling spread from south to north.

It would be impossible in a chapter of this size to provide a full account of all the sources available for the study of British dialects in the later modern period. Instead, I have chosen to concentrate on providing instances where such sources provide insight into processes which have been observed by twentieth and twenty-first-century socio-linguists. I hope that these glimpses will inspire some readers to undertake a more thorough study of some of these sources.

8.3   Beyond the British Isles

8.3.1   An apology

Watts and Trudgill, in the introduction to *Alternative Histories of English,* provide the following critique of earlier histories of English:

> Generally, histories of English have concentrated, as far as the modern period is concerned, on Standard English in England, with an occasional nod in the direction of the USA and with no acknowledgement of the simple fact that during roughly the last 200 years English has also been spoken, and written in a standard form, by sizeable communities of native speakers in Australia, New Zealand and South Africa, to name only the three most populous areas (2002: 1).

If, in the course of this volume, I have concentrated on developments in the Standard English of England, it is because efforts to 'fix' that standard loom so large in this period, and the interplay of standard and non-standard varieties is so important. I hope that I have given at least a 'nod' to other varieties, but it would be a huge undertaking to include the histories of all these varieties of English in one single-authored volume. The *Cambridge History of the English Language* has separate volumes for 'English in Britain and Overseas' (Burchfield, 1994) and 'English in North America' (Algeo, 2001), and the volume edited by Watts and Trudgill is not a seamless whole, but a collection of papers, some of which present research on varieties which have only recently become the object of scholarly interest. All that I can hope to achieve in this last section is a sense of the burgeoning of new varieties of English in the course of the later modern period, and the increasing autonomy of these varieties.

8.3.2 'Divided by a common language': American English and British English

We saw in Chapter 3 that, as early as 1789, just 13 years after the Declaration of Independence and six years after the Peace of Versailles, Webster declared independence for American English: 'customs, habits and *language*, as well as government should be national. America should have her *own* distinct from all the world' (1789: 179). Of course, American English had been developing ever since the first English-speaking colonists arrived at the beginning of the seventeenth century. New lexical items, coined to describe the flora, fauna and landscape of the new country, were very soon arriving back in Britain through the vehicles of reports, letters and travellers' tales. Mencken points out that, 'as early as 1621, Alexander Gill was noting in his "Logonomia Anglica" that *maize* and *canoe* were making their way into English' (Mencken, 1936: 3). The contact between the various regional dialects of the English-speaking colonists and the languages of the Native Americans and of other European colonists would also have been influencing the separate development of English in America for many years before the Revolution. However, it is only after America's political independence from Britain that American English, or 'American', begins to be 'ascertained' and 'fixed' according to its own standards set out in works such as Webster's *Compendious Dictionary* (1806) and *American Dictionary* (1832). The *OED*'s first citation for the word *Americanism* in the sense of 'a word or phrase peculiar to, or extending from, the United States' is from John Witherspoon, a Scottish clergyman who became president of Princeton. The first edition of the *OED* gives the date of this as 1794, but Mencken dates the same citation as having been printed in *The Pennsylvania Journal and Weekly Advertiser*. Witherspoon defines *Americanism* as 'an use of phrases or terms, or a construction of sentences, even among people of rank and education, different from the use of the same terms or phrases, or the construction of similar sentences in Great Britain' (cited in Mencken, 1936: 5–6). Witherspoon goes on to tell us how he invented the term: 'the word *Americanism*, which I have coined for the purpose, is exactly similar in its formation and significance to the word *Scotticism*' (Mencken, 1936). The analogy here is apt, for Witherspoon had brought with him to America all the linguistic baggage of the Scottish Enlightenment. Just as we saw in Chapters 5 and 7 that Scottish authors such as Buchanan and Hume took it upon themselves to rid their fellow countrymen of Scotticisms, so Witherspoon adopted the same attitude to the language of his newly adopted compatriots. The language used by Witherspoon in his condemnation of Americanisms is exactly the same as that of British normative texts of the same period:

> I have heard in this country, in the senate, at the bar, and from the pulpit, and
> see daily in dissertations from the press, errors in grammar, improprieties and
> vulgarisms which hardly any person of the same class in point of rank and
> literature would have fallen into in Great Britain (Mencken, 1936).

In the above paragraph, I have unwittingly used one of the 'Americanisms' condemned by Witherspoon: *fellow countrymen* was, he asserted 'an evident tautology'. However, as Mencken points out, 'Witherspoon's strictures ... fell upon deaf ears' (1936: 7). The political agenda in post-revolutionary America favoured Webster's 'linguistic Declaration of Independence' (1936: 11). This did not mean that a less prescriptive attitude to language prevailed in the new nation: on the contrary, America's alliance with France brought calls for an academy for 'correcting, improving and ascertaining the English language' in America, reminiscent of Swift's *Proposal* of 1712. John Adams made such a plea in a letter to the president of Congress:

> It will have a happy effect upon the union of States to have a public standard
> for all persons in every part of the continent to appeal to, both for the signifi-
> cation and pronunciation of the language ... English is destined to be in the
> next and succeeding centuries more generally the language of the world than
> Latin was of the last or French is in the present age. The reason of this is
> obvious, because the increasing population of America, and their universal
> connection and correspondence with all nations will, aided by the influence of
> England in the world, whether great or small, force their language into general
> use, in spite of all the obstacles that may be thrown in their way, if any such
> there should be (1780, cited in Mencken, 1936: 8).

We saw in Chapter 3 that Webster took up this theme of American English as the future world language and that, with hindsight, the confidence of these citizens in the future influence of their country and their language was not misplaced. Webster's dictionaries gave the stamp of approval to thousands of 'Americanisms', and introduced the moderately reformed spelling which is the most obvious distinguishing feature of written American English to this day. Throughout the nineteenth century, and much of the twentieth, the attitude to American English of British, and especially English, commentators has been deprecatory, ranging from the patronizing to the downright hostile. An example of the former is an article in the *Edinburgh* on John Quincy Adams's *Letters on Silesia*: 'The style of Mr Adams is in general very tolerable English; which, for an American composition, is no moderate praise' (1804, cited in Mencken, 1936: 14). The more hostile comments often combine condemnation of Americans' use of English with that of their morals and politics. The extract from Alford cited in Chapter 5 (p. 100) is one example of this, but Mencken cites a much earlier one from the *European Magazine and London Review* of 1797. Here, the author objects to Thomas Jefferson's use of the term *to belittle*:

> '*Belittle!*' What an expression! It may be an elegant one in Virginia, and even perfectly intelligible; but, for our part, all we can do is to *guess* at its meaning. For shame, Mr. Jefferson! Why, after trampling upon the honour of our country, and representing it as little better than a land of barbarism – why, we say, perpetually trample upon the very grammar of our language, and make that appear as Gothic as, from your description, our manners are rude? Freely, good sir, will we forgive all your attacks, impotent as they are illiberal, upon our *national character*; but for the future spare – O spare, we beseech you, our mother-tongue! (cited in Mencken, 1936: 14).

Criticism of American English by British commentators takes on a more urgent tone in the twentieth century, when improved transport and communications and, above all, the availability of phonographic recordings and films, brings the two varieties into closer contact. Mencken cites a report of the London bureau of Associated Press from 1920:

> England is apprehensive lest the vocabularies of her youth become corrupted through incursions of American slang. Trans-Atlantic tourists in England note with interest the frequency with which resort is made to 'Yankee Talk' by British song and play writers seeking to enliven their productions. Bands and orchestras throughout the country when playing popular music play American selections almost exclusively. American songs monopolize the English music hall and musical comedy stage. But it is the subtitle of the American moving picture film which, it is feared, constitutes the most menacing threat to the vaunted English purity of speech (cited in Mencken, 1936: 38).

A more neutral tone is taken by the linguistic scholars of the period, who likewise note the influx of American vocabulary into British English. Craigie, in the preface to the second edition of the *OED*, writes:

> For some two centuries, roughly down to 1820, the passage of new words or senses across the Atlantic was regularly westward; practically the only exceptions were terms which denoted articles or products peculiar to the new country. With the Nineteenth Century, however, the contrary current begins to set in, bearing with it many a piece of driftwood to the shores of Britain, there to be picked up and incorporated in the structure of the language. The variety of these contributions is no less notable than their number (1927, cited in Strang, 1970: 35).

Even here, the metaphor of driftwood seems slightly derogatory, but it is evident that, in the twentieth century, the term 'Americanism' is understood primarily as a word or sense imported into British English from American English rather than, in Witherspoon's sense, an 'error, impropriety or vulgarism' peculiar to American usage. Foster devotes the first chapter, and approximately one-fifth of the pages of his (1968) *The Changing English Language* to 'the impact of America'. He notes that 'the Annual Register for 1922 records that Sinclair Lewis's *Babbitt* had a glossary appended to it in the British edition in order to explain certain Americanisms', but the author commented that 'the cinematograph, and the theatre . . . will have given the ordinary man a sufficiently large American vocabulary for his needs' (1968: 17). The *Dictionary of Modern American Usage* was first published in 1935, designed 'to assist English people who visit the United States, or who meet American friends, or who read American books and magazines, or who listen to American "talkies"' (Foster, 1968). Of course, the introduction of 'talkies' from 1927 meant that the majority of British people could hear an American accent for the first time, but perhaps the greatest period of American influence on British English came during and after World War II, when American servicemen were stationed in Britain and came into direct contact with British civilians. Strang cites a number of examples from a 'Short Guide to Britain' produced by the American War Department as a guide to its servicemen stationed here during World War II. This is a glossary in which American terms are 'translated' into British English. Strang marks a number of terms which, according to her recollection, were 'already in British usage during the war years': *battery* (for British *accumulator*), *brief-case* (*portfolio*), *cheese-cloth* (*butter-muslin*), *dessert* (*sweet course*), *farm-hand* (*agricultural labourer*), *junk* (*rubbish*), *peanut* (*monkey-nut*), *scrambled eggs* (*buttered eggs*) and *sweater* (*pullover*) (1970: 37). All of these American terms are now normal British usage, and some of the 'British' terms, such as *buttered eggs* now sound totally alien. The same can be said for some of the pairs of terms not marked by Strang, such as American *weather man* versus British *clerk of the weather* and *thriller* to describe a genre of novel, as opposed to the British *shocker*. Objections to 'Americanisms' continue to be expressed by British commentators throughout the twentieth century (and indeed into the twenty-first), but, with a few years' hindsight, these objections seem amusingly fusty. Foster notes that the word *teenager* was 'well-established by the late nineteen-forties', but that 'a contributor to the *Daily Mail* voiced the opinion of many when he wrote that "our daughter is what is hideously termed a teen-ager" (25 March 1954)' (1968: 56, 64). Foster goes on to suggest that the vehemence of objections to 'Americanisms' in the immediate post-war period may reflect British resentment of the 'relative decline of the military and economic power of Britain, as contrasted with those of the U.S.A. and the Soviet Union'. He cites a correspondent to the *Radio Times*, who asks: 'Why has the B.B.C. succumbed to the use of the word "Britisher"? . . . Britons never shall be slaves, not even to American forms of diction' (17 June 1955) (1968: 64). Webster had predicted that a number of circumstances would 'produce, in course of time, a language in North America as different from the future language of England as the modern Dutch, Danish or Swedish are from the German, or from one another' (1789: 22). In the immediate aftermath of the American Revolution, he was not in a position to predict either the effects of the 'special relationship' between Britain and the USA or the astonishing developments in transport and communication which would bring the speakers of these two branches of English into increasingly close contact with one another. He would probably have been pleased by the eventual autonomy of American English, and its influence over what he saw as the degenerate language of Britain. Today, it is acknowledged that the history of American English, like that of British English, is not that of a single homogeneous entity, and that its history is made up of many influences. Dillard notes at the end of his *A History of American English*:

> Our language history unites us with Great Britain, it is true, and also with Europe; the contact varieties which have figured so much in our language history link us more than we had suspected with the so-called Third World.

Canadian English developed initially as a result of Americans who opposed the Revolution fleeing from the Eastern USA to Ontario and New Brunswick from 1776. This migration of Americans to Canada continued until 1812, so that Priestley could state that 'the greater part of the English-speaking population in Canada was American in origin' (1951: 73). This, together with the proximity to, and influence of, the USA accounts for the similarity between these two varieties. Immigrants from the British Isles, especially Scotland and Ireland, came in large numbers during the nineteenth century, and the greater concentration of Scots and Irish migrants to the maritime provinces of Nova Scotia. New Brunswick and Prince Edward Island led to the development of distinctive dialects in these areas. Newfoundland did not even join the Canadian federation until 1949 and its extreme isolation, divided from the rest of Canada by Francophone Quebec, and settlement pattern of Irish and south-western English have led to the development of a variety distinctive enough to have its own dictionary (Story, Kirwin and Widdowson, 1982). Awareness of Canadian English as a distinctive national variety comes later than that of American English. Canadian English has, until very recently, been discussed in terms of the influences from America on the one hand and Britain on the other.

Bloomfield, for instance, asserted that 'Canadian English is basically eighteenth-century American English modified by Southern Standard English and the English taught by Scots schoolteachers' (1947: 4). General awareness of distinctions between American and Canadian English tends to focus on a few Canadian shibboleths, such as the tendency to end sentences with *eh* (a feature also found in Scots and some northern English dialects); 'Canadian Raising' whereby /au, ai/ are pronounced /ʌu, ʌi/ before voiceless consonants as in *house, right*; and a few lexical oppositions such as (Canadian first) *chesterfield/sofa; pop/soda; blinds/shades; cellar/basement; tin/can; braces/suspenders;* and *tap/faucet*. In most of these cases, the 'Canadian' word is also used in Britain. However, the publication of *A Dictionary of Canadianisms on Historical Principles* (Avis, 1967) drew attention to lexical innovations that are Canadian in origin, such as the many compounds with *snow* including *snowbird; snow-buggy; snow-water* and *snow-bunny*. Writing at the end of our period, Priestley suggests that 'Canadian speech has tended to preserve a national identity' (1951: 76). He suggests that Canadian participation in the two world wars brought a renewed appreciation of British culture and language as a counterbalance to the influence of America, and that 'the half-century [1900–50] has ... brought about the emergence of a distinct Canadian national character, and a distinct Canadian language'. Much more research has been conducted on Canadian English in the second half of the twentieth century, but within the period covered by this volume we can see this variety emerging from the twin shadows of British and American English.

8.3.3   English transported: the development of Australian English

One consequence of the American Revolution was that Britain no longer had the option of transporting its convicts to Virginia. In order to relieve the overcrowded jails of the home country, a penal settlement was founded at Port Jackson in 1788. Between this date and the end of transportation in 1852, 160,000 convicts were transported to Australia from various parts of the British Isles, including Ireland. As well as the convicts, small numbers of wardens and military personnel were sent to oversee and govern the colony, and, from 1820, free settlers came in increasing numbers, even more so after the 'gold rushes' of the 1850s. According to Horvath (1985), the division between convicts and free settlers created the social stratification of early Australian society and, eventually, the variation in Australian English between the 'Broad Australian' of convicts and their descendants, the 'Cultivated Australian' of the governing class, and the 'General Australian' of free settlers. It is generally agreed that the distinguishing characteristics of Australian English are largely a result of dialect contact, with the predominant dialects amongst convicts and free settlers being those of urban areas in the south of England (notably London), and to a lesser, but not insignificant extent, of Ireland (Gordon and Sudbury, 2002). The stigma of the penal colony was to affect perceptions of Australian English, from within and outside Australia, until very recently. Baker, whom Turner refers to as 'the Mencken of Australian English Studies' (1994: 327), draws a parallel between the development of American English and Australian English:

> It is scarcely necessary to emphasize that the history of this country is in many ways similar to that of the United States. The original white inhabitants were English-speaking and many of them had little love for the England they had left behind. They were faced with new modes of life, new environments and the heartbreak of carving out a livelihood out of countries they did not under-stand or know. Both countries were distant from their joint motherland; and, since it was impossible for them to be industrial, both countries were close to the earth and all that grew from it (1966: 4).

As Turner's comment suggests, Baker's was the first serious historical study of Australian English, but, from early in the nineteenth century, derogatory comments were made about the language of the colony. Baker cites Edward Gibbon Wakefield writing in 1829 that 'terms of slang and flash are used, as a matter of course, everywhere, from the gaols to the Viceroy's palace, not excepting the Bar and the Bench. No doubt they will be reckoned quite parliamentary, as soon as we obtain a parliament' (1966: 8). 'Flash' was one of the terms used for criminal slang or cant, and, well into the twentieth century, the distinctive vocabulary of Australian English is treated as slang, and a matter for humorous comment. Turner notes that 'a serious dictionary of Australian usage is likely to be reviewed under a heading such as "Fair dinkum cobber, take a dekko at this yabber"' (1994: 320). Indeed, the first dictionaries written on Australian soil were dictionaries of slang: the *Vocabulary of the Flash Language* was compiled by James Hardy Vaux, a convict in Newcastle, New South Wales, and is really a record of criminal slang rather than Australianisms as such. Baker notes that *The Australian Slang Dictionary* (c. 1880), described on the cover as 'comprising all the Quaint Slang Words and Flash Dialogues in use in the Australian shadows of life' (1966: 26), is mainly made up of English slang. The first serious attempt at a dictionary of Australian English was Morris, whose (1898) *Austral English* is unjustly criticized by Baker for including words such as *Christmas* on the grounds that the word must have different connotations in a land where the festival takes place in the summer. In the same year, Lake produced a supplement to Webster's *International Dictionary* of over 700

Australasian words and phrases. Clearly, by the end of the nineteenth century, there was an awareness of Australian English as distinct from British and American Englishes, but the impetus to create an independent national variety came much later to Australia than it did to the USA, probably because, to this day, Australia's head of state is still the British monarch: there has not been an Australian Revolution. As late as 1966, Baker could write, albeit disparagingly, of 'the philistines who still talk of England as *Home*, though they have lived in Australia all their lives, and who scorn things Australian because they happen to belong to this country' (1966: 21). He cites a plea from Norman Bartlett in 1941:

> Australians need to be increasingly aware of themselves as a people with distinct characteristics and distinct duties towards themselves and others ... The Australian future should be worked out as a natural extension of Australian characteristics, an expression of our robust, sardonic, masculine egalitarianism (1966: 21).

Fifteen years earlier, Partridge and Clark, in what now seems a quaintly named chapter on 'Dominions English', write of what they term 'nationalist movements' which advocate linguistic independence for certain territories. They suggest that of the 'Dominions Australia is the only country in which such a movement is both strong and vocal' (1951: 64). In a supplementary article included as an appendix, A. K. Thompson suggests that the two world wars were instrumental in creating a sense of Australian patriotism and 'a heightened interest of Australians in Australia' (1951: 334). British perceptions of Australia were changed during these periods too, for, just as ordinary Britons and Americans came into contact when American service-men were stationed in Britain, British men also served alongside Australian 'diggers', particularly during World War II. It would be interesting to see whether Australianisms entered British servicemen's slang at this point. The experience of the two world wars seems to have turned the tide of Australian opinion concerning the distinct identity of their nation and language, but, until very recently, there was still a tendency for at least some Australians to view the RP-like 'Cultivated Australian' as superior to 'Broad Australian'. Thompson wrote that 'in Australia there is still a strong tendency to think that speech which approaches most closely to Southern English is the best' but that 'it is inevitable that before very long some form of Educated Australian will become standard Australian speech' (1951: 336). His words were to prove partly true: by the end of the twentieth century, Australian English was to become an aspirational variety for young Britons, just as American English had been. This was largely due to the influence of television (mainly soap operas such as *Neighbours* and *Home and Away*) and the interaction of young, backpacking Britons and Australians in both hemispheres. Australian terms such as *uni* ('university') and *barbie* (barbecue) have become established in British usage. However, the variety which is becoming the norm in Australia is General Australian: both the Broad and the Cultivated varieties are, according to Horvath (1985), increasingly rare.

8.3.4   Other varieties of English

It may seem strange to be placing under this heading what have become major national varieties of English such as New Zealand English, as well as less-researched varieties. I refer any reader offended by this treatment of his or her variety to the apology in Section 8.3.1 above. This volume is intended to deal with developments in the history of English up to the end of World War II and, whilst all the varieties referred to in this section were certainly evolving during this period, there is neither as much research on these varieties conducted before 1950, nor as much of a sense within these areas of separate varieties with endogenous standards until much more recently. To gain an insight into the way these varieties were regarded in the immediate post-war period, we can turn again to Partridge and Clarke's chapter on 'Dominions English'. Partridge and Clarke were conscious of being quite avant-garde in even including such a chapter: they protest that 'certain Englishmen . . . speak as if the only kind of English with a right to exist were the English spoken by those who, born in England, have spent most of their lives there' (1951: 64). They go on to state that 'the most English of the Dominions, New Zealand does not wish to be linguistically different' and that 'South Africa, despite its intense political nationalism . . . has no strong linguistic nationalism' (1951: 65). Both these countries were not colonized by English speakers in any great numbers until the nineteenth century, and so the resulting varieties of English are 'younger' than American, Canadian or even Australian English. In the case of South Africa, the variety known as 'South African English', defined by Gordon and Sudbury as that 'spoken as a first language by white South Africans', is a minority variety but is, as they acknowledge, that which has 'been the focus of most studies of English in South Africa' (2002: 72). The British annexed the Cape of Good Hope from the Dutch in 1795, but the first significant wave of English-speaking settlers did not arrive until 1820. A second wave came to Natal in the 1850s and a third group of European settlers, some of whom were English-speaking, arrived in the Transvaal and Witwatersrand regions when diamonds and gold were discovered in the 1880s. The variety of English that developed in the Cape was less prestigious than that of

Natal, mainly because of the lower-class origins of the earlier settlers and the tendency for Natal settlers to maintain links with Britain. By the end of the nineteenth century, when the discovery of gold and diamonds brought more European settlers and greater prosperity, white South African society was stratified with new settlers at the top, Natalians in the middle, and Cape colonists at the bottom, and their varieties of English were likewise stratified. Gordon and Sudbury tell us that 'RP was quickly established as the most prestigious accent in this increasingly hierarchical society. Since Natal English shared similarities with RP, it was recognised as not being significantly different from British English by other settlers ... For that reason it gained the status of an acceptable, local informal standard, (2002: 75). For many years after World War II, RP was still the prestige accent of white South African English. Lanham cites the BBC correspondent John Simpson as commenting on this in 1973:

> Listening to the radio is like switching on the BBC Home Service in the days before Suez ... the accents of the English services are impeccably upper middle-class. It's only when people are interviewed that you hear the authentic South African being spoken (1996: 24).

Since then, though, 'respectable' South African English, based largely on Natal English, has increasingly taken over as the reference variety. Serious academic study of South African English is relatively recent, with Lanham's work published from the late 1970s onwards and dictionaries of South African English appearing in 1987 (Branford) and 1996 (Silva).

New Zealand English is the youngest of what we might call the 'major' varieties of English, as the first sizeable settlement by English speakers dates from 1840. The first settlers were 'respectable' British people who came to seek a better life. Gordon and Sudbury comment that 'their aim was to create a new Britain in the South Pacific in the context of British law, religion, education, social values and practices' (2002: 78). A second wave of immigrants arrived in the 1860s, when gold was discovered: these came from all over the world, including a sizeable number from Australia. Bauer (1994: 386) points out that, in the early days of settlement, communications between New Zealand and Australia were better than those between different parts of New Zealand. The third wave of settlement came between 1870 and 1885, when migrants from the British Isles were actively recruited with, according to Gordon and Sudbury, over 100,000 arriving in the 1870s. Although earlier writers stress the continuity between educated New Zealand English and RP/Standard English, recent research on an archive of recordings of the first New Zealand-born 'Pakeha' has demonstrated that a distinct New Zealand accent had already evolved by the 1870s. What has changed in the course of the later twentieth century is that, as in Australia and South Africa, an endogenous prestige variety has taken over from RP and the national variety has become an object of serious historical and socio-linguistic study. The ONZE (Origins and Evolution of New Zealand English) project is currently under way, and a *Dictionary of New Zealandisms on Historical Principles* was published in 1997 (Orson).

If research into New Zealand English is of relatively recent origin, then this is even more the case for what Trudgill terms the 'lesser-known varieties of English' (2002: 29–44). In the course of the later modern period, English was to expand into most parts of the world, with distinctive varieties evolving in each territory. Trudgill's chapter provides a résumé of the histories of these varieties, and points to ongoing research, much of which is marked as forthcoming. Trudgill's sweep of history and geography invokes a sense of the expansion of English in this period, and of the exciting projects still to be undertaken in the study of 'extraterritorial' varieties of English:

> In the nineteenth century ... English expanded to Hawaii, and into the southern hemisphere – not only to Australia, New Zealand and South Africa, as is well known, but also to the South Atlantic Islands of St Helena, Tristan da Cunha and the Falklands, and in the Pacific to Pitcairn Island and Norfolk Island. There was also expansion from the Caribbean islands to eastern coastal areas of Costa Rica and Panama; and the repatriation of African Americans to Sierra Leone and Liberia, as well as an African-American settlement in the Dominican Republic. During this time also, Caribbean islands which had hitherto been Francophone started on a slow process of becoming anglophone to different degrees: Dominica, St Lucia, Trinidad and Tobago, Grenada and St Vincent and the Grenadines. Other little-known anglophone colonies which still survive today were also established during the nineteenth century in southern Brazil, by American southerners fleeing the aftermath of the Civil War, and in the Benin islands of Japan, by New England and Hawaiian Whalers and seamen, and on one of the Cook Islands in the South Pacific. There are also today long-standing indigenous groups of British-origin native anglophones in Namibia, Botswana, Zimbabwe and Kenya (2002: 29–30).

I am conscious that I have not even begun to discuss here the development of second-language varieties of English in areas such as India, Pakistan and West Africa, or of creole varieties. Such coverage would be beyond the scope of this book, but it is important to remember that most of these varieties, like those discussed above, had their origins in the later modern period. Whilst much of this book has been concerned with the attempts of British writers to create a uniform standard variety, it is fitting that it should end with an assertion of the increasing diversification of Englishes in 'modern times'.

References

Aarsleff, H. (1967). *The Study of Language in England 1780–1860*. London: Athlone Press; 2nd edition, 1983.

Abercrombie, D. (1965). 'RP and local accent', in *Studies in Phonetics and Linguistics*. London: Oxford University Press, pp. 10–15.

Adams, J. (1799). *The Pronunciation of the English Language Vindicated from Imputed Anomaly and Caprice*. Edinburgh: J. Moir for the Author.

Aitchison, J. (1981). *Language Change: Progress or Decay?* London: Fontana; 2nd edition, 1991.

Alford, H. [1864] (1870). *The Queen's English: Notes on Speaking and Writing*. London: Strahan.

Algeo, J. (ed.) (2001). *The Cambridge History of the English Language*, volume VI: *English in North America*. Cambridge: Cambridge University Press.

Alston, R. C. (ed.) (1967–70). *English Linguistics 1500–1800*. London: Scolar Press.

Andresen, J. T. (1990). *Linguistics in America 1769–1924: A Critical History*. London: Routledge.

Anon (1759). 'Review of M. Le Blond *The Military Engineer*'. *The Critical Review* 8: 177–8.

Anon (1789). 'Review of E. Hugill (translation) *The Field Engineer*'. *The Critical Review* 67: 328–30.

Anon (1878). *Enquire Within upon Everything, to which is added Enquire Within upon Fancy Needlework*. London: Houlston and Sons.

Arnaud, R. (1983). 'On the progress of the progressive in the private correspondence of famous British people (1800–1880)', in S. Jacobson (ed.), *1982 Papers from the Second Scandinavian Symposium on Syntactic Variation, Stockholm 15–16 May*. Stockholm: Almqvist and Wiksell, pp. 83–94.

Arnaud, R. (1998). 'The development of the progressive in 19th century English: a quantitative survey'. *Language Variation and Change* 10: 123–52.

Ash, J. (1763). *Grammatical Institutes: or an Easy Introduction to Dr Lowth's Grammar*. London: E. and C. Cilly.

Austin, F. (1984). 'Double negatives and the eighteenth century'. *English Historical Linguistics* 3: 138–48.

Avis, W. S. (1967). *A Dictionary of Canadianisms on Historical Principles*. Toronto: W. G. Gage.

Bailey, N. (1721). *Universal Etymological English Dictionary*. London: E. Bell et al.

Bailey, N. (1730). *Dictionarium Britanicum*. London: T. Cox.

Bailey, R. W. (1996). *Nineteenth-Century English*. Ann Arbor: University of Michigan Press.

Bailey, R. W. (2003). 'The ideology of English in the long nineteenth century', in Dossena and Jones (eds) (2003), pp. 21–44.

Baker, S. J. (1945). *The Australian Language*. Sydney and London: Angus and Robertson Ltd.

Baker, S. J. (1966). *The Australian Language*, 2nd edition. Sydney: Angus and Robertson.

Barber, C. (1964). *Linguistic Change in Present–day English*. Edinburgh: Oliver and Boyd.

Barber, C. (1976). *Early Modern English*. London: Deutsch.

Barber, C. (1981). 'Thou and you in Shakespeare's Richard III'. *Leeds Studies in English*, n.s. XII: 273–89. Reprinted in V. Salmon and E. Burness (eds), *Reader in the Language of Shakespearean Drama*. Amsterdam: Benjamins, pp. 163–79.

Barnes, William (1878). *An Outline of Speech-Craft*. London: Kegan Paul.

Batchelor, T. (1809). *An Orthoëpical Analysis of the English Language*. London.

Bauer, L. (1994). *New Zealand English*, in Burchfield (ed.) (1994), pp. 382–429.

Baugh, A. C. and T. Cable (1978). *A History of the English Language*, 3rd edition. London: Routledge and Kegan Paul.

Beal, J. C. (1993). 'The grammar of Tyneside and Northumbrian English', in J. and L. Milroy (eds), *Real English: The Grammar of English Dialects in the British Isles*. London: Longman, pp. 187–242.

Beal, J. C. (1997). 'Syntax and morphology', in C. Jones (ed.), *The Edinburgh History of the Scots Language*. Edinburgh: Edinburgh University Press, pp. 355–77.

Beal, J. C. (1999), *English Pronunciation in the Eighteenth Century: Thomas Spence's 'Grand Repository of the English Language'*. Oxford: Clarendon Press.

Beal, J. C. (2000). 'From Geordie Ridley to Viz: popular literature in Tyneside English'. *Language and Literature* 9(4): 343–59.

Beal, J. C. (2000). 'HappY-tensing: a recent innovation?', in R. Bermudez-Ortero, D. Denison, R. M. Hogg and C. B. McCully, (eds), *Generative Theory and Corpus Studies*. Berlin: Mouton de Gruyter, pp. 483–97.

Beal, J. C. (2002). 'Out in left field: spelling reformers of the eighteenth century', *Transactions of the Philological Society* 100(1): 5–23.

Beal, J. C. (2004). '"Marks of disgrace": attitudes to non-standard pronunciation in eighteenth-century pronouncing dictionaries', in R. Lass and M. Dossena (eds), *Historical Dialectology*. Bern: Lang, pp. 1–21.

Beal, J. C. (forthcoming). 'Geordie nation: language and identity in the north-east of England'. To appear in *Lore and Language* 17, 2004.

Beal, J. C. and K. P. Corrigan (2000). 'Comparing the present with the past to predict the future for Tyneside English'. *Newcastle and Durham Working Papers in Linguistics*, ed. M. Akita and K. Oga, 6: 13–30.

Beal, J. C. and K. P. Corrigan (forthcoming). 'A tale of two dialects: relativisation. in Newcastle and Sheffield', in M. Filppula, M. Palander, J. Klemola and E. Penttilä (eds), *Dialects across Borders*. Amsterdam: Benjamins.

Beattie, J. (1787). *Scoticisms, Arranged in Alphabetical Order*. Edinburgh.

Blackbourn, D. (1998). *The Long Nineteenth Century: A History of Germany, 1780–1918*. Oxford: Oxford University Press.

Blake, N. F. (1996). *History of the English Language*. Basingstoke: Macmillan.

Blank, Paula (1996). *Broken English: Dialects and the Politics of Language in Renaissance Writings*. London: Routledge.

Bloomfield, M. W. (1947). 'Canadian English and its relationship to eighteenth-century American speech'. *Journal of English and Germanic Philology* 47: 59–66.

Blount, T. (1656). *Glossographia*. London: T. Newcombe for H. Moseley.

Bolton, W. F. (1966). *The English Language: Essays by English and American Men of Letters*, volume I: *1490–1839*. Cambridge: Cambridge University Press.

Bolton, W. F. and D. Crystal (1969). *The English Language. Essays by English and American Men of Letters*, volume II: *1858–1964*. Cambridge: Cambridge University Press.

Bourcier, G. (1981). *An Introduction to the History of the English Language*, English adaptation by Cecily Clark. Cheltenham: Stanley Thomas.

Branford, J. (1987). *A Dictionary of South African English*. Cape Town: Oxford University Press.

Breen, H. H. (1857). *Modern English Literature: Its Blemishes and Defects*. London: Longman, Brown, Green and Longmans.

Brewer, C. (1993). 'The second edition of the Oxford English Dictionary'. *Review of English Studies*, n.s. 44: 313–42.

Brewer, C. (2000). 'OED sources', in Mugglestone (ed.) (2000), pp. 40–59.

Bronstein, A. J. and E. K. Sheldon (1951). 'Derivatives of Middle English O in eighteenth- and nineteenth-century dictionaries'. *American Speech* 24: 81–9.

Brown, G. (1823). *The Institutes of English Grammar*. New York: Samuel S. and William Wood.

Brown, R. (1700). *The English School Reformed*. London.

Brown, R, and C. Gilman (1960). 'The Pronouns of Power and Solidarity', in T. A. Sebeok, *Style in Language*. Cambridge, MA: MIT Press, pp. 253–76.

Brown, R. and C. Gilman (1989). 'Politeness theory and Shakespeare's four major tragedies'. *Language in Society* 18: 159–212.

Bryant, M. M. (1962). *Modern English and its Heritage*, 2nd edition. New York: Macmillan.

Buchanan, J. (1753). *The Complete English Scholar*. London.

Buchanan, J. (1757). *Linguae Britannicae Vera Pronuntiatio*. London: A. Millar.

Buchanan, J. (1762). *The British Grammar*. London: A. Millar.

Buchanan, J. (1766). *Essay Towards Establishing a Standard for an Elegant and Uniform Pronunciation of the English Language, Throughout the British Dominions*. London: A. Millar.

Buchanan, J. (1769). *A Regular English Syntax. Wherein is exhibited, the whole variety of English construction, properly exemplified*. London: printed for G. Keith, J. Johnson and J. Payne, G. Pearch, F. Blyth and G. Burnett.

Bullokar, W. (1580). *The Booke at Large*. London.

Bullokar, W. (1586). *Bref Grammar for English*. London.

Burchfield, R. (ed.) (1994). *The Cambridge History of the English Language*, volume V: *English in Britain and Overseas, Origins and Development*. Cambridge: Cambridge University Press.

Burchfield, R. (1996). *Fowler's Modern English Usage*, 3rd edition. Oxford: Clarendon Press.

Burke, P. (1978). *Popular Culture in Early Modern Europe*. London: Temple Smith.

Burn, J. (1786). *A Pronouncing Dictionary of the English Language*, 2nd edition. Glasgow: Alex Adam for the Author and James Duncan.

Burney, Fanny (1789). Letter to Esther Burney, in *The Journals and Letters of Fanny Burney (Madame D'Arblay)*, volume 2: *Courtship and Marriage, 1793; Letters 40–121*, edited by Joyce Hemlow. Oxford: Clarendon Press.

Butt, J. (ed.) (1965). *The Poems of Alexander Pope*. London: Methuen.

Campbell, G. (1776). *The Philosophy of Rhetoric*. Edinburgh.

Cameron, D. (1995). *Verbal Hygiene*. London: Routledge.

Carew, Richard. (1595). *The Excellency of the English Tongue*, in William Camden, *Remaines concerning Britaine: But Especially England, and the Inhabitants Thereof*, 1614.

Carroll, J. (ed.) (1964). *Selected Letters of Samuel Richardson*. Oxford: Clarendon Press.

Cave, A. (2001). 'Language Variety and Communicative Style as Local and Subcultural Identity in a South Yorkshire Coalmining Community'. Ph.D. thesis, University of Sheffield.

Cawdrey, R. (1604). *A Table Alphabetical*. London: I.R. for E. Weaver.

Censor (*c.* 1880). *Don't: A Manual of Mistakes and Improprieties More or Less Prevalent in Conduct and Speech*. London: Field and Tuer; facsimile edition Whitstable: Prior Publications, 1990; revised and enlarged edition London: Ward, Lock and Co. Ltd, *c.* 1950.

Cheshire, J., V. Edwards and P. Whittle (1993). 'Non-standard English and dialect levelling', in James and Lesley Milroy (eds), *Real English*. London: Longman, pp. 53–96.

Chomsky, N. and M. Halle (1968). *The Sound Pattern of English*. New York: Harper and Row.

Cobbett, W. (1818). *A Grammar of the English Language*. London.

Cobbett, W. (1819). *A Grammar of the English Language, in a Series of Letters*, 2nd edition. London: printed for John M. Cobbett.

Cobbett, W. (1823). *A Grammar of the English Language, in a Series of Letters, to which are added Six Lessons, intended to prevent Statesmen from using false grammar, and from writing in an awkward manner*. London: printed for John M. Cobbett. Reprinted with an introduction by R. Burchfield. Oxford: Oxford University Press, 1984.

Cobbett, W. (1830). *Rural Rides* London: A. Cobbett.

Cochrane, J. and J. Humphreys (2003). *Between You and I: A Little Book of Bad English*. London: Icon.

Cohen, M. (1977). *Sensible Words: Linguistic Practice in England, 1640–1785*. London and Baltimore: Johns Hopkins University Press.

Coleridge, H. (1859). *A Glossarial Index to the Printed English Literature of the 13th Century*. London: Trübner.

Coles, E. (1674). *The Compleat English Schoolmaster*. London: Peter Parker.

Coles, E. (1676). *An English Dictionary*. London: S. Crouch.

Cooper, C. (1685). *Grammatica Linguae Anglicanae*, see Sundby (1953).

Cooper, C. (1687). *The English Teacher*, see Sundby (1953).

Coote, E. (1596). *The English Schoole Maister*. London: Widow Olwyn for Ralph Jackson and Robert Dexter.

Corfield, P. (1991). *Language, History and Class*. Oxford: Basil Blackwell.

Craigie, W. A. (1927). *English Spelling, its Rules and Reasons*. New York.

Craigie, W. A. (1933). Preface to the 1933 edition of the *Oxford English Dictionary* ed. J. A. H. Murray, H. Bradley, W. A. Craigie, W. A. and C. T. Onions. Oxford: Clarendon Press.

Crowley, T. (1989). *The Politics of Discourse: The Standard Language Question in British Cultural Debates*. London: Macmillan.

Crowley, T. (1991). *Proper English? Readings in Language, History and Cultural Identity*. London: Routledge.

Crowley, T. (1996). *Language in History: Theories and Texts*. London: Routledge.

Crowley, T. (2003). *Standard English and the Politics of Language*. London: Palgrave.

Curme, G. O. and H. Kurath (1931). *A Grammar of the English Language*, Volume III: *Syntax*. New York, Boston: D. C. Heath and Co.

Daines, S. (1640). *Orthoepia Anglicana*. London: Robert Young and Richard Badger for the Company of Stationers.

Defoe, Daniel [1724–7] (1927). *A Tour Through the Whole Island of Great Britain*, introduced by G. D. H. Cole. London: Peter Davies.

De Maria, R. (1986). *Johnson's Dictionary and the Culture of Learning*. Oxford: Clarendon Press.

Denison, D. (1993). *English Historical Syntax*. London: Routledge.

Denison, D. (1998). 'Syntax', in S. Romaine (ed.), *The Cambridge History of the English Language*, Volume IV: *1776–1997*. Cambridge: Cambridge University Press, pp. 92–326.

Dennis, L. (1940). 'The progressive tense: frequency of its use in English'. *Proceedings of the Modern Language Association of America* 55: 855–65.

Dillard, J. L. (1992). *A History of American English*. London: Longman.

Dobson, E. J. (1955). 'Early Modern Standard English'. *Transactions of the Philological Society*, 25–54.

Dobson, E. J. (1957). *English Pronunciation 1500–1700*, 2 vols. Oxford: Clarendon Press.

Dobson, S. (1969). *Larn Yersel Geordie*. Newcastle: Frank Graham.

Dolezal, F. (2000). 'Charles Richardson's New Dictionary and Literary Lexicography, being a rodomontade upon illustrative examples'. *Lexicographica* 16: 104–51.

Dossena, M. and C. Jones (eds) (2003). *Insights into Late Modern English*. Bern: Peter Lang.

Drake, Glendon (1977). *The Role of Prescriptivism in American Linguistics, 1820–1970*. Amsterdam: Benjamins.

Dryden, J. [1672] (1978). 'Defence of the epilogue'. Epilogue to his *The Conquest of Granada*, ed. H. T. Swedenberg. Berkeley and London: University of California Press.

Durkin, P. (2002). 'Changing documentation in the Third Edition of the *Oxford English Dictionary*: sixteenth-century vocabulary as a test-case', in Teresa Fanego, Belén Méndez-Naya and Elena Seoane (eds), *Sounds, Words, Texts and Change*. Current Issues in Linguistic Theory 224. Amsterdam: John Benjamins, pp. 65–82.

Dyche, T. and W. Pardon (1735). *A New General English Dictionary*. London: R. Ware.

Easther, A. (1883). *Glossary of the Dialect of Almondbury and Huddersfield*. London: Trübner for the English Dialect Society.

Ellegård, A. (1953). *The Auxiliary 'do': The Establishment and Regulation of its Use in English*. Gothenburg Studies in English 2. Stockholm: Almquist and Wiksell.

Ellis, A. J. (1869–89). *On Early English Pronunciation*. London: Asher and Trübner and Co.

Elphinston, J. (1786). *Propriety Ascertained in Her Picture*, volume I. London: John Water.

Elphinston, J. (1787). *Propriety Ascertained in Her Picture*, volume II. London: John Water.

Elphinston, J. (1790). *Inglish Orthoggraphy Epittomized*. London: W. Richardson, J. Deighton, W. Clark et al.

Engblôm, V. (1938). *On the Origin and Early Development of the Auxiliary 'do'*. Lund: C. W. K.Gleerup.

Entick, John (1764). *A New Spelling Dictionary of the English Language*. London.

Fabricius, A. (2002). 'Weak vowels in modern RP: an acoustic study of happy-tensing and KIT/ schwa shift'. *Language Variation and Change* 14(2): 211–38.

Fiennes, Celia (1888). *Through England on a Side-Saddle in the Time of William and Mary*, ed. Hon. Mrs Griffiths. London: Field and Tuer.

Finegan, E. (1998). 'English grammar and usage', in Romaine (ed.) (1998), pp. 536–87.

Finkenstaedt, T., E. Leisi and D. Wolff (1970). *A Chronological English Dictionary: Listing 80,000 Words in Order of their Earliest Known Occurrence*. Heidelberg: Winter.

Fisher, A. (1750). *A New Grammar: Being the Most Easy Guide to Speaking and Writing the English Language Properly and Correctly*, 2nd edition. Newcastle: J. Gooding for I. Thompson.

Fisher, A. (1754). *A New Grammar*. Newcastle: I. Thompson.

Fitzmaurice, Susan (1998). 'The commerce of language in the pursuit of politeness in the eighteenth century'. *English Studies* 79: 309–28.

Fitzmaurice, Susan (forthcoming). 'The meanings and uses of the progressive construction in an early eighteenth-century English network' in Anne Curran and Kimberly Emmons (eds), *Studying the History of English: Conversations about the Past and Present*. Berlin: Mouton de Gruyter.

Foster, B. (1968). *The Changing English Language*. London: Macmillan.

Foulkes, P. and G. Docherty (2000). 'Another chapter in the story of /r/: "Labiodental" variants in British English'. *Journal of Sociolinguistics* 4(1): 30–59.

Fowler, H. W. and F. G. Fowler (1906). *The King's English*. Oxford: Clarendon Press.

Fowler, H. W. (1930). *Modern English Usage*. Oxford: Clarendon Press.

Fowler, R. (forthcoming). 'Text and meaning in Richardson's Dictionary', in J. Coleman and A. McDermott (eds), *Dictionary History and Historical Lexicography*. Lexicographica Series Major. Tübingen: Neumeyer.

Freeborn, D. (1992). *From Old English to Standard English*. London: Macmillan.

Gaskell, Elizabeth [1854] (1973). *North and South* ed. A. Easson. London: World's Classics.

Gaskell, W. (1854). *Two Lectures on the Lancashire Dialect*. London: Chapman and Hall.

Gildon, C. and J. Brightland (1711). *A Grammar of the English Tongue*. London.

Gimson, A. C. (1962). *An Introduction to the Pronunciation of English*. London: Arnold.

Gordon, E. and A. Sudbury (2002) 'The history of southern hemisphere Englishes', in Watts and Trudgill (eds) (2002), pp. 67–86.

Görlach, M. (1991). *Introduction to Early Modern English*. Cambridge: Cambridge University Press.

Görlach, M. (1999). *English in Nineteenth-Century England*. Cambridge: Cambridge University Press.

Görlach, M. (2001). *Eighteenth-Century English*. Heidelberg: Winter.

Graham, G. F. (1869). *A Book about Words*. London: Longman and Green.

Grant, W. and J. Main Dixon (1921). *Manual of Modern Scots*. Cambridge: Cambridge University Press.

Greenleaf, Jeremiah (1821). *Grammar Simplified*, 3rd edition. New York: C. Starr.

Greenwood, J. (1711). *An Essay Towards a Practical English Grammar*. London: R. Tookey.

Greig, J. Y. T. (ed.) (1932). *The Letters of David Hume*. Oxford: Oxford University Press.

Grose, F. (1787). *Provincial Glossary*. London: T. Hooper.

Grund, P. and T. Walker (2001). 'The subjunctive in adverbial clauses in nineteenth-century English'. Paper presented at Later Modern English Conference, Edinburgh.

Hall, F. (1872). *Recent Exemplifications of False Philology*. New York : Scribner, Armstrong and Co.

Hall, F. (1873). *Modern English*. London: Trübner.

Harker, D. (ed.) (1972). *Allan's Tyneside Songs*. Newcastle: Frank Graham.

Hart, J. (1589). *An Orthographie*. London: Seres.

Hartmann, R. R. K. (1983). *Lexicography: Principles and Practice*. London: Academic Press.

Haugen, Einar (1971). 'The ecology of language'. *The Linguistic Reporter* supplement 25 (winter): 19–26.

Heslop, R. O. (1892). *Northumberland Words*. London: English Dialect Society.

Heslop, R. O. (1903). 'Dialect Notes from Northernmost England'. *Transactions of the Yorkshire Dialect Society* 5: 7–31.

Hoare, M. R. and V. Salmon (2000). 'The language of science in the OED', in Mugglestone (ed.) (2000), pp. 156–71.

Hodgson, W. B. (1882). *Errors in the Use of English*, American revised edition. New York: D. Appleton.

Holmberg, B. (1964). *On the Concept of Standard English and the History of Modern English Pronunciation*. Lund: Gleerup.

Honey, J. (1988). '"Talking Proper": schooling and the establishment of English "Received Pronunciation"', in *An Historic Tongue: Studies in English Linguistics in Memory of Barbara Strang*. London: Routledge, pp. 209–27.

Hope, Jonathan (1990) 'Applied historical linguistics: sociohistorical linguistic evidence for the authorship of Renaissance plays'. *Transactions of the Philological Society* 89: 201–26.

Horgan, A. D. (1994). *Johnson on Language: An Introduction*. Basingstoke: Macmillan.

Horn, W. and M. Lehnert (1954). *Laut und Leben. Englische Lautgeschichte der neueren Zeit (1400–1950)*, 2 volumes. Berlin: Deutsche Verlag der Wissenschaften.

Horvath, B. (1985). *Variation in Australian English*. Cambridge: Cambridge University Press.

Hughes, A. and P. Trudgill (1996). *English Accents and Dialects*, 3rd edition. London: Arnold.

Hughes, E. (1952). *North Country Life in the Eighteenth Century*, volume 1: *The North East 1700–1750*. London: Oxford University Press.

Hulbert, J. R. (1947). 'On the origin of the grammarians' rules for the use of *shall* and *will'*. *Proceedings of the Modern Language Association of America* 62: 1178–82.

Hunter, J. (1829). *Hallamshire Glossary.* London: William Pickering.

Jacobson, S. (ed.) (1986). *Papers from the Second Scandinavian Symposium on Syntactic Variation: Stockholm, May 15–16 1982*. Stockholm: Almqvist and Wiksell.

Jespersen, O. (1909–49). *A Modern English Grammar on Historical Principles*, 2 vols. Heidelberg: Winter; Copenhagen: Munksgaard.

JK (1702). *New English Dictionary*. London: H. Bonwicke.

Johnson, S. (1747). *The Plan of a Dictionary of the English Language*. London.

Johnson, S. (1755). *A Dictionary of the English Language*. London: W. Strahan for J. and P. Knapton, T. and T. Longman et al.

Johnston, W. (1764). *Pronouncing and Spelling Dictionary.* London: the Author.

Jones, B. (1962). *The Poems of William Barnes*. London: Centaur Press.

Jones, C. (1989). *A History of English Phonology*. London: Longman.

Jones, C. (ed.) (1991). *Sylvester Douglas: A Treatise on the Provincial Dialect of Scotland (1779)*. Edinburgh: Edinburgh University Press.

Jones, C. (1993). 'Scottish Standard English in the late eighteenth century'. *Transactions of the Philological Society* 91 (1): 95–131.

Jones, C. (1995). *A Language Suppressed*. Edinburgh: John Donald.

Jones, C. (1997). 'An early 18th century Scottish spelling book for ladies'. *English Studies* 78 (5): 430–50.

Jones, D. (1907). *Phonetic Transcriptions of English Prose*. Oxford: Clarendon Press.

Jones, D. (1917). *An English Pronouncing Dictionary (on Strictly Phonetic Principles)*. London: J. M. Dent.

Jones, D. (1937). *An English Pronouncing Dictionary (on Strictly Phonetic Principles)*. London: J. M. Dent.

Jones, D. (1960). *The Pronunciation of English*. Cambridge: Cambridge University Press.

Jones, D. (1967). *Everyman's English Pronouncing Dictionary*, ed. A. C. Gimson, 13th edition. London: Dent.

Jones, J. (1701). *Practical Phonography.* London: Richard Smith.

Jones, R. F. (1953). *The Triumph of the English Language*. Oxford: Oxford University Press.

Jones, S. (1798). *Sheridan Improved. A General Pronouncing and Explanatory Dictionary of the English Language*, 3rd edition. London: Vernor and Hood, J. Cushell, Ogilvie and Son and Lackington, Allen and Co.

Jonson, B. (1640), 'The English Grammar', in *The Works of Benjamin Jonson*, volume II, pp. 31–84. London.

Joyce, P. (1991). 'The people's English: language and class in England *c.* 1840–1920', in P. Burke and R. Porter, *Language, Self and Society: A Social History of Language*. Cambridge: Polity Press, pp. 154–90.

Kenrick, W. (1773). *A New Dictionary of the English Language*. London: John and Francis Rivington, William Johnston et al.

Kerswill, P. and A. Williams (2002). '"Salience" as an explanatory factor in language change: evidence from dialect levelling in urban England', in M. C. Jones and E. Esch (eds), *Language Change: The Interplay of Internal, External and Extra-Linguistic Factors*. Berlin: Mouton, pp. 81–110.

Kirkby, J. (1746). *A New English Grammar*. London: R. Manby and H. S. Cox.

Kirkham, S. A. (1825). *Compendium of English Grammar*. Fredericktown: Herald Press.

Kökeritz, H. (1953). *Shakespeare's Pronunciation*. New Haven: Yale University Press.

Kruisinga, E. (1932). *Handbook of Present-Day English*, 3 volumes. Groningen: Noordhoff.

Kytö, M., J. Rudanko and E. Smitterberg (2000). 'Building a bridge between the present and the past: a corpus of 19th-century English'. *ICAME Journal* 24: 85–97.

Labov, W. (1966). *The Social Stratification of English in New York City*. Washington, DC: Center for Applied Linguistics.

Labov, W. (1972). *Sociolinguistic Patterns*. Oxford: Basil Blackwell.

Labov, W. (1975). 'On the use of the present to explain the past', in *Proceedings of the Eleventh International Congress of Linguists*, Bologna, volume 2, pp. 825–51. Reprinted in P. Baldi and R. N. Werth (eds) (1978), *Readings in Historical Phonology*. Philadelphia: Pennsylvania State University Press.

Lang, A. (1890). *Life, Letters and Diaries of Sir Stafford Northcote*, 2 vols. Edinburgh: W. Blackwood and Sons.

Lanham, L. W. (1996). 'A history of English in South Africa', in V. De Klerk (ed.), *Focus on South Africa*. Amsterdam: Benjamins, pp. 18–34.

Lass, R. (ed.) (1999). *The Cambridge History of the English Language*, volume III: *1476–1776*. Cambridge: Cambridge University Press.

Leonard, S. A. (1929). *The Doctrine of Correctness in English Usage 1700–1800*. Wisconsin: Madison.

Lloyd, R. J. (1894). 'Standard English'. *Die Neueren Sprachen* 2: 52–3.

Locke, J. [1690] (1823). *The Works of John Locke, a new edition corrected*. London: printed for Thomas Tegg.

Lowth, R. (1762). *A Short Introduction to English Grammar*. London: R. Dodsley.

Macafee, C. (1982). 'Glasgow dialect in literature'. *Scottish Language* I: 45–53.

Macaulay, R. (1991). *Locating Dialect in Discourse: The Language of Honest Men and Bonny Lasses in Ayr*. Oxford: Oxford University Press.

Mackay, C. (1867). 'Inroads upon English'. *Blackwood's* 102: 399–417.

Mackie, W. S. (1936). 'Shakespeare's English and how far it can be investigated with the help of the NED'. *Modern Language Review* 31: 1–10.

McArthur, T. (1992). *The Oxford Companion to the English Language.* Oxford: Oxford University Press.

McKnight, G. H. (1928). *Modern English in the Making.* Reprinted as *The Evolution of the English Language.* New York: Dover Publications, 1968.

MacMahon, M. (1998). 'Phonology', in Romaine (ed.) (1998), pp. 373–535.

Marsh, G. P. (1860). *Lectures on the English Language.* New York: Burchfield.

Marshall, W. (1787). *The Rural Economy of Norfolk.* London: T. Cadell.

Martin, B. (1749). *Lingua Britannica Reformata.* London: J. Hodges, J. Austen, J. Newberry et al.

Martin, T. (1824). *A Philological Grammar of the English Language.* London: Rivingtons.

Mencken, H. L. (1936). *The American Language*, 4th edition. London: Kegan Paul, Trench, Trubner and Co.

Michael, I. (1970). *English Grammatical Categories and the Tradition to 1800.* Cambridge: Cambridge University Press.

Miller, J. (1993). 'The Grammar of Scots', in J. Milroy and L. Milroy (eds), *Real English: The Grammar of English Dialects in the British Isles.* London: Longman.

Milroy, J. (1992). *Linguistic Variation and Change.* Oxford: Blackwell.

Milroy, J. and J. Harris (1980). 'When is a merger not a merger? The MEAT/MATE problem in a present-day English vernacular'. *English World-Wide* 1 (2): 199–210.

Milroy, J. and L. Milroy (1991). *Authority in Language: Investigating Standard English.* London: Routledge; 2nd edition, 1999.

Mitchell, H. (1799). *Scotticisms, Vulgar Anglicisms and Grammatical Improprieties Corrected.* Glasgow.

Moorman, F. W. (1918). *Songs of the Ridings.* London: Elkin Matthews.

Morris, E. E. (1898). *Austral English: A Dictionary of Australian Words, Phrases and Usage.* London: Macmillan.

Mugglestone, L. C. (1991). 'The fallacy of cockney rhyme: from Keats and earlier to Auden'. *Review of English Studies*, n.s. 42: 57–66.

Mugglestone, L. (1995). *Talking Proper.* Oxford: Clarendon Press.

Mugglestone, L. (2000a). 'An historian not a critic: the standard of usage in the OED', in Mugglestone (ed.) (2000b), pp. 189–206.

Mugglestone, L. (ed.) (2000b). *Lexicography and the OED: Pioneers in the Untrodden Forest.* Oxford: Oxford University Press.

Mulcaster, Richard [1582] (1925). *Elementarie*, ed. E. T. Campagnac. Oxford: Oxford University Press.

Mulholland, J. (1967). 'Thou and you in Shakespeare: a study in the second person pronoun'. *English Studies* 48: 34–43.

Murray, J. A. H. (1873). *The Dialect of the Southern Counties of Scotland.* London: Philological Society.

Murray, J. A. H. (1880). 'Ninth annual address delivered at the anniversary meeting of the Philological Society, Friday 21 May 1880'. *Transactions of the Philological Society*: 131–2.

Murray, J. A. H. (1888). *A New English Dictionary on Historical Principles.* Oxford: Clarendon Press. This later becomes known as the *Oxford English Dictionary.* The 1933 edition with supplement was edited by J. A. H. Murray, H. Bradley, W. A. Craigie and C. T. Onions. Oxford: Clarendon Press. The second edition (1989) was prepared by J. A. Simpson and E. S. C. Weiner. Oxford: Clarendon Press. OED online is at www.oed.com.

Murray, J. A. H. (1888). 'Preface' to *A New English Dictionary on Historical Principles*, volume I. Oxford: Clarendon Press.

Murray, J. (1900). *The Evolution of English Lexicography* (The Romanes Lectures 1900). Oxford: Clarendon Press.

Murray, J. (1928). *A New English Dictionary on Historical Principles.* Oxford: Clarendon Press.

Murray, K. M. E. (1977). *Caught in the Web of Words: James A. H. Murray and the Oxford English Dictionary*, preface by Robert W. Burchfield. New Haven and London: Yale University Press.

Murray, L. (1798). *English Grammar, Adapted to the Different Classes of Learner.* York: Wilson, Spence and Mawman.

Nares, R. (1784). *Elements of Orthoepy.* London: T. Payne and Son.

Nelson, W. (1952). 'The teaching of English in Tudor grammar schools'. *Studies in Philology* 49: 19–143.

Nevala, M. (2001). 'Private and public: on the use of address and endorsement formulae in eighteenth-century correspondence'. Paper presented at Late Modern English Conference, University of Edinburgh, August 2001.

Nevalainen, T. and M. Rissanen (1986). 'Do you support the *do* support? Emphatic and non-emphatic DO in affirmative sentences in present-day spoken English', in S. Jacobson (ed.) (1986), pp. 35–50.

Nicholson, J. (1889). *The Folk Speech of East Yorkshire.* London: Simpkin, Marshall and Co.; Hull: A. Brown and Sons; Driffield: T. Holderness.

O'Connor, J. D. (1947). 'The phonetic system of a dialect of Newcastle upon Tyne'. *Le Maître Phonetique* 89: 6–8.

Oldireva, L. (2001). 'On variation and standardisation processes in public and private writing: preterite and past participle forms in English 1680–1790'. Paper presented at Later Modern English Conference, Edinburgh.

Olsson, Y. (1961). *On the Syntax of the English Verb, with Special Reference to 'have a look' and Similar Complex Structures.* Goteborg: Elanders.

Orson, H. W. (1997). *A Dictionary of New Zealandisms on Historical Principles.* Auckland: Oxford University Press.

Orton, H. and W. J. Halliday (1963). *Survey of English Dialects, the Basic Material,* volume 1: *The Six Northern Counties and Man.* Leeds: E. J. Arnold.

Osselton, Noel E. (1983). 'On the history of dictionaries', in Hartmann (1983), pp. 13–21.

Osselton, Noel E. (1986). 'The first English dictionary: a compiler at work' in R. R. K. Hartmann (ed.), *The History of Lexicography. Papers from the Dictionary Research Centre Seminar at Exeter, March 1986.* Amsterdam: John Benjamins, pp. 175–84.

Osthoff, H. and K. Brugmann (1878). *Morphologische Untersuchungen auf dem Gebiete der indogermanischen Sprachen.* Leipzig: S. Hirzel.

Påhlsson, C. (1972). *The Northumbrian Burr.* Lund: C. W. K. Gleerup.

Palsgrave, T. (1530). *L'esclarcissement de la langue francoyse*. London: Richard Pynson.

Parish, W. D. (1875). *A Dictionary of the Sussex Dialect*. Lewes: Farncombe and Co.

Parrish, T. (2002). *The Grouchy Grammarian: A How-not-to Guide to the 47 Most Common Mistakes in English Made by Journalists, Broadcasters, and Others who Should Know Better*. London: J. Wiley.

Partridge, E. and J. W. Clark (1951). *British and American English Since 1900*. London: Andrew Dakers Ltd.

Pegge, S. (1844). *Anecdotes of the English Language; Chiefly Regarding the Local Dialect of London and its Environs*, ed. H. Christmas. London: J. B. Nichols and Sons.

Percy, C. (1994). '"Paradigms for their sex?" Women's grammars in late eighteenth-century England'. *Histoire Epistemologie Langage* 16 (II): 121–41.

Percy, C. (forthcoming). 'Plane English: the orthography of opposition in mid-eighteenth-century England'. To appear in *The Age of Johnson*, 15 (2004).

Perry, W. (1775). *The Royal Standard English Dictionary*. Edinburgh: David Willison for the Author.

Phillips, K. C. (1970). *Jane Austen's English*. London: Deutsch.

Phillips, K. C (1984). *Language and Class in Victorian England*. London: Deutsch.

Philological Society (1859). *Proposal for the Publication of a New Dictionary by the Philological Society*. London: Trübner and Co.

Poole, J. (1646). *The English Accidence; or, a Short, Plaine and Easy Way, for the more speedy attaining to the Latin tongue, by the help of the English*. London.

Pope, A. (1924). *The Rape of the Lock*, ed. Bonamy Dobrée. London: Everyman.

Pope, R. (1990). *Atlas of British Social and Economic History Since c. 1900*. London: Routledge.

Porter, R. (2000). *Enlightenment: Britain and the Creation of the Modern World*. London: Penguin.

Poutsma, H. (1914). *A Grammar of Late Modern English*. Groningen: Noordhoff.

Price, O. (1655). *The Vocal Organ*. Oxford.

Priestley, F. E. L. (1951). 'Canadian English', in Partridge and Clark (1951), pp 72–9.

Priestley, J. (1761). *The Rudiments of English Grammar*. London: Griffiths; 2nd edition, 1768.

Priestley, J. B. (1933). *English Journey*. London: Heinemann.

Przedlacka, J. (2001). 'Estuary English and RP: some recent findings. *Studia Anglica Posneniansa* 36: 35–50.

Pullum, G. K. (1974). 'Lowth's Grammar: a re-evaluation', *Linguistics* 137: 63–78.

Puttenham, G. (1589). *The Art of English Poesie*. London.

Quirk, R., S. Greenbaum, G. Leech and J. Svartvik (1985). *A Comprehensive Grammar of the English Language*. London: Longman.

Ray, J. (1674). *A Collection of English Words, not Generally Used*. London: for C. Wilkinson.

Raybould, E. (1998). 'How far was English syntax affected by Latin in the age of Dr Johnson?', in M. Ryden et al. (eds), *A Reader in Early Modern English*. Frankfurt am Main: University of Bamberg Studies in English Linguistics, pp. 187–99.

Richardson, C. (1835). *A New Dictionary of the English Language*. London: Bell and Daldy.

Rippmann, W. (1906). *The Sounds of Spoken English: A Manual of Ear Training for Students*. London: J. M. Dent.

Rissanen, M. (1999). 'Syntax', in Lass (ed.) (1999).

Robinson, F. J. G. (1972). 'Trends in Education in Northern England During the Eighteenth Century: A Biographical Study'. Unpublished doctoral dissertation, University of Newcastle.

Robinson, M. (1973). 'Modern Literary Scots: Fegusson and after', in A. J. Aitken (ed.), *Lowland Scots*. Occasional Papers no. 2. Edinburgh: Association for Scottish Literary Studies, pp. 38–55.

Rodriguez-Gil, M. (2002). 'Teaching English Grammar in the Eighteenth Century: Ann Fisher'. Unpublished doctoral dissertation, University of Las Palmas.

Rohdenburg, G. (2001). 'Mechanisms of syntactic change: the rise and fall of prepositional constructions in late Modern English'. Paper presented at the Later Modern English Conference, Edinburgh.

Romaine, S. (1982). *Socio-historical Linguistics: Its Status and Methodology*. Cambridge: Cambridge University Press.

Romaine, S. (ed.) (1998). *The Cambridge History of the English Language*, volume IV: *1776–1997*. Cambridge: Cambridge University Press.

Rosewarne, D. (1994). 'Estuary English – tomorrow's RP?' *English Today 37*: 3–8.

Ross, A. S. C. (1970). *How to Pronounce It*. London: Hamish Hamilton.

Rush, J. [1827] (1855). *The Philosophy of the Human Voice*, 4th edition. Philadelphia: J. Maxwell.

Rydén, M. (1981). 'The study of eighteenth-century English syntax', in W. Winter and J. Fisiak (eds), *Trends in Linguistics*, Studies and Monographs 23: *Historical Syntax*. Berlin: Mouton.

Schäfer, J. (1980). *Documentation in the OED: Shakespeare and Nashe as Test Cases*. Oxford: Oxford University Press.

Schäfer, J. (1989). *Early Modern English Lexicography*. Oxford: Clarendon Press.

Scheffer, J. (1975). *The Progressive in English*. Amsterdam: North Holland.

Schlauch, M. (1959, reprinted 1968). *The English Language in Modern Times (Since 1400)*. Warsaw: Pan'stwowe Wydawnictwo Naukowe.

Seoane-Posse, E. (2002). 'On the evolution of scientific American and British English, with special reference to recent and ongoing changes in the use of the passive voice'. Paper presented at 12th International Conference on English Historical Linguistics, Glasgow.

Sheldon, E. K. (1938). 'Standards of English Pronunciation according to the Grammarians and Orthoepists of the 16th, 17th, and 18th Centuries'. Unpublished doctoral dissertation, University of Wisconsin.

Sheldon, E. K. (1946). 'Pronouncing systems in eighteenth-century dictionaries'. *Language* 22: 27–41.

Sheldon, E. K. (1947). 'Walker's influence on the pronunciation of English'. *Proceedings of the Modern Language Association of America* 62: 130–46.

Sheldon, E. K. (1967). *Thomas Sheridan of Smock Alley 1719–1788*. Princeton, NJ: Princeton University Press.

Sheridan, T. (1756). *British Education, or the Source of the Disorders of Great Britain*. London.

Sheridan, T. (1761). *A Dissertation on the Causes of the Difficulties, which Occur, in Learning the English Tongue.* London: R. and J. Dodsley.

Sheridan, T. (1762). *A Course of Lectures on Elocution.* London.

Sheridan, T. (1775). *Lectures on the Art of Reading.* London.

Sheridan, T. (1780). *A General Dictionary of the English Language.* London: J. Dodsley, C. Dilly and J. Wilkie.

Sheridan, T. (1789). *A General Dictionary of the English Language,* 3rd edition. London: Charles Dilly.

Shields, A. F. (1973). 'Thomas Spence and the English Language'. Unpublished MA dissertation, University of Newcastle upon Tyne.

Shields, A. F. (1974). 'Thomas Spence and the English Language'. *Transactions of the Philological Society:* 33–64.

Shorrocks, G. (1991). 'Ellis as dialectologist: a reassessment'. *Historiographia Linguistica* 18 (2–3): 321–34.

Shorrocks, G. (1999). *A Grammar of the Dialect of the Bolton Area.* Frankfurt: Peter Lang.

Silva, P. (ed.) (1996). *A Dictionary of South African English on Historical Principles.* Oxford: Oxford University Press.

Simpson, D. (1986). *The Politics of American English, 1760–1850.* Oxford: Oxford University Press.

Sinclair, J. (1782). *Observations on the Scottish Dialect.* Edinburgh.

Sledd, H. and G. J. Kolb (1955). *Dr Johnson's 'Dictionary': Essays in the Biography of a Book.* Chicago: University of Chicago Press.

Smart, B. H. (1836). *Walker Remodelled: A New Critical Pronouncing Dictionary of the English Language.* London: T. Cadell.

Smart, B. H. (1842). *The Practice of Elocution,* 4th edition. London: Longman, Brown, Green and Longmans.

Smith, J. (1996). *An Historical Study of English: Function, Form and Change.* London: Routledge.

Smith, O. (1984). *The Politics of Language 1791–1819.* Oxford: Clarendon Press.

Smith, R. (1824). *The Productive Grammar.* Boston: Richardson, Lord and Holbrook; New York: Collins and Hannay.

Söderlind, J. (1951–8). *Verb Syntax in John Dryden's Prose.* Cambridge, MA: Harvard University Press.

Spence, T. (1775). *The Grand Repository of the English Language.* Newcastle: T. Saint.

Spence, T. (1814). *The Giant Killer, or Anti-Landlord,* numbers 1, 2. London.

Starnes, De W. and G. E. Noyes (1946). *The English Dictionary from Cawdrey to Johnson 1604–1755.* Reprinted with an introduction by Gabriele Stein, Amsterdam: John Benjamins, 1991.

Story, G. M., W. J. Kirwin and J. Widdowson (1982). *A Dictionary of Newfoundland English.* London and Toronto: University of Toronto Press.

Strang, B. M. H. (1970). *A History of English.* London: Methuen.

Strang, B. M. H (1982). 'Some aspects of the history of the *be + ing* construction', in J. Anderson (ed.), *Language Form and Linguistic Variation: Papers Dedicated to Angus McIntosh.* Current Issues in Linguistic Theory 15. Amsterdam: Benjamins, pp. 427–74.

Stuart-Smith, J. (1999). 'Glasgow: accent and voice quality', in P. Foulkes and G. Doherty (eds), *Urban Voices: Accent Studies in the British Isles*. London: Edward Arnold, pp. 201–22.

Sundby, Bertil (ed.) (1953). *English Teacher (1687)*. Lund, Copenhagen and Gleerup: Munksgaard.

Sweet, H. (1873–4). 'The history of English sounds'. *Transactions of the Philological Society*, 461–623.

Sweet, H. (1877). *A Handbook of Phonetics*. Oxford: Clarendon Press.

Sweet, H. (1882). *The Elementary Sounds of English*. Oxford.

Sweet, H. (1890). *A Primer of Phonetics*. Oxford.

Sweet, H. (1891–8). *A New English Grammar, Logical and Historical*. Oxford: Clarendon Press.

Swift, J. (1710). Letter to Isaac Bickerstaff, Esq. *The Tatler*, 26 September 1710.

Swift, J. (1712). *A Proposal for Correcting, Improving and Ascertaining the English Tongue*. London: Benjamin Tooke.

Taglicht, J. (1970). 'The genesis of the conventional rules for the use of *shall* and *will*'. *English Studies* 51: 191–213.

Taylor, F. E. (1901). *The Folk Speech of South Lancashire*. Manchester: John Heywood.

Tieken Boon Van Ostade, I. (1982). 'Double negation and eighteenth-century grammars'. *Neophilologus* LXVI: 278–85.

Tieken Boon Van Ostade, I. (1987). *The Auxiliary 'do' in Eighteenth-Century English: A Sociohistorical-Linguistic Approach*. Dordrecht: Foris.

Tieken Boon Van Ostade, I. (2000). 'Of norms and networks: the language of Robert Lowth'. Paper presented to the 11th International Conference for English Historical Linguistics.

Tieken Boon van Ostade, I. (forthcoming). 'Eighteenth-century prescriptivism and the norm of correctness', to appear in A. van Kemenade and B. Los, (eds), *Handbook of the History of English*. Oxford: Blackwell.

Trench, R. C. (1851). *English Past and Present: Eight Lectures*. London: Macmillan.

Trench, R. C. (1851). *On the Study of Words*. London: J. Parker.

Trench, R. C. (1857). *On some Deficiencies in our English Dictionaries*. London: Philological Society.

Trench, R. C. (1860). *On some Deficiencies in our English Dictionaries*, revised edition. London: John W. Parker and Son.

Trench, R. C. et al. (1860). *Canones Lexicographici; or, Rules to be Observed Editing the New English Dictionary*. London: Philological Society.

Trudgill, P. (1974). *The Social Differentiation of English in Norwich*. Cambridge: Cambridge University Press.

Trudgill, P. (2002). 'The history of the lesser-known varieties of English', in Watts and Trudgill (eds) (2002), pp. 29–44.

Truss, L. (2003). *Eats, Shoots and Leaves: A Zero-Tolerance Guide to Punctuation*. London: Profile Books.

Tucker, A. (1773). *Vocal Sounds*. London: T. Jones.

Tucker, S. (1967). *Protean Shape: A Study in Eighteenth-Century Vocabulary and Usage*. London: Athlone.

Tulloch, G. (1980). *The Language of Walter Scott: A Study of his Scottish and Period Language*. London: Deutsch.

Turner, G. W. (1994). 'English in Australia', in Burchfield (ed.) (1994), pp. 277–327.

Unger, H. G. (1998). *Noah Webster: The Life and Time of an American Patriot.* New York: Wiley.

Ussher, G. N. (1785). *The Elements of English Grammar.* Gloucester: R. Raines.

Vicinius, M. (1974). *The Industrial Muse: A Study of Nineteenth-Century British Working-Class Literature.* London: Croom Helm.

Viereck, W. (1965). 'Zur Entstehung und Wertung des Uvularen r unter besonderen Berücksichtigunge der Situation in England', *Jahrbuch des Marburger Universitätsbundes* 65: 125–34.

Visser, Fr. T. (1963–73). *An Historical Syntax of the English Language*, in three parts. Leiden: Brill.

Wales, K. (2002). 'North of Watford Gap: a cultural history of Northern English (from 1700)', in Watts and Trudgill (eds) (2002), pp. 45–66.

Walker, J. (1791). *A Critical Pronouncing Dictionary.* London: G. G. J. and J. Robinson and T. Cadell.

Walpole, H. [1753] (1941). *Correspondence*, volume 10: *With George Montagu*, ed. W. S. Lewis and Ralph S. Brown. London: Oxford University Press.

Wang, W. S.-Y. (1969). 'Competing sound changes as a cause of residue'. *Language* 45: 9–25.

Warburton, W. and A. Pope (eds) (1747). *The Works of Shakespear in Eight Volumes.* London: printed for J. and P. Knapton, [and] S. Birt [etc.].

Ward, I. (1945). *The Phonetics of English.* Cambridge: Heffer.

Ward, W. (1765). *An Essay on Grammar, as it may be applied to the English Language.* London: Robert Horsfield.

Warkentyne, H. (1965). 'The Phonology of the Dialect of Hexham in Northumberland'. Unpublished MA dissertation, University College, London.

Watts, R. and P. Trudgill (2002). *Alternative Histories of English.* London: Routledge.

Webster, N. (1784). *Grammatical Institutes.* Hartford, CT.

Webster, N. (1790). *A Collection of Essays and Fugitiv Writings on Moral, Political, Historical and Literary Subjects.* Boston.

Webster, N. (1789). *Dissertations on the English Language.* Boston.

Webster, N. (1806). *A Compendious Dictionary of the English Language.* Hartford, CT: Sidney's Press for Hudson and Goodwin; New Haven: Increase Cooke and Co.

Webster, N. (1828). *The American Dictionary of the English Language.* New York: S. Converse.

Webster, N. (1832). *A Dictionary of the English Language. Reprinted by E. H. Barker ... from a Copy Communicated by the Author, and Containing Many Manuscript ... Additions*, 2 vols. London: Black and Co.

Webster's International Dictionary of the English Language, ed. W. T. Harris and F. S. Allen (1909); W. A. Neilson, T. A. Knott and F. W. Carhart (1934); Philip Babcock Gove (1961). New York: Merriam-Webster.

Wells, J. (1982). *Accents of English*, 3 volumes. Cambridge: Cambridge University Press.

Wells, R. A. (1973). *Dictionaries and the Authoritarian Tradition.* The Hague: Mouton.

Wharton, J. (1654). *The English Grammar; or, the Institution of Letters, Syllables, and Words in the English-Tongue.* London: William Du Gard.

White, R. G. (1871). 'Words and their Uses'. *The Galaxy* 11 (6).

Whitney, W. D. (1875). 'The elements of English pronunciation', in *Oriental and Linguistic Studies*, second series. London: Trübner and Co.

Whitney, W. D. (1889–91, supplement 1909). *Century Dictionary and Cyclopedia*. New York: Century.

Willinsky, J. (1994). *Empire of Words: The Reign of the OED*. Princeton: Princeton University Press.

Wilson, J. (1926). *The Dialects of Southern Scotland*. Oxford: Oxford University Press.

Withers, Philip (1788). *Aristarchus*. London: J. Moore.

Wright, J. (1892). *A Grammar of the Dialect of Windhill*. London: F. Trübner for the English Dialect Society.

Wright, J. (1896–1905). *The English Dialect Dictionary*. London: Kegan Paul for the English Dialect Society.

Wright, J. (1905). *The English Dialect Grammar*. Oxford: Henry Frowde.

Wyld, H. C. (1927). *A Short History of English*, 3rd edition. London: Murray; 1st edition, 1914.

Wyld, H. C. (1936). *A History of Modern Colloquial English*, 3rd edition. Oxford: Basil Blackwell; 1st edition, 1920.

Zandvoort, R. W. (1957). *Wartime English: Materials for a Linguistic History of World War II*. Groningen: J. B. Wolters.

Zgusta, L. (1989). 'The *Oxford English Dictionary* and other dictionaries'. *International Journal of Lexicography* 2: 188–230.

Name and Subject Index

Lexical Index

Lightning Source UK Ltd.
Milton Keynes UK
05 June 2010

155164UK00001B/27/P